# The Original Sceptics

# The Original Sceptics
## A Controversy

Edited by
MYLES BURNYEAT
AND
MICHAEL FREDE

Hackett Publishing Company, Inc.
Indianapolis/Cambridge

Copyright © 1997 by Hackett Publishing Company

Printed in the United States of America

00  99  98  97       1  2  3  4  5

For further information, please address

Hackett Publishing Company, Inc.
P.O. Box 44937
Indianapolis, Indiana 46244-0937

Cover design by John Pershing
Text design by Dan Kirklin


Library of Congress Cataloging-in-Publication Data

The original sceptics/edited by Myles Burnyeat and Michael Frede.
        p.      cm.
    Includes bibliographical references.
    ISBN 0-87220-348-4 (alk. paper).   ISBN 0-87220-347-6 (pbk.: alk. paper)
    1. Scepticism.   2. Sextus Empiricus.   3. Cicero, Marcus Tullius.
Academica.   I. Burnyeat, Myles.   II. Frede, Michael.
b525.075   1996
186—dc20                                           95-51451
                                                   CIP


The paper used in this publication meets the minimum requirements of American
National Standard for Information Sciences—Permanence of Paper for Printed
Library Materials, ANSI Z39.48-1984.

                              ∞

# CONTENTS

Preface     ix
Note on the Abbrevations     xiii

1. The Sceptic's Beliefs     1
   Michael Frede

2. Can the Sceptic Live His Scepticism?     25
   Myles Burnyeat

3. The Beliefs of a Pyrrhonist     58
   Jonathan Barnes

4. The Sceptic in His Place and Time     92
   Myles Burnyeat

5. The Sceptic's Two Kinds of Assent and the Question of the
   Possibility of Knowledge     127
   Michael Frede

Select Bibliography     153

# Previous Publication Details

Chapter 1: Michael Frede, 'The Sceptic's Beliefs', first appeared as 'Des Skeptikers Meinungen' in *Neue Hefte für Philosophie*, Heft 15/16 (1979), 102–29; reprinted in English as 'The Skeptic's Beliefs' in Michael Frede, *Essays in Ancient Philosophy* (University of Minnesota Press 1989), chapter 10.

Chapter 2: Myles Burnyeat, 'Can the Sceptic Live His Scepticism?', first appeared in *Doubt and Dogmatism: Essays in Hellenistic Epistemology*, edited by Malcolm Schofield, Myles Burnyeat, and Jonathan Barnes (Clarendon Press 1980), chapter 2; reprinted in *The Skeptical Tradition*, edited by Myles Burnyeat (University of California Press 1983), chapter 6.

Chapter 3: Jonathan Barnes, 'The Beliefs of a Pyrrhonist', first appeared in *Proceedings of the Cambridge Philological Society* N.S. 28 (1982), 1–29; reprinted in *Elenchos* 4 (1983), 5–43, and incorporated into Jonathan Barnes, 'Pyrrhonism, Belief and Causation: Observations on the Scepticism of Sextus Empiricus', *Aufstieg und Niedergang der Römischen Welt* Band 36.4 (1990), 2608–95.

Chapter 4: Myles Burnyeat, 'The Sceptic in His Place and Time', first appeared in *Philosophy in History: Essays on the Historiography of Philosophy*, edited by Richard Rorty, J. B. Schneewind, and Quentin Skinner (Cambridge University Press 1984), chapter 10; reprinted in the expanded version printed here in *Scepticism from the Renaissance to the Enlightenment*, edited by Richard H. Popkin and Charles B. Schmitt (Wolfenbütteler Forschungen Band 35, Wiesbaden 1987), 13–43, and in Spanish translation in *Anales del Seminario de Metafísica* 27 (1993), 273–306.

Chapter 5: Michael Frede, 'The Sceptic's Two Kinds of Assent and the Question of the Possibility of Knowledge', first appeared in *Philosophy in History: Essays on the Historiography of Philosophy*, edited by Richard Rorty,

J. B. Schneewind, and Quentin Skinner (Cambridge University Press 1984), chapter 11; reprinted in Michael Frede, *Essays in Ancient Philosophy* (University of Minnesota Press 1989), chapter 11, and in Spanish translation in *Anales del Seminario de Metafísica* 27 (1993), 247–71.

# Preface

The five essays gathered in this volume have a single aim: to understand and evaluate ancient scepticism.

Sceptical arguments and sceptical ideas have had an enduring role in modern philosophy. When you embark on a philosophical education, scepticism is one of the first topics you meet. Consequently, scepticism is one of the few things that every philosopher thinks they know a good deal about. But the scepticism they know about—scepticism as it is discussed in modern philosophy—is in many ways a pale and impoverished version of the ancient original. Our hope is that this volume will help students and scholars get to know the richness, depth, and systematic power of the ancient philosophical movements which originally gave scepticism its name.

There were two such movements, each with its own history: the Academics, who did not call themselves sceptics, and the Pyrrhonists, who did. In each case, our main source is an author writing towards the end of the movement's history. Cicero's *Academica,* begun in 45 B.C., takes stock of some two hundred years of debate and development in the sceptical Academy. The works of Sextus Empiricus, written around 200 A.D., provide a compendious summing up of some two hundred years of Pyrrhonist argument and polemic. As the Academics declined, the Pyrrhonists emerged to renew the sceptical scrutiny of the claims of dogmatic philosophy.

These two movements, their history, and the relation between them are the subject of the following chapters. The first four essays are mainly concerned with Pyrrhonian scepticism as formulated by Sextus Empiricus. Cicero and the Academics come to the fore in Chapter 5.

When we began, each of us independently, to take an interest in ancient scepticism, the scholarly literature on the subject was small, and concentrated more on historical than on philosophical issues. The Select Bibliography at the end of this volume shows a dramatically different situation today. The issues and controversies first raised in the five essays collected here are at the centre of current discussion.

It is, we think, appropriate that a book on two philosophical movements which lived by controversy and debate should itself be full of debate between the three authors—a debate that continued, and developed, in private as well as public discussion over a number of years. The disagreements are systematic. They have to be, because in the debate about Pyrrhonian scepticism what is at stake between us is how to understand a sceptical philosophy which offers a systematic approach to all questions whatsoever (Chapters 1–4). But Academic scepticism was systematic too, and it will become clear to the reader that the debate over Pyrrhonian scepticism ramifies into delicate issues about what, if anything, differentiates the Pyrrhonist's outlook from this or that form of Academic scepticism (Chapter 5).

The Pyrrhonists say they have found that if you follow the sceptical approach, if you take the sceptical arguments to their final conclusion, if you become habituated to suspending judgement on all issues, then your life is transformed. You gain the tranquillity that other philosophical schools promise, but fail to deliver. Scepticism is a philosophy for the whole of life. Consequently, a proper understanding of scepticism must include an understanding of the life it offers, as well as the arguments. That makes for a richer conception of what scepticism is than modern philosophers are used to. But it also means that the interpretation of ancient scepticism is a complicated task, demanding the most careful combination of textual and philosophical skills. There is much to debate, and plenty of room for disagreement. We hope that this collection will encourage readers to study the ancient sceptical writings—they are quite accessible to Greekless readers in the translations recommended in the Bibliography—and try to make up their own minds on the issues involved.

But there is one thing that all the contributors to this volume agree upon. Scepticism, properly understood, is not just about knowledge. The central sceptical question is not 'How do you know?', as so many modern philosophy books make out, but the more fundamental question 'Have you any reason to believe?'

When the earliest of these papers were written, it was commonly assumed that to be a sceptic is to believe that nothing can be known for certain. It was supposed that the philosophical question raised by the sceptic was whether we do or even can know anything for certain, either in general or in some particular domain, about the external world, or about other minds, or about the past. Scepticism is still widely understood in such terms in philosophy today. But as readers will discover, originally scepticism had a much broader and more challenging scope.

A preface is not the place to try to explain why people came to think of scepticism as narrowly concerned with knowledge and certainty. That would require a complicated historical investigation, the outcome of which would be yet further disagreement between the two editors of this volume. Disagreement is inevitable because what has to be investigated is how the ideas of the original sceptics were transmitted, interpreted, and assessed in later antiquity, the Middle Ages, and the early modern period, both before and after Descartes. Any description of these processes will be shaped by the author's view of what the original ideas in fact were, as readers can see when Frede tells his version of the story in Chapter 5. It is equally true of Burnyeat's account of Descartes's dealings with scepticism in his paper 'Idealism and Greek Philosophy: What Descartes Saw and Berkeley Missed', listed in the Bibliography.

Meanwhile, we invite our readers to go back to the original sceptics to explore the wide range of philosophical possibilities they explored. The papers reprinted here were written, as we have said, not to present a new scholarly consensus, let alone a new dogma, on ancient scepticism, but to break unjustified preconceptions about it and to encourage a new look at the ancient evidence. We are glad that these essays have been received with so much interest, for we think that the questions they raise continue to be some of the main questions to be faced not only by historians of ancient philosophy, but also by contemporary philosophers.

# Note on Abbreviations

The bulk of the material discussed in the following chapters derives from a handful of main sources, all readily available in English translation, as indicated in the Bibliography.

The works concerned, introduced by the abbreviations which will be used in referring to them, are as follows:

DL: Diogenes Laertius, *Lives of the Philosophers*
PH: Sextus Empiricus, *Outlines of Pyrrhonism*
M: Sextus Empiricus, *Adversus Mathematicos*
Cic. *Acad.:* Cicero, *Academica*

To these may be added some of the essays in Plutarch's *Moralia*, in particular *Adversus Colotem* (Plu. *Col.*) and *De Stoicorum repugnantiis* (Plu. *Stoic. rep.*).

For the minority of references which fall outside this list, the abbreviations are based on those in Liddell-Scott-Jones, *A Greek-English Lexicon* (9th edn., Oxford, 1940) and the *Oxford Latin Dictionary* (Oxford, 1968–).

# 1

# The Sceptic's Beliefs

## Michael Frede

There are no views or beliefs that define Pyrrhonean Scepticism. Nor are there any specific doctrines or dogmas which a sceptic, rather than a member of one of the 'dogmatic' schools, would have. Even the phrase, "nothing is to be known," is not accepted by the sceptical philosopher as expressing a sceptical doctrine (*PH* I 200). According to Photius (Bibl. cod. 212, 169b 40ff.), Aenesidemus argued that the Academic sceptics really were dogmatists, since some of them did, in fact, claim that nothing is knowable (cf. *PH* 2–3). There are no specifically Pyrrhonean doctrines, no views which any Pyrrhonist, just by being a Pyrrhonist, would have to accept. Still less is Pyrrhonean scepticism characterized by specifically sceptical views that rely on 'deeper' insights into the true nature of things. It is the dogmatists, not the sceptics, who claim to have such insights (*PH* I 2–3).

The usual interpretation of Pyrrhonean scepticism, of course, ascribes a far more radical stance to these sceptics. According to this interpretation, the sceptic not only claims to have no deeper insight into things, he also claims not to know anything at all; not only does he maintain no specifically sceptical doctrines, he also has no views or beliefs about anything. Such a characterization of Pyrrhonism typically relies on the following: as far as knowledge is concerned, the Pyrrhonist, as a full-blooded sceptic, can hardly assume that he knows anything without undermining his scepticism; and, as for beliefs, the ancient sceptics assure us that they are withholding judgment on whatever issue is under consideration. The sceptic refuses to assent to any proposition.

Any interpretation along these lines, however, seems fundamentally mistaken to me. No matter how ingenious he may be, the sceptic cannot avoid knowing many things. It might even turn out that, with great effort, imagination, and cleverness, he could bring about that he knows less and less.

There is, however, no reason to suppose that the sceptic is pursuing such a strategy. If he, then, simply cannot avoid knowing many things, he will also often be aware of knowing, and not merely supposing, certain things. And if we turn from our own conception of scepticism to the words of Sextus Empiricus, we can see clearly that the sceptic, in many instances, does think of himself as knowing something. I can, in fact, see no reason why he should not think this; it is perfectly compatible with his scepticism. Yet, whatever the case may be with regard to knowledge, it seems clear to me both that there are many things the sceptic thinks or believes are the case and that it is perfectly compatible with his scepticism for him to have all sorts of views and beliefs. And it is just this last point which shall be our concern here—can the sceptic have beliefs?

Given how much speaks in its favor, it is hardly surprising that the received interpretation has won almost universal acceptance; indeed so much speaks in its favor that its defenders have not even been deterred by the fact that, on this interpretation, the sceptical position turns out to be inconsistent. For it is generally assumed that ordinary, everyday life is simply not possible without any beliefs or views; and so it is generally assumed that the sceptic refutes himself, when he insists on total suspension of judgment while, at the same time, constantly relying on all sorts of judgments in his actual life. Hume's version of this objection is perhaps the most familiar; without a doubt, it has contributed substantially to the standard picture of the sceptic as a person who, if only he took his own views seriously, would be completely helpless in ordinary life.

Of course, the ancient sceptics, starting with Arcesilaus at the latest, were quite familiar with this objection. Clearly, they felt it did not really tell against their position. Since the issue was raised again and again over the course of centuries, it seems reasonable to suppose that the sceptics had, in fact, considered the matter quite carefully, when they claimed that this objection did not tell against them. That in turn should lead us to suspect that the sceptics' position is more complicated than the objection would have it, that the objection somehow overlooks some crucial aspect of their position. Still, it is hardly a coincidence that, all their protests to the contrary notwithstanding, the sceptics find themselves faced with basically the same objection time and again. The sceptical position must be one that positively provokes such an objection. Yet it seems to me that one violates the canons of interpretation if one does not take the sceptics' constant protests—that this objection does not really tell against their position—at least as seriously as the fact that they were constantly confronted by it.

If we, then, take seriously the sceptics' protestations and try to understand how they could think that this objection somehow misses the mark, there seem to be basically two lines along which the sceptics could argue, in defending themselves against this objection. The objectors claim that the sceptics, in theory, suspend judgment on all matters, but that, in practice, they simply cannot avoid making all kinds of judgments. Thus, one could argue against the objection by (i) trying to show that the sceptics denied that one could not avoid making judgments in practice, in everyday life—judgments like 'it is very hot today' or 'this car is about to run me over'. The sceptics could grant that it is extraordinarily difficult to bring oneself into such a state that one no longer even feels any temptation to have any view but insist that it is, in principle, possible and, indeed, is compatible with living a life worth living. Or, (ii) one could argue that the sceptics thought that even if one suspended judgment on all matters, at least suspended judgment in the sense in which they recommend that one suspend judgment, one would still have many beliefs and views, quite enough, at any rate, to lead a worthwhile life.

For various reasons—which I shall come to—it seems as if the sceptics opted for the second line. Since, however, there are some indications that they pursued the first line, to meet the standard objection, I want to consider this interpretation of their position at least briefly. There are basically three points that make this interpretation seem attractive: (i) As I have already indicated, there are a large number of passages that seem to show that the sceptic suspends judgment about everything and hence has no views or beliefs. Precisely because this part of their position is so well attested, one might suppose that the only way out was for the sceptic to hold that one could go through life without any views or beliefs; (ii) there are at least some reasons for thinking that Pyrrho himself attempted to lead a life entirely without beliefs or views—and Pyrrho is generally thought to have been the source for Pyrrhonean scepticism; (iii) quite a number of sceptical arguments survive that seem to set out to show that human action and human life is possible even without beliefs, that acting does not presuppose that one believes this or that is the case. And this third point seems to fit in very well with the first two.

For the time being, I want to pass over (i) and note that it will turn out that it is only true in a restricted sense that the sceptics suspend judgment on all matters and that everything depends on how one construes this restriction. As for (ii) it may well be that Antigonus of Carystus, virtually a contemporary of Pyrrho's, thought that Pyrrho undertook leading a life without beliefs. Diogenes Laertius, whose report ultimately derives from

Antigonus' biography, writes: "In his life he followed [his scepticism]; he avoided nothing, took no precautions, but faced all risks, carts, precipices, dogs or whatever else it happened to be; he left nothing to the guidance of the senses; but he was . . . saved from harm by his friends who always accompanied him" (DL IX 61). We cannot rule out that Antigonus' remarks, on which this report depends, were intended as a sort of critical caricature of sceptical philosophers. In that case we would have here yet another instance of the standard objection that scepticism and normal life are incompatible. Still, it is clear that Diogenes Laertius himself does not take his source in this way, and so we must, with all due caveats, perhaps suppose that Antigonus did see Pyrrho's life as an attempt at leading a life without beliefs. This interpretation is compatible with his regarding that attempt as a failure; for the comment about Pyrrho's friends suggests that Pyrrho leads his life under false pretenses, that the appearance of living like a serious sceptic is achieved only by relying on the judgments of his friends. Whatever Antigonus' view may have been, it is this passage of Diogenes Laertius' that one will turn to, if one wants to claim that Pyrrho did attempt to live his life without any beliefs, even without beliefs of the sort we rely on in our ordinary, everyday life. However straightforward and simple, non-theoretical and nonphilosophical these beliefs may be, the serious followers of Pyrrho, on this view of scepticism, will seek to manage without them. He will not even think things like, e.g., that he has forgotten his watch or that he must do some shopping.

If our main interest, however, is in the position that later goes under the name of Pyrrhonean scepticism, we need not be especially interested in what Pyrrho actually thought about this matter; and that for at least two reasons:

(A) It is striking that Pyrrho is the only ancient sceptic to whom the doxographers ascribe a life that can easily be regarded as at least an attempt at a life without beliefs. All the other sceptics seem to have led conventional lives; Sextus Empiricus even emphasizes that the sceptical life is, and should be expected to be, a conventional one. It seems clear that the later sceptics all sought a life which—on any ordinary criterion—would count as a satisfactory life. Their lives cannot readily be construed as lives without beliefs or even as attempts at lives without beliefs, rather they seem like lives guided by beliefs, whatever the sceptics may say. It is revealing that Aenesidemus, the philosopher presumably most responsible for Pyrrhonism, seems to have objected to those features of Pyrrho's life we found described by Antigonus of Carystus. According to Aenesidemus, Pyrrho did not act as foolishly as Antigonus had said he did (DL IX 62). An indication of how Pyrrhonists after Aenesidemus viewed Pyrrho's life is provided by Galen (*De subfiguratione empirica* XI, p. 82, 23ff. Deichgräber): Here Pyrrho is described in the way the Pyrrhonists see themselves—in practical life, the Pyrrhonist follows what seems evident to him. That, precisely, is what the Pyrrho of Antigonus' biography had not done; otherwise, he would not have needed his friends to save him from harm. Thus, when later sceptics, both Pyrrhonists and Academics, do recommend a life without beliefs, this surely is not the sort of life that the historical Pyrrho had recommended, but a life that at any rate superficially looked like a life led by someone who was guided by ordinary, everyday beliefs.

(B) I also think that it might very well be the case that Pyrrho's influence on Pyrrhonean scepticism is far less than generally assumed. The ancient doxographers already failed in their attempts to construct a continuous tradition linking Aenesidemus and Sextus with Pyrrho (DL IX 115ff.). Menodotus, a prominent Pyrrhonist himself, pointed out that the tradition was broken after Pyrrho. Since Pyrrho left no writings, later authors had to rely on the testimony of Timon, Pyrrho's student, a testimony of dubious value, as I have tried to show elsewhere (*J. Phil.* 70, 1973; p. 806). How badly matters stood when it came to reconstructing Pyrrho's views is shown by these lines of Diogenes', which are clearly meant to give the sources for reports about Pyrrho: "Pyrrho himself left no writings, but those who knew him, Timon, Aenesidemus, Numenius, Nausiphanes and others like them, did" (DL IX 102). Aenesidemus here seems in all likelihood to be the familiar Pyrrhonist; and if that is so, we cannot conclude, from the "those who knew him," that Numenius is not the well-known Platonist. If that is correct, it is clear just how bad the situation with respect to sources on Pyrrho really is.

Not surprisingly, then, it seems as if later Pyrrhonists were unclear about how their position was related to that of the historical Pyrrho. When Sextus (*PH* I 7) tells us that scepticism is sometimes called 'Pyrrhonean' because Pyrrho seems to have turned to scepticism "more than his predecessors," it is difficult to avoid the impression that Sextus has certain doubts about the position of the historical Pyrrho. When we hear of Theodosius' suggestion (DL IX 70) that the label 'Pyrrhonists' be dropped, since one cannot know what another person is thinking and hence cannot know what Pyrrho had actually intended, we ought not to see this primarily as raising an epistemological worry about other minds; rather, Theodosius seems to want to distance himself from the position of the historical Pyrrho or at least to leave open the question, to what extent was Pyrrho already a Pyrrhonist.

Thus, for these two reasons, it seems of relatively little significance for our question, what Pyrrho himself thought. Even if Pyrrho had really thought that a proper sceptic has no beliefs, this would have few implications for Pyrrhonean scepticism.

Finally (iii), there are whole series of sceptical arguments that purport to show that human action is possible without beliefs, that suspension of judgment does not lead to complete inactivity. Arcesilaus, for example, argued that human action requires nothing more than that things appear to us in a certain way and that we be so constructed that when things do appear to us in a certain way, a drive or instinct leading to action is triggered and that this does not require our also assenting to the appearances (see Plut. *Col. 1122 B–D;* Plu. *Stoic. rep.* 1057 A–B). Put more simply, if not as precisely, the point is just this: suppose someone is, say, hungry and is given his favorite food; why should he need—in addition to his hunger and the impression that he is being given his favorite food—the judgment that, in fact, he is being given his favorite food, to lead him to actually eat?

Given such arguments, one might think that we now have the solution to our problem: the sceptics *do* have an argument which—though we may not accept it—allows us to see why they thought that it is possible to manage without judgments or beliefs even in everyday life. Such a diagnosis of the situation, however, involves overlooking that the sceptic, in this case, would be doing precisely what he usually criticizes the dogmatist for doing: he would be trying to deny what quite obviously is the case, viz., that actions presuppose beliefs, by relying on a theoretical, dogmatic argument which purports to show that action is possible even without assent to appearances, even without judgments. The claim that actions do not presuppose beliefs, especially if based on an argument like the one outlined above, is no less dogmatic than the dogmatic claim that actions do presuppose beliefs. As soon as one sees this, it also becomes clear that the sceptics do not offer these arguments to try to show that we could act without beliefs. That would be pure dogmatism. These arguments are rather offered to counterbalance the weight of the dogmatic arguments which tend to make us believe that it is not possible to act without beliefs (cf. Cic. *Acad.* II 34, 108). We cannot, then, assume, on the basis of such arguments, that the sceptics really did think that life is possible without beliefs, and thus they cannot escape the charge of self-refutation in this way. Indeed, it seems as if in this case, too, the sceptics are simply following their usual strategy of providing equipollent arguments on both sides of every issue.

Closer examination, thus, shows that the considerations which might have led us to defend the sceptic on these grounds—that he supposes, perhaps correctly, that it is possible to manage without beliefs even in everyday life—are, in light of the historical facts, unconvincing. But a sceptical position grounded in this way would itself also be scarcely plausible. Roughly speaking, the claim that it is possible to live without beliefs involves both a theoretical and a practical problem. If we suppose, as it seems we must, that all humans, in the course of their normal development, come to have a large number of beliefs, the practical question is whether or not it is possible, in practice, for a person both to rid himself of these beliefs as well as to prevent himself from acquiring any new ones, and this in such a way that he does not so diminish his capacity for acting that it no longer seems appropriate to speak of human action and a human life. Even if this practical question could be answered affirmatively, it is difficult to see what, besides sheer dogmatism, would lead someone to make use of this possibility. The dogmatist, who has certain views about what real knowledge is and who rejects everything else as mere belief, who believes that everything depends on his beliefs not being merely beliefs and who, like the Stoics, thinks mere beliefs are sinful—such a dogmatist will also believe that he must somehow resist the ordinary way of doing things, of thinking about things, and that he must get rid of his beliefs, once he has been shown that even what he had previously taken for certain knowledge has turned out to be, by his own dogmatic criteria, merely belief. The dilemma—either one must have certain knowledge or one must manage in life without beliefs—is not a dilemma with which the sceptic is confronted; on the contrary, he confronts the dogmatist with it, the dogmatist who rejects our ordinary beliefs and even our ordinary knowledge as 'unscientific' or 'unphilosophical', hence as irresponsible.

It will be objected that it is not dogmatism but experience that leads the sceptic to resist the ordinary way of thinking about things, in particular, the surprising experience that suspending judgment is accompanied by what he had hoped for from right reason, from judging correctly, namely, peace of mind.

Against this, we can say that it is only suspension of judgment understood in a special, qualified sense, alluded to above, that leads the sceptic to his goal. I shall have more to say about this sense later. However, by looking at *PH* I 12 and I 29, we can already see that the sceptic's experience, his discovery, is not that it is entirely possible to live without beliefs but that, if one considers things only on the basis of theory and reflection, one finds that, for every proposition, as much speaks in its favor as against it; thus, one cannot but suspend judgment, because the arguments always end up balancing each other, and, surprisingly, it turns out that it does not matter that one cannot form any judgments in *this* way; one even finds oneself in a wonderful state of calm. It seems to me that we can imagine ourselves in the situation of someone who thinks he has made such a discovery, but it also seems to me that this situation is not at all like that of someone who thinks he has discovered that a life without beliefs is accompanied by peace of mind.

Furthermore, the objection, that it is not dogmatism but his discovery (that a life without beliefs brings peace of mind) that leads the sceptic to give up all of his beliefs, does not solve our problem. For while this objection could perhaps explain why the sceptic leads a life without beliefs, once he has discovered that a life without beliefs is a tranquil one, our problem was seeing what would lead the sceptic to discover this in the first place. For the sceptic to make this discovery, however, he must either bring it about that he is in a state in which he has no beliefs or somehow be put into such a state. What, though, could bring him into such a state, on what grounds could he bring himself into such a state; they could only be dogmatic ones. It is relatively easy, though, to see how someone could find himself more and more able at contriving arguments for and against any position and thus also find it ever harder to reach a decision or make a judgment, and we can see how someone might end up in the sceptic's position without particularly trying to end up in such a position.

Perhaps, someone could, in practice, come to live without beliefs by acting *as if* he had a belief that something was the case in every situation in which he previously would have believed that something was the case? What, though, is he now supposed to do in those cases where, previously, he only would have acted as if he believed that something was the case? Is not the very distinction, between acting as if one believed something was the case and acting because one believes something to be the case, a dogmatic one, with no content, no implications for practice? For reasons of this sort, a sceptical position relying on the claim that it is possible, in practice, to live without beliefs, seems quite unsatisfactory to me; and a sceptical position relying on a *theory* of action which implied that human action does not presuppose beliefs would, of course, be still more unsatisfactory. Thus, for philosophical as well as historical reasons this sort of defense for the sceptic seems unattractive to me.

Fortunately, the problem is solved for us by Sextus Empiricus' own words. In *PH* I 13ff., Sextus explains in what sense the sceptic is not dogmatic. What is not in question, at least if we follow Sextus, is whether the sceptic has no dogmas, no beliefs at all but whether he has no beliefs of a certain sort. Sextus distinguishes between a wider (*koinoteron*) and a narrower sense of 'belief'; and only beliefs in the narrower sense count as dogmatic. Hence, there can be no doubt whatsoever that, according to Sextus, a serious Pyrrhonean sceptic can have beliefs.

What needs to be asked is what sorts of beliefs these are, and how is the fact that the sceptic does have beliefs compatible with the claim that the sceptic suspends judgment about every issue. Those who incline toward an interpretation according to which the sceptic has no beliefs even in everyday life have the following answer. They will say that it is necessary to distinguish between how things are and how they appear. The sceptic will suspend judgment on how things are, and, if he wants to be consistent, he will also have no beliefs on how things are. This, however, by no means rules out that he should have beliefs about how things appear to him.

As a matter of fact, various passages seem to support this view. We find Sextus, for example, saying, "no one, presumably, disputes that the underlying thing appears to be such or such; what is in question is whether the thing is as it appears to be" (*PH* I 22). This second question, whether the thing is as it appears to be, is the one the dogmatists think they have the answer to, while the sceptic suspends judgment. So it seems as if the sceptic has no beliefs about how things are and thus not really any beliefs at all. Of course, one can, if one wants to, say that the sceptic has beliefs about how things appear to him; and it is with reference to these beliefs that Sextus (in *PH* I, 13ff.) speaks as if there were nondogmatic beliefs.

Against this interpretation, I want to maintain that, although there is a sense in which the sceptic has no beliefs about how things are—namely, he has no beliefs about how things *really* are—there is a perfectly good sense in which he does have beliefs about how things are—namely, to the extent that it seems to be the case that things are so or so. Obviously, this distinction needs textual support as well as some clarification. Sextus repeatedly points out that when the sceptic uses expressions of the form '. . . is . . .', these are to be construed as '. . . appears . . .' (*phainetai*—cf. *PH* II 135; 198; 200; *M* XI 19); but '. . . is . . .' is also used in the sense of '. . . is in reality (or, in the nature of things) . . .' (*physei, pros tēn physin, kata tēn physin*—cf. *PH* I 27, 78, 140). This second use of '. . . is . . .', Sextus in one passage at least, seems to gloss as follows: "but if [honey] also *is* sweet, to the extent that this is a question for reason, we [i.e., the sceptics] call into question" (*PH* I 20).

The explanation for this distinction depends, above all, on the following: it is characteristic of the dogmatists that they believe it is possible to go behind the surface phenomena to the essence of things, to the nature of things, to true reality. We believe that the objects around us are colored; in reality, however, they only reflect light of certain wave-lengths that makes them appear colored. The dogmatists further believe that it is reason—if only we would follow it—that can lead us beyond the world of appearances to the world of real being; and thus for them it is a matter of reason, what is to count as real and as true, and what is to count as appearance. It is in the sense of *this* distinction that the sceptic suspends judgment on how things really are. He has discovered by experience that he can reach no decision, if he leaves a question to reason. When all that is at issue, however, is whether something seems to him to be the case, the sceptic too will not deny that something seems to him to be the case. It may well seem to him that something is red, or sweet. What he does suspend judgment on is whether it really, in the nature of things, is red, or sweet. And so, the sceptic will also have beliefs about how things are, not only about how they appear to him. Against this, it will be urged that the sceptic uses "seem" or "appears" (*phainesthai*) in a nonepistemic sense; when he says, "it seems to me that p," this does not mean that he thinks or believes that p is the case, only that things appear as if p were the case. If, for example, we see a partially submerged oar, while it may appear as if the oar were bent, we do not believe that it is. According to this objection, it is just in this nonepistemic sense of "appears" that many things appear to be the case for the sceptic; for he suspends judgment on how things are.

Three things, it seems to me, tell against this objection: (i) the assumption that the sceptics use "appears" only in this nonepistemic sense is based on the false presupposition that it is true, without qualification, that the sceptic suspends judgment about how things are; (ii) the objection relies on an inadequate understanding of the contrast between appearance and reality, between how things seem and how they are; (iii) it ultimately leads to what I take to be a disastrous misunderstanding of the epistemological problem, the misunderstanding that certain mental contents (ideas or representations) are directly accessible and that the problem is only how to get from these representations to knowledge of the things that the representations represent. This division into the inner world of the I with its immediately accessible contents and a problematic outer world which needs to be reconstructed, strikes me as dogmatic and philosophically problematic; certainly this division is not just a matter of common sense; it would require some argument to see things in this way.

(i) It is true only with qualifications that the sceptic suspends judgment on how things are. At *PH* I 215, Sextus distinguishes between the stance of the Pyrrhonists and that of the Cyrenaics with these words: "as for the objects in the external world, we suspend judgment insofar as it is a matter of reason" (*epechomen hoson epi to logo*). Sextus does indeed say that the sceptic suspends judgment on how things are. Yet, it is important to note how he qualifies this claim—insofar as it is a matter of reason. The qualification or restriction is not that the sceptic suspends judgment about how things are but not about how they appear; the restriction, rather, is that the sceptic suspends judgment about how things are in a certain respect. That, however, implies that there is another respect in which the sceptic does not suspend judgment about how things are. Once we have noticed this curious restriction here, we can see that such restrictions, "*hoson epi +* dative," occur again and again in the *Outlines of Pyrrhonism* (e.g., III 65, *hoson epi to philosopho logo,* cf. also II 26; 104; III 6; 13; 29; 65; 81; 135; 167). This construction also occurs in the gloss on the one sense of '. . . is . . .' which we considered above. There we had, "if [honey] also is sweet, to the extent that this is a matter of reason, we call into question" (*PH* I 20). We may, thus, assume that the import of this restriction is that the sceptic suspends judgment on how things really are; but that is not the same as claiming that the sceptic suspends judgment on how things are without any restriction.

Sextus' discussion of the sign, at *PH* II 97ff. and *M*, 141ff., illustrates this nicely. Suppose that the question arises, are there signs, i.e., can anything count as the sign of another thing? The dogmatists, of course, believe that there are signs; they have a theory of signs, and they construct arguments which supposedly show that there are signs. The sceptic will, as usual, produce a whole series of arguments, which purports to show that there are no signs, in order to neutralize the persuasive force of the dogmatists' arguments. With plausible arguments on both sides of the question, an equilibrium is reached; one no longer knows which argument to trust. Sextus proceeds in exactly this way. Yet, despite all of his arguments against the existence of signs, it is clear that Sextus himself thinks that there are signs, namely, the so-called commemorative ones (*PH* II 104; *M* VIII 151–58). Sextus does not say that it only seems as if there were signs, that the sceptic only has the idea of signs but does not think that there actually are any; his point, rather, is that even the sceptic takes certain things as signs of other things, e.g., smoke as a sign of fire. Sextus' discussion of signs, thus, is a good example of how, in a certain sense, the sceptic does suspend judgment about how things are—namely, to the extent that one considers this matter for arguments, for reason—but also of how, despite his suspension of judgment, the sceptic does think that, given how things are, there are signs.

When the sceptic reports that he regards the existence of signs as a phenomenon, that it seems to him that there are signs, this report does not merely indicate that it appears to him that there are signs, though he does not believe there actually are any; rather, this report indicates that it appears to him that there are signs in the sense that he thinks there are signs. How this is supposed to be compatible with the claim that the sceptic does not believe that there are really, in the nature of things (*physei, ontōs alēthōs*), may be a difficult question. But it would be naive to suppose that one cannot make out a meaningful contrast between how things are and how things really are and thus think that someone who has no view about how things really are can only have a view about how things seem (nonepistemically) to him.

(ii) It is necessary, then, to get a clearer understanding of the contrast between appearance and reality, at least sufficiently clear to see how it is possible that someone can really believe something to be the case without believing this is how things are in reality.

If something seems to us to be the case, we can, at least in some cases, come to regard the matter differently, if we are, say, given an explanation of why the thing only appears that way. It is necessary to distinguish between two quite different sorts of cases: (a) it can happen that something no longer seems to be the case. If, for example, it is pointed out that we have not properly seen the thing, that we falsely presupposed this or that, that we inferred something incorrectly etc., we shall no longer think that what seemed to be the case is so. In certain especially interesting cases, an impression that things are thus or thus persistently recurs, despite the fact that we know quite well that things are not as they appear; the illusions of the senses are a good example of this type of case.

For example, I might, when I see an oar partially submerged in water, say that 'it appears bent to me,' where 'appears to me' has the sense that I believe that the oar is bent; if, however, someone explains to me why it only appears bent to me, I shall no longer think that the oar is bent. Nonetheless, the oar still *looks* bent. And thus I can still say that the oar appears to be bent, but now I shall be using 'appears' nonepistemically. (b) It can, however, also happen that, even after we have been given an explanation of why something only appears a certain way and even after we have accepted this explanation, we still think the thing is as it appears to be. Suppose, for example, that a particular wine seems quite sweet to me. Someone might explain, it only seems sweet, because I had eaten something sour just before tasting the wine. If I accept this explanation, I shall no longer think that the wine is sweet; at most, I shall think the wine only seems to be sweet. Yet, someone might also try to provide a quite different explanation. He might say that there is, in reality, no such thing as sweetness, no such thing as sweetness in wine; the wine, rather, has certain chemical properties which, in normal circumstances, make it taste such that we call it sweet. It may even be that I am convinced by an explanation of this sort and come to view how things taste in an entirely new light. Nonetheless, such an explanation might seem rather puzzling, because it is not entirely clear how it is supposed to bear on my claim that the wine is quite sweet. Even if I accept this explanation, the wine will still seem sweet, and I shall still think that it is. Thus, in a sense, it will still be true that it does not merely seem as if the wine is sweet, even if I believe that, in reality, there is no such thing as sweetness.

Cases of the second sort, it seems to me, show that the contrast between how things really are and how they appear nonepistemically is insufficient. If one does not think that something is so and so in the true nature of things, this does not yet mean it only seems as if the thing were so and so. Thus, if the sceptic suspends judgment on how things are in reality, this does not mean that he only has impressions, but no beliefs, about things.

That, in fact, something like this more complex contrast is what is involved here seems clear to me not only from the problem itself but also from the situation of the sceptic. Ancient scepticism is essentially a reac-tion to dogmatism, to the attempt to get behind the phenomena, with the aid of reason, to true reality and, thus, to dissolve the real or apparent contradictions among the phenomena, the contradictions in the world as it appears to us (cf. *PH* I 12). However, it is characteristic of dogmatism that this attempt, to move beyond the phenomena, calls into question the status of the phenomena themselves. Parmenides and Plato are particularly clear examples of this, but, in the last analysis, the same is true of all the other dogmatic philosophers. But in calling into question the status of the phe-nomena, they also call into question the status of our ordinary beliefs and claims, as these are beliefs and claims that reflect how things appear to us. Since, however, the dogmatists, generally speaking, do not deny that the phenomena have at least some objective status, it does not follow that if someone suspends judgment about how things really are, he only has impressions about how things are, and, no beliefs. Plato, for example, ascribes a precarious intermediate status to the objects of belief or *doxa* in the *Republic;* they come between what really is, the objects of reason and knowledge, and what does not exist at all. He does not say that what we ordinarily call 'reality' is nothing but appearance, that our ordinary beliefs and impressions are no better than hallucinations. Though they fail to capture true being and, thus, are not really true, this does not mean that they are simply false in the way that it is simply false that Socrates died in 398. Another example is the role the assumption that, in the case of an ordinary object, for any predicate F, it is never really F, plays in so many interpretations of Plato. Obviously, the import of this assumption is not that for some reason or other water, say, is never heated long enough to be really hot. To put the point rather simply, what is at issue is not whether or not Socrates died in 399, but whether it is appropriate, given the true nature of things, whether it correctly mirrors reality, to speak of Socrates' having died in 399. This question is not at all settled by the fact that it is clear that we ordinarily do say Socrates died in 399. For it might be that, given the true nature of things, it is inappropriate to speak of persons and times. Yet, even if someone believed this, that would not mean that he could not continue to think and say that Socrates died in 399; and there is no reason to suppose that his belief would differ from anyone else's who believes that Socrates died in 399. Thus, there is a perfectly good sense in which someone who suspends judgment about how things really are can have beliefs about how things are.

What is to stop the sceptic from having such beliefs? It is the dogmatists who talk endlessly about the need to go beyond the phenomena, who insist on the need to rely on reason and reason alone, which is also why, at least in medicine, they are called *logikoi*, i.e., rationalists (cf. *M* VIII 156). For they think that reason and reason alone has access to how things really are. It is the dogmatists who believe that it is necessary for us to revise our beliefs, or at least all the important and central ones, in the light of reason. The Stoics even think we ought to give up all beliefs that do not meet the strict criteria of reason and thus are not validated by reason. They, thus, expect us to rid ourselves of all the beliefs we have acquired in ordinary ways, if these should fail to meet the rigorous criteria of reason. Beliefs that do meet these criteria are beliefs about how things are, to the extent that this is a matter of reason, i.e., beliefs about how things really are. The sceptic indeed has no such beliefs; and if he followed the dogmatists' strictures—to accept only those beliefs validated by reason—he would, in fact, have no beliefs about how things are.

Yet why should he accept their strictures? What could lead him to follow only reason? It has been his experience that whenever he tries to rely only on reason, he fails to reach a decision; this past experience could hardly motivate him to follow only reason. We can imagine someone being faced with the following conflict: he has certain beliefs, acquired in some ordinary way which not only cannot be validated by reason but which turn out to conflict with certain insights of reason. If we believe the Eleatics, or the Atomists, or Plato, or Aristotle, or the Stoics, we should expect to be faced with conflicts of this sort rather often. In such a case, we would need to choose whether to follow reason or our ordinary beliefs. The sceptic, however, is not in this situation. Whenever he follows reason seriously and fully, he can form no judgment, hence also no judgment that conflicts with his ordinary beliefs. Thus, he is not even faced with the choice, should he follow only reason (against his ordinary beliefs), at least not in this way.

Since he has not been dissuaded from doing so, the sceptic will continue to rely on how things appear to him, on what seems to him to be the case. He will not think that it only seems as if things were so and so; for that thought presupposes that he believes what the dogmatists believe, namely, that, in reality, things are quite different from the way they seem to be. For him, of course, nothing rules out the possibility that, in reality, things should be exactly as they appear to be. Since he suspends judgment on how things are in reality, he will not think that it merely seems to him that things are thus or thus. If it had been his discovery that, in every instance, it only seems to him that this or that is the case, he would indeed have no beliefs on how things are. When the sceptic, however, speaks of what seems to him to be the case, and when he says that he is only reporting how it appears to him, he cannot be speaking of something which he thinks *only seems* to be the case; and that for the reasons indicated.

Thus, it seems to me that if we properly construe the contrast between how things really are and how they seem to us, it does not follow that the sceptic has no beliefs about how things are just in virtue of his suspending judgment about how they are in reality.

(iii) As a matter of fact, Sextus often does speak as if ideas or impressions (*phantasiai*) were directly accessible and the problem was to determine whether or not to assent to these impressions, that is, whether or not one should think that things are the way our impressions represent them as being. The conventional interpretation holds that the sceptic does indeed have such impressions but that he consistently refuses to assent to them and, hence, has no beliefs about how things are.

The question, though, is does Sextus Empiricus speak this way because this is how *he* sees the problem of knowledge or because he needs to tailor his argument to his dogmatic opponents' way of regarding matters. After all, his goal is to get the dogmatist to suspend judgment on the basis of his own principles and theories. This much at least is clear: it is the dogmatists, especially the Stoics, who assume that certain impressions arise in us, impressions which we voluntarily either do or do not assent to, which we—

if we proceed responsibly—need to judge by a criterion of truth, before we assent to them and form a judgment. Such a view seems wholly dogmatic, because it presupposes a theory about what beliefs actually are, how they arise and how they *ought* to arise. I very much doubt that Sextus shares the view that our beliefs are formed thus: certain impressions arise in us, and, by some means or other, we decide whether or not to assent to them. At any rate, it is conspicuous that Sextus himself, whenever he speaks of the circumstances in which the sceptic, too, will give his assent, avoids speaking as if the sceptic were assenting to an impression. The explanation for this does not seem to be Arcesilaus' criticism of this way of talking (cf. *M* VII 154) but, rather, something deeper. Moreover, the sceptic has no criterion, on the basis of which he could decide whether or not to assent to an impression. In fact, certain things just seem to him to be the case; the sceptic has no theory on how or why this is so. If, however, someone insists on using dogmatic terminology, he can say that things affect the sceptic in such a way that he comes to assent to something (cf. *PH* I 19; 113, 193). Yet, it is hardly plausible that Sextus, when he speaks this way, means to commit himself to the view that there are mental acts of assenting which, together with the appropriate impressions, constitute having beliefs and forming judgments. For these reasons, I am inclined to believe that the sceptic has beliefs not only about how things seem to him but also about how they are, and to believe that things appear to him to be the case, in the sense that he believes they are the case without, of course, believing this is the way they are in reality, this is the way they are insofar as it is a matter for reason to determine what is true and what is real.

If Sextus believes that a sceptic can have beliefs about how things are, we would expect to be able to see this in the passage already mentioned, where Sextus explains in what sense the sceptic can have beliefs (*dogmata*). Conversely, if it really were true that the sceptic can only have beliefs about how things seem to him, this too we should be able to see from this passage. At any rate, it strikes me as methodologically sound to base one's interpretation of an author's views primarily on those passages where he explicitly sets them out and not rest content with indirect indications of what they might be. Since Sextus Empiricus explicitly considers our question in *PH* I 13, let us turn to this passage: "We say that the sceptic does not dogmatize, not in the sense of 'belief' (dogma) in which some say, speaking quite generally, a belief consists in consenting to a thing (*eudokein tini pragmati*); for the sceptic does assent to such affections which necessarily result when things appear to him in certain ways; he would not, for example, when he is hot or cold, say, 'I believe I am not hot (cold)'; We rather say, he does not dogmatize, in the sense of 'belief', in which some say a belief consists in assenting to one of the nonevident things which the sciences have as their objects of inquiry; for the Pyrrhonean assents to nothing nonevident."

The expression on which a lot depends here is, "consenting to something." *Eudokein*, to judge from its frequent occurrence in papyri, is quite a common word, especially in legal contexts. It also occurs frequently in Hellenistic literature, e.g., in Polybius. On the other hand, it hardly appears at all in philosophical texts; as a philosophical term, it occurs nowhere else. Thus, it has no philosophical or technical meaning, no philosophical associations and is connected with no special philosophical claims; presumably, it is exactly this fact that leads Sextus to choose the word. *Eudokein* and *eudokeisthai* are used in the sense of 'be content with', 'assent to', 'agree', 'consent to', 'recognize', 'accept', or 'suppose'. The *Suida* has, s.v. *eudokein*, the following entry: "*synkatatithesthai. 'ho de ephē eudokein tois legomenois, ei laboi pisteis,' anti tou areskesthai.*" First we are given a synonym, then a quote from Polybius, finally a gloss on his use of the term. In the *Etymologicum Magnum* (ed. Gaisford), there is an entry for *eudokein*, which is of no interest for us here, but also a gloss on *eudokoumenos*, which we encounter again in the *Lexeis rhētorikai* (*Anecdota Graeca Bekkeri*, v. I, p. 260); it runs as follows: "*ho synkatatithemenos kai mē antilegōn.*" This gloss seems to fit in very well with our Sextus passage, because its two parts seem to correspond to the two parts of Sextus' explanation of how the sceptic consents to something: (a) the sceptic assents to something (*synkatatithetai*), (b) he does not oppose it and does not protest.

Precisely which meaning of *eudokein*, however, should we ascribe to Sextus here? The following sentence from Polybius (I, 8, 4) provides a good example of the ordinary use of *eudokein: hōste . . . pantas . . . eudokēsai stratēgon hauton hyparchein Hierōna.* Out of context, this sentence could mean any number of things—they decided, voted, decreed, agreed, that Hiero was to be their *stratēgos*, they all thought it would be a good thing, would be proper, if Hiero would be their *stratēgos*. In fact, the sentence means that they accepted the fact that Hiero was to be their *stratēgos*, they recognized (in the legal sense) that Hiero was their *stratēgos*.

Obviously, in our passage, beliefs, not decisions, are being discussed. Therefore, our task is to find an interpretation on which *eudokein* has its usual meaning even though it is beliefs which are being talked about.

It seems as if the following interpretation would satisfy this condition: what the sceptic literally accepts, what he is content with, what he has no objection to is whatever seems to him to be the case, whatever seems evident to him. He accepts the judgment of *phantasia;* at least he raises no objection against its verdict; if it says things are thus or thus, he does not challenge this. The gloss and Sextus' explanation (*hoion oun an* . . . ) do indeed suggest that the principle, that one consents if one does not object, is at work here. Such an interpretation fits in well with our observations on the question whether Sextus accepts the dogmatists' views about the origin of beliefs. The dogmatists see assent as a voluntary act, a judgment about the impression which presents itself to us; it is only this judgment that leads to a belief. Sextus, to judge by the passage at hand, sees things differently: something which can count as a belief, a judgment, arises in us when we do not object and consequently consent. In the case of those illusions of the senses familiar to us, we do object; otherwise we would falsely believe that the oar was bent. That what the sceptic does not object to is what seems evident to him, what seems to him to be the case, is clear from the next bit of our passage; for there Sextus says that the sceptic refuses to assent to anything nonevident. If he does not refuse to assent to something, it will be a phenomenon, something evident, something that seems to him to be the case.

Why is the sceptic content with what seems to him to be the case; why does he raise no objection? If he were a dogmatist, he certainly would not be content; the dogmatist is so concerned that things might, in reality, be quite different, that he does not accept the verdict of *phantasia;* instead, he relies on reason in order to find out how things really are (cf. *PH* I 12). He is also not disturbed by the fact that his reason, in its reckless haste, contradicts the phenomena (cf. *PH* I 20). The sceptic, on the other hand, has learned from experience, that reason, if he tries to follow it seriously and fully, gets him no further and, thus that, he must rest content with how things appear (cf. *PH* I 12). It may be objected that sceptics will also argue against what seems evident to them, since they argue against everything; but Sextus himself explains that the sceptic only argues against phenomena for dialectical reasons (*PH* I 20).

In the second part of our passage, Sextus tells us the sense in which the sceptic has no beliefs. The relevant sense of 'belief' seems surprisingly narrow at first, especially if one assumes that the sceptic has no beliefs about how things are. Only those beliefs will count as dogmatic which involve an assumption or claim about one of the nonevident objects of scientific inquiry. Sextus clearly has the theorems of philosophers and scientists in mind, theorems which they attempt to establish in their efforts to go beyond the phenomena and what is evident in order to get a grip on true reality. These are the doctrines which serve to characterize the various dogmatic schools and allow us to distinguish among them. Menodotus apparently has the same sense of belief in mind when he says that all of Asclepiades' beliefs are false (*omnia eius dogmata esse falsa*—Galen *De subf. emp.* 84, 21–22 D). If Sextus had only such typical school doctrines in mind here, it would be clear that the sceptic could have all sorts of beliefs about how things are. For our ordinary, everyday beliefs are, in general, not theoretical doctrines, not assumptions that are part of any science. The sceptic would thus be free to have such 'unscientific' beliefs. Actually, however, matters are presumably more complicated. Since the sceptic suspends judgment—either in a restricted or in an unrestricted sense—on every matter, even those things that are evident to him must, in a certain respect, be nonevident. Presumably, we need to understand this as follows: everything, if considered only as an object for reason, can be called into question; every question can be regarded as a question to be answered by reason, a question requiring a theoretical answer derived from first principles which are immediately evident to reason. Nothing, looked at in this way, will be evident to the sceptic, not even the most lowly, ordinary belief. Any belief, whatever its content may be, can be a dogmatic belief; conversely, every belief can be an undogmatic one. Thus, it is not the content of theoretical views (though, as we shall see, content is not entirely irrelevant) that makes them dogmatic views; it is, rather, the attitude of the dogmatist who believes his rationalist science actually answers questions, actually gives him good reasons for believing his theoretical doctrines. Sextus probably does have primarily the doctrines of the dogmatic schools in mind here, but it would presumably be a mistake to construe the notion of dogmatic belief so narrowly that it could not, in principle, apply to any belief, regardless of content.

What then, does this passage tell us about our question? It seems to me that the text does not even so much as suggest that the sceptic can have beliefs but only ones about how things seem to him not ones about how things are. As far as the second part of our passage is concerned, it says only that the sceptic may not have beliefs of a certain kind, viz., philosophical or scientific ones which depend on reasoned grounds (here, of course, he is presupposing a dogmatic notion of knowledge and science; if there can be such a thing as sceptical science remains to be seen). Whichever way we choose to interpret the text, there will be a large number of beliefs about things which are not dogmatic beliefs. As far as the first part of our passage is concerned, here too the claim is not that the beliefs which the sceptic may have are only ones about his own impressions. On the contrary, the text says, at least on the interpretation suggested, that the sceptic will be content with what seems to him to be the case; surely, that will include a large number of observations about the world around him.

Whoever wants to find the claim, that the sceptic only accepts such beliefs as are about his own impressions, in this passage, will refer to two details: (a) Sextus says that the sceptic assents to certain affections (*pathe*); (b) the example he provides seems—if translated in the usual way—to show that the sceptic will not deny that he feels so or so, if that is how he does feel. As for (a), we need to get clearer about what Sextus means by affections, when he says the sceptic assents to them. There are two main possibilities (though it is not clear that, from a sceptical perspective, they do not collapse into one): (1) Referring to, say, *PH* I 22, we could say Sextus means to talk of impressions (*phantasiai*) when he speaks of affections here. In that case, Sextus would be using only a slight variant of the dogmatists' way of speaking; the dogmatists talk as if (and Arcesilaus criticizes them for this—cf. *M* VII 154) what we assent to is an impression, a way of talking which, as we have noted, Sextus seems to take pains to avoid. These impressions, however, are impressions of things which appear thus or thus to us; and assenting to them is assuming that things are the way they appear to be. (2) Sextus might, when talking of affections, be referring to the disposition to be affected by things in a certain way, whether one wants to be so affected or not. And assenting to these affections would consist in acquiescing: that it is *this* that seems to be the case, this and nothing else, and *that* it seems to be the case. Neither (1) nor (2), however, gives us any reason to think that the belief will only be about the sceptic's own impressions. In any event, "assenting to such impressions" cannot mean "assenting to the claim that one is affected in this way, that one has such impressions." Yet, such a meaning is required, if the first detail is to bear on the issue at hand.

So, only the example remains. A precise analysis of the example is difficult for both linguistic and intrinsic reasons. For example, how exactly is "I am hot" to be understood; how is "*thermainesthai*" to be translated—'to be heated' or perhaps 'to feel hot'? Fabricius, in his revision of Henricus Stephanus' translation, opts for the first, literal meaning; Bury and Hossenfelder opt for the second one. It is by no means clear if the word can even have this second meaning. It can mean 'having a fever'; and the dictionary (LSJ) refers to at least one passage (Plato *Theaet.* 186 D) where it unquestionably means 'feel heat' or 'sense heat', a meaning we perhaps also find in one place in Sextus (*PH* II 56). If we followed ordinary usage, we would be inclined to think that here as well "*thermainesthai*" is to be translated by 'be heated', especially since this seems to conform to Sextus' usual usage. The context certainly provides no reason not to translate it so; one will, thus, translate it differently only under the influence of a preconceived notion of what Sextus' position is.

Nevertheless, let us suppose that "*thermainesthai*" does refer here to the subjective feeling, to sensation. In that case, the expression "*dokō mē thermainesthai*" ('I do not think I am feeling any warmth') creates difficulties. Now the translation presumably must read, when the sceptic feels warmth he will not say, 'I do not think I am feeling any warmth'. Presumably now the "*thermainomenos*," in the previous line, refers to the affection of the sceptic, the affection which he does not refuse to assent to by objecting to it. If the sceptic, however, feels or notices warmth, the objection should not be, "I do not think I am feeling warmth," but it should rather be, "I do not think that there is any warmth," or, "it seems to me that it is not warm." For, as we have just seen, assenting to an affection does not consist in assuming that it exists. What the sceptic does not deny, when he senses warmth, is that something is warm. Perhaps, however, we should still assume that *thermainomai* can mean 'I am hot' or 'I feel hot'. One passage in Sextus (*M* I 147) shows that the transition to this meaning would be easy. In that case, we could say that the affection consists in the impression that one is feeling hot; and the sceptic will not go against this impression by saying, 'I do not think that I am feeling hot'. Perhaps nothing rules out this interpretation. Yet, it is worth considering that (1) it assumes a very strange meaning for *thermainesthai*, (2) the text does not suggest this meaning, and (3) even if translated this way, the passage still will not yield the intended interpretation. Sextus is interested in providing an especially clear example of something that is evident even to the sceptic. If Sextus chooses the example of feeling hot, this by no means implies that only his own impressions will be evident to the sceptic; rather, it is just an exceptionally clear example of the sort of thing that could be evident to someone.

In summary, we can say that the passage, in which Sextus explicitly discusses what sorts of beliefs the sceptic can have without being dogmatic, not only does not come out and say, but does not even suggest, that the sceptic can have beliefs only about his own impressions, only about how things seem to him.

It might be objected that what, on our interpretation, Sextus is prepared to call '*dogmata*' are not even beliefs. We might, for example, think that the mere feeling that something is the case is not to be regarded as a belief just because we do not object to this feeling or impression. It may very well be the case that the sceptic's beliefs do not satisfy some specific, dogmatic definition of 'belief.' If, however, we stay with the ordinary use of verbs like 'believe', 'think', or 'suppose' (or the ordinary use of "*dokein*"), it is clear that the conditions for employing these verbs are so weak that the sceptic's beliefs will satisfy them without any difficulty. If someone steps into the house, and we ask him if it is still raining outside, and he, without hesitating, answers that it is, we would regard this as an expression of his belief that it is still raining. One would need to have a dogmatic view about what is to count as a belief to be prepared to deny this. There is no reason to suppose that the sceptic, if asked such a question, would not answer either yes or no; and there is no reason to suppose that the sceptic would mean anything different by his answer than anyone else (cf. also Cicero *Acad.* II 104).

It is true that the sceptic does not believe that it is *really* still raining. His answer is not grounded in some insight into the true nature of things, an insight such that reason could not but give the answer it does. For reason throws up an unlimited number of possibilities about how it might, after all, be the case that it is no longer raining, without itself being able, as the sceptic has discovered all too often, to eliminate these possibilities. His answer, rather, tells us only what seems to him to be the case; if we ask *him*, that is how it strikes him. In this respect, however, his answer does not differ from that of the man on the street. He, too, only reports his impressions and does not also think that things *really* are the way he takes them to be, the way they appear to him.

How then does the sceptic differ from the man on the street? He differs, it seems to me, in two respects: (i) presumably the average person is quite dogmatic about some of his views, especially moral or ethical ones. As far as scientific speculation is concerned, he may be quite content to leave that to others, but when moral or political questions are at stake, he will tend to claim that he does have some deeper insight, even if his experience seems to tell against it, he has views about what is really good or really bad (cf. *PH* I 27; 30). (ii) In contrast to the man on the street, the sceptic is acutely aware of the fact that in all sorts of ways things might, in reality, be quite different from how they appear to be. He takes the phenomena as they come, but he knows better than anyone else that nothing rules out the possibility that things could really be radically different.

Does the sceptic differ from other people in regard to what he believes or thinks? We might think that the sceptic only believes what is evident to him, what is a phenomenon, and that only those things are evident to him which are accessible through observation and experience; and so we might go on to think that the sceptic will refuse to believe anything that is not accessible through observation. Any interpretation along these lines, however, seems false to me. I shall leave aside the fact that experience is extraordinarily complicated and that perception and observation, in the ordinary sense, play a comparatively subordinate role in experience. The sceptic simply has no general answer to the question, 'What is evident?'. There are things that are evident to him, and he could list any number of them. There is no reason, however, why the same things should be evident to other people, or to most people, much less to all people; there is also no reason to suppose that only things which can be perceived or observed should be evident to the sceptic. The text of Sextus Empiricus shows that he believes many things are the case which cannot be observed. Even if it should turn out that all the things that seem evident to a sceptic are also things that can be observed, this could not be because the sceptic only considers things that can be observed as true. For if he thought that, he would be, just like the dogmatists, using a criterion to distinguish between true and false impressions. But the sceptic does not rely on any criterion for his beliefs.

This, of course, does not mean that his scepticism will have no influence on the content of his beliefs. There are, for example, large numbers of views which one in all likelihood would not have unless one relied on reason dogmatically, unless one thought one had arguments which justified these views. It is not very likely that someone would think that there is no motion or no change without also thinking he had some special insight and some good reason for thinking this. Not very likely, but not impossible. For we can imagine someone who has been raised by Stoics and who thus has the Stoic concept of God. As a sceptic, he no longer believes that the Stoic proofs of God's existence entail their conclusion; since, however, his belief was not induced by these arguments, nothing about his belief need change even when the arguments no longer carry conviction. On the whole, though, the sceptic will mostly believe what experience suggests to him.

What fundamentally distinguishes the sceptic from other people are not the beliefs he has but his attitude toward them. He no longer has the more or less naive and partially dogmatic attitude of the 'ordinary' man; his relation to his beliefs is permeated by the awareness that things are quite possibly different in reality, but this possibility no longer worries him. This distinguishes him from the dogmatist who is so worried by the question, how are things in reality, that he succumbs to the illusion that reason could guarantee the truth of his beliefs, could give him the knowledge which would be secure because of his awareness that things could not, in reality, be different from the way reason says they are. This dogmatic craving for the security of true belief as a necessary, perhaps even a sufficient condition for the tranquility and healing of the soul strikes the sceptic as, at best, futile, perhaps even pathological and harmful. As the passage quoted at the end of this paper shows, the sceptics were not alone in this view; but it was a view that quickly lost ground during the second and third centuries. We know of only one successor of Sextus in the third century, Saturninus (DL IX 116). The temptation had become too great: if mere reason could not lead us to the truth we need for our salvation and beatitude, it would require cleansed, purified, and illuminated reason, perhaps even reason in the light of some revelation; but whatever it takes, we must have the real truth if our lives are not to fail.

These are the introductory sentences to Hero's treatise on artillery: "The largest and most important part of philosophical activity is that which is devoted to peace of mind. Those who want to attain wisdom have carried out and, indeed, carry out to this very day a large number of investigations concerned with peace of mind. In fact, I believe that theoretical inquiry about this will never end. In the meantime, however, mechanics has progressed beyond the theoretical study of peace of mind, and it has taught all men, how, with the help of part of it—a very small part indeed—to live with peace of mind, I mean the part concerned with artillery." (Hero's *Belopoiika* ed. by H. Diels and E. Schramm; Abh. Preuss. Akad. d. Wiss., Berlin, 1918, p. 5.). The sceptic saw his task as, on the one hand, not giving in to the temptation to expect more from reason and philosophical thinking than these can provide without, on the other hand, coming to hold reason in contempt.[1]

1. With this paper, compare Myles Burnyeat's "Can the Sceptic Live His Scepticism" (= chap. 2), in: *Doubt and Dogmatism* ed. M. Schofield et al., (Oxford, 1980).

# 2

# Can the Sceptic Live His Scepticism?

## Myles Burnyeat

### Hume's Challenge

A Stoic or Epicurean displays principles, which may not only be durable, but which have an effect on conduct and behaviour. But a Pyrrhonian cannot expect that his philosophy will have any constant influence on the mind: or if it had, that its influence would be beneficial to society. On the contrary, he must acknowledge, if he will acknowledge anything, that all human life must perish, were his principles universally and steadily to prevail. All discourse, all action would immediately cease; and men remain in a total lethargy, till the necessities of nature, unsatisfied, put an end to their miserable existence. It is true; so fatal an event is very little to be dreaded. Nature is always too strong for principle. And though a Pyrrhonian may throw himself or others into a momentary amazement and confusion by his profound reasonings; the first and most trivial event in life will put to flight all his doubts and scruples, and leave him the same, in every point of action and speculation, with the philosophers of every other sect, or with those who never concerned themselves in any philosophical researches. When he awakes from his dream, he will be the first to join in the laugh against himself, and to confess, that all his objections are mere amusement, and can have no other tendency than to show the whimsical condition of mankind, who must act and reason and believe; though they are not able, by their most diligent enquiry, to satisfy themselves concerning the foundation of these operations, or to remove the objections, which may be raised against them (David Hume, *An Enquiry Concerning Human Understanding*, § XII, 128).[1]

---

1. Cited from the third edition of Selby-Bigge's edition, with text revised by P. H. Nidditch (Oxford, 1975). One of Nidditch's revisions is restoring the word 'only' to the first sentence of the quoted passage.

I begin with Hume, both in deference to the vital influence of Pyrrhonian scepticism on modern thought, following the rediscovery and publication of the works of Sextus Empiricus in the sixteenth century,[2] and because Hume is so clear on the philosophical issues I wish to discuss in connection with Sextus Empiricus. Pyrrhonism is the only serious attempt in Western thought to carry scepticism to its furthest limits and to live by the result, and the question whether this is possible, or even notionally coherent, was keenly disputed in ancient times and had been a major focus of renewed debate for some two hundred years before Hume wrote. My purpose is to return to those old controversies from the perspective of a modern scholarly understanding of Sextus Empiricus.

The background to the passage I have quoted is Hume's well-known contention that our nature constrains us to make inferences and to hold beliefs which cannot be rationally defended against sceptical objections. He has particularly in mind the propensity for belief in external bodies and for causal inference, but not only these. And he has a particular purpose in showing them to be rationally indefensible. Since exposure to the sceptical objections does not stop us indulging in belief and inference, it does not appear that we make the inferences and hold the beliefs on the strength of the reasons whose inadequacy is shown up by the sceptical arguments; for when a belief or a practice is genuinely based on reasons, it is given up if those reasons are invalidated. Since we do not give up the inferences and the beliefs in the face of overwhelming sceptical objections, there must be other factors at work in our nature than reason—notably custom and imagination—and it is to these, rather than to man's much-vaunted rationality, that the beliefs and the inferences are due.[3] In the passage quoted Hume's claim is a double one: first, that what the sceptic invalidates when his arguments are successful, and hence what he would take from us if such arguments could have a 'constant influence on the mind', is nothing less than reason and belief; second, that what makes it

2. The exciting story of this influence has been pursued through the ins and outs of religious and philosophical controversy in a series of studies by Richard H. Popkin. See, in particular, *The History of Scepticism, from Erasmus to Descartes* (revised edn., New York, Evanston and London, 1968); 'David Hume: His Pyrrhonism and His Critique of Pyrrhonism', *Philosophical Quarterly I* (1951), 385–407; 'David Hume and the Pyrrhonian Controversy', *Review of Metaphysics* 6 (1952/3), 65–81.

3. On the role and importance of this argument within Hume's general programme for a naturalistic science of man, see Barry Stroud, *Hume* (London, Henley, and Boston, 1977), esp. chap. 1.

impossible to sustain a radical scepticism in the ordinary business of life is that 'mankind . . . must act and reason and believe'. A brief comment on each of these claims in turn will give us a philosophical context in which to consider what Sextus Empiricus has to say in defence and advocacy of his Pyrrhonist ideal.

All too often in contemporary discussion the target of the sceptic is taken to be knowledge rather than belief. Sceptical arguments are used to raise questions about the adequacy of the grounds on which we ordinarily claim to know about the external world, about other minds, and so on, but in truth there are few interesting problems got at by this means which are not problems for reasonable belief as well as for knowledge. It is not much of an oversimplification to say that the more serious the inadequacy exposed in the grounds for a knowledge-claim, the less reasonable it becomes to base belief on such grounds. To take a well-worn, traditional example, if the evidence of our senses is really shown to be unreliable and the inferences we ordinarily base on this evidence are unwarranted, the correct moral to draw is not merely that we should not claim to know things on these grounds but that we should not believe them either. Further, in the normal case, that which we think we should not believe we do not believe: it takes rather special circumstances to make intelligible the idea that a man could main-tain a belief in the face of a clear realization that it is unfounded. If scepticism is convincing, we ought to be convinced, and that ought to have a radical effect on the structure of our thought.

It is very clear that Hume appreciated this. He presses the Pyrrhonist not on the matter of knowledge-claims, which are easily given up, but on the question whether he can stop holding the beliefs which his arguments show to be unreasonable. Sextus appreciated the point also. The objection that a man cannot live without belief was familiar, indeed much older than the Pyrrhonist movement, since it goes right back to the time when Arcesilaus in the Academy first urged *epochē* about everything.[4] Accordingly, Sextus

4. Witness the title of the polemical tract by Arcesilaus' contemporary, the Epicurean Colotes, 'On the fact that the doctrines of the other philosophers make it impossible to live' (Plu. *Col.* 1107 d, 1108 d). The section dealing with Arcesilaus borrowed the Stoic argument that total *epochē* must result in total inaction (ibid. 1122 ab)—essentially, Hume's charge of total lethargy. For the controversy around this issue in the period of Academic scepticism, see the references and discussion in Striker 1980. Subsequently, the Pyrrhonist *epochē* encountered similar criticism: (1) Aristocles *apud* Eus. *PE* XIV 18, 23–4 argues that judgement, hence belief, is inseparably bound up with the use of the senses and other mental faculties; (2)

defends exactly the proposition Hume challenged the Pyrrhonist to defend, the proposition that he should, can, and does give up his beliefs in response to the sceptical arguments; and out of this continuing resignation of belief he proposes to make a way of life. Likewise with the Pyrrhonist's abandonment of reason: that too, according to Sextus, is not only desirable but practicable, subject to the complication that the abandonment of reason is itself the result of argument, i.e. of the exercise of reason. Consequently— and here I come to my second point of comment—Hume has no right to assume without argument that it is impossible to live without reason and belief. No doubt it seems an obvious impossibility, but Sextus claims otherwise, and he purports to describe a life which would substantiate his claim. That description ought to be examined in detail before we concede Hume's dogmatic claim that the Pyrrhonist cannot live his scepticism.[5] We ought to try to discover what the life without belief is really meant to be.

## Belief, Truth, and Real Existence

We may begin, as the sceptic himself begins, with the arguments. *Skepsis* means enquiry, examination, and Pyrrhonian scepticism is in the first instance a highly developed practice of argumentative enquiry, formalized according to a number of modes or patterns of argument. The Ten Modes of Aenesidemus (*PH* I 36 ff., DL IX 79 ff.) and the Five of Agrippa (*PH* I 164–77, DL IX 88–9) are the most conspicuous of the patterns, but there are others besides, all of which recur with quite remarkable regularity on page after page of the sceptic literature, and always with the same result: *epochē*, suspension of judgement and belief. These patterns of argument, with this outcome, constitute the essence of scepticism (*skepsis*, enquiry) as that is defined by Sextus Empiricus in the *Outlines of Pyrrhonism;* it is, he states, 'a capacity for bringing into opposition, in any way whatever, things that appear and things that are thought, so that, owing to the equal strength of the opposed items and rival claims, we come first to suspend

---

Galen, *De dignosc. puls.* VIII 781, 16–783, 5 K = Deichgräber, K. *Die griechische Empirikerschule* (Berlin, 1930), frag. 74, p. 133, 19–p. 134, 6, asks scoffingly whether the Pyrrhonist expects us to stay in bed when the sun is up for lack of certainty about whether it is day or night, or to sit on board our ship when everyone else is disembarking, wondering whether what appears to be land really is land; (3) Sextus has the lethargy criticism in view at *M* XI 162–3.

5. I call it dogmatic because Hume offers no argument to support his claim against the alternative, Pyrrhonist account of life and action, available in Sextus or in modern writers like Montaigne.

judgement and after that to *ataraxia* (tranquillity, freedom from disturbance)' (*PH* I 8; cp. 31–4). The definition delineates a journey which the
sceptic makes over and over again from an opposition or conflict of opinions
to *epochē* and *ataraxia*.

The journey begins when he is investigating some question or field of
enquiry and finds that opinions conflict as to where the truth lies. The hope
of the investigation, at least in the early stages of his quest for enlightenment, is that he will attain *ataraxia* if only he can discover the rights and
wrongs of the matter and give his assent to the truth (*PH* I 12, 26–9, *M* I 6).
His difficulty is that, as sceptics through the ages have always found, in any
matter things appear differently to different people according to one or
another of a variety of circumstances, all catalogued in great detail by the
Ten Modes of Aenesidemus. We are to understand, and sometimes it is
explicitly stated (e.g. *M* VII 392, VIII 18, IX 192, XI 74), that conflicting
appearances cannot be equally true, equally real. Hence he needs a criterion
of truth, to determine which he should accept. But the sceptic then argues,
often at some length, that there is no intellectually satisfactory criterion we
can trust and use—this is the real backbone of the discussion, corresponding to a modern sceptic's attempt to show we have no adequate way of telling
when things really are as they appear to be, and hence no adequate insur-
ance against mistaken judgements. Assuming the point proved, the sceptic
is left with the conflicting appearances and the conflicting opinions based
upon them, unable to find any reason for preferring one to another and
therefore bound to treat all as of equal strength and equally worthy (or
unworthy) of acceptance. But he cannot accept them all, because they
conflict. Hence, if he can neither accept them all (because they conflict) nor
make a choice between them (for lack of a criterion), he cannot accept any.
That is the standard outcome of the sceptic discovery of the equal strength
(*isostheneia*) of opposed assertions. So far as truth is concerned, we must
suspend judgement. And when the sceptic does suspend judgement, *ataraxia* follows—the tranquillity he sought comes to him, as if by chance,
once he stops actively trying to get it; just as the painter Apelles only
achieved the effect of a horse's foam when he gave up and flung his sponge
at the painting (*PH* I 26–9).

All this is compressed into Sextus' definition of scepticism. The sequence
is: conflict—undecidability—equal strength—*epochē*, and finally *ataraxia*.
The arguments bring about *epochē*, suspension of judgement and belief,
and this, it seems, effects a fundamental change in the character of a man's
thinking and thereby in his practical life. Henceforth he lives *adoxastōs*,
without belief, enjoying, in consequence, that tranquillity of mind (*ataraxia*,

freedom from disturbance) which is the sceptic spelling of happiness (*eudaimonia*).[6] But note: the conflict of opinions is inconsistency, the impossibility of being true together (cf. *M* VII 392); the undecidability of the conflict is the impossibility of deciding which opinion is true; the equal strength of conflicting opinions means they are all equally worthy (or unworthy) of acceptance as true; *epochē* is a state in which one refrains from affirming or denying that any one of them is true; even *ataraxia* is among other things a matter of not worrying about truth and falsity any more. All these notions depend on the concept of truth; no stage of the sequence would make sense without it. And it is a fact of central importance that truth, in the sceptic's vocabulary, is closely tied to real existence as contrasted with appearance.[7]

When the sceptic doubts that anything is true (*PH* II 88 ff., *M* VIII 17 ff.), he has exclusively in view claims as to real existence. Statements which merely record how things appear are not in question—they are not called true or false—only statements which say that things are thus and so in reality. In the controversy between the sceptic and the dogmatists over whether any truth exists at all, the issue is whether any proposition or class of propositions can be accepted as true of a real objective world as distinct from mere appearance. For 'true' in these discussions means 'true of a real objective world'; the true, if there is such a thing, is what conforms with the real, an association traditional to the word *alēthēs* since the earliest period of Greek philosophy (cf. *M* XI 221).[8]

Now clearly, if truth is restricted to matters pertaining to real existence, as contrasted with appearance, the same will apply right back along the sequence we traced out a moment ago. The notions involved, consistency and conflict, undecidability, *isostheneia*, *epochē*, *ataraxia*, since they are

6. The claim that sceptic *ataraxia* alone is *eudaimonia* is argued at length in *M* XI 110–167.

7. Cf. Stough 1969, 142 ff.

8. If the modern reader finds this an arbitrary terminological narrowing, on the grounds that if I say how things appear to me my statement ought to count as true if, and only if, things really do appear as I say they do (cf. Stough 1969, loc. cit.), the answer is that his objection, though natural, is anachronistic. The idea that truth can be attained without going outside subjective experience was not always the philosophical commonplace it has come to be. It was Descartes who made it so, who (in the second *Meditation*) laid the basis for our broader use of the predicates 'true' and 'false' whereby they can apply to statements of appearance without reference to real existence. See Burnyeat 1982.

defined in terms of truth, will all relate, via truth, to real existence rather than appearance. In particular, if *epochē* is suspending belief about real existence as contrasted with appearance, that will amount to suspending all belief, since belief is the accepting of something as true. There can be no question of belief about appearance, as opposed to real existence, if statements recording how things appear cannot be described as true or false, only statements making claims as to how they really are.

This result is obviously of the first importance for understanding the sceptic's enterprise and his ideal of a life without belief. Sextus defines 'dogma'—and, of course, the Greek word *dogma* originally means simply 'belief' (cf. Pl. *Rep.* 538 c, *Tht.* 158 d)—as assent to something non-evident, that is, to something not given in appearance (*PH* I 16).[9] Similarly, to dogmatize, as Sextus explains the term, is what someone does who posits the real existence of something (*hōs huparchon tithetai*, *PH* I 14, 15, from a context where it has been acknowledged that not everyone would use the word in this restricted sense).[10] Assent is the genus; opinion, or belief, is that species of it which concerns matters of real existence as contrasted with appearance. The dogmatists, the endless variety of whose opinions concerning real existence provides the sceptic with both his weapons and his targets, are simply the believers; to the extent that it is justified to read in the modern connotation of 'dogmatist', viz. person with an obstinate and unreasonable attachment to his opinions, this belongs not to the core meaning of the Greek term but to the sceptic's argued claim, to which we

9. The notion of that which is evident (δῆλον, πρόδηλον, ἐναργές) is a dog-matist's notion in the first instance. Things evident are things which come to our knowledge of themselves (*PH* II 97, *M* VIII 144), which are grasped from themselves (*PH* II 99), which immediately present themselves to sense and intellect (*M* VIII 141), which require no other thing to announce them (*M* VIII 149), i.e. which are such that we have immediate non-inferential knowledge of them, directly from the impression (*M* VIII 316). Examples: it is day, I am conversing (*M* VIII 144), this is a man (*M* VIII 316). Sextus declares that this whole class of things is put in doubt by the sceptic critique of the criterion of truth (*PH* II 95, *M* VIII 141–2). Consequently, any statement about such things will be dogma in the sense the sceptic eschews.

10. The reader should be warned that some interpretations take *PH* I 13–15 as evidence that 'dogma' and 'dogmatize' are still more restricted than I allow, with the consequence that the sceptic does not eschew all belief. It will be best to postpone controversy until the rest of my interpretation has been set out, but meanwhile the examples in the previous note will serve as well as any to illustrate the sorts of thing about which, in my view, the sceptic suspends judgement.

shall come, that *all* belief is unreasonable. All belief is unreasonable precisely because, as we are now seeing, all belief concerns real existence as opposed to appearance.

## Historical Interlude

We can trace this polemic against belief at least as far back as Aenesidemus, the man who was chiefly responsible for founding, or at any rate reviving, Pyrrhonism in the first century B.C.—some two hundred years or more before Sextus compiled his *Outlines of Pyrrhonism*. Aenesidemus' own *Outline Introduction to Pyrrhonism* was presumably the first work to bear such a title, and we know something of it from a report in Diogenes Laertius (IX 78 ff.; cf. also Aristocles *apud* Eus. *PE* XIV 18, 11). Aenesidemus set out to classify the various modes or ways in which things give rise to belief or persuasion[11] and then tried to destroy, systematically, the beliefs so acquired by showing that each of these modes produces conflicting beliefs of equal persuasiveness and is therefore not to be relied upon to put us in touch with the truth.[12] Most obviously, where our senses deliver consistent reports we tend to be persuaded that things really are as they appear to be,[13] but if we take full account of the different impressions which objects produce on different animals and different people and people in different conditions or circumstances, and all the other considerations adduced under the Ten Modes, we will see that in any such case as much evidence of the same kind, or as good, can be adduced for a contrary opinion; each type of evidence can be matched by evidence of the same sort but going the other way, each source of belief is a source of conflicting beliefs.[14] The moral, naturally, is *epochē* about what is true (DL IX 84); but this is also expressed by saying we must accept our ignorance concerning the real nature of things (DL IX 85, 86), which confirms once again the intimate connection of truth and reality. Then there is the additional

11. DL IX 78: καθ’ οὓς τρόπους πείθει τὰ πράγματα.

12. DL IX 79: ἐδείκνυσαν οὖν ἀπὸ τῶν ἐναντίων τοῖς πείθουσιν ἴσας τὰς πιθανότητας.

13. DL IX 78: πείθειν γὰρ τά τε κατ’ αἴσθησιν συμφώνως ἔχοντα.

14. Note the partial overlapping between the τρόπους in DL IX 78 and the δέκα τρόπους, καθ’ οὓς τὰ ὑποκείμενα παραλλάττοντα ἐφαίνετο in 79 ff.: cp τά τε κατ’ αἴσθησιν συμφώνως ἔχοντα with Modes I–IV, VII, τὰ νόμοις διεσταλμένα with Mode V, τὰ μηδέποτε ἢ σπανίως γοῦν μεταπίπτοντα and τὰ θαυμαζόμενα with Mode IX.

consideration that some of the modes in which beliefs are acquired have little or no bearing on truth and falsity, as when we believe something because it is familiar to us or because we have been persuaded of it by an artful speaker. In sum

> We must not assume that what persuades us (*to peithon*) is actually true. For the same thing does not persuade every one, nor even the same people always. Persuasiveness (*pithanotēs*) sometimes depends on external circumstances, on the reputation of the speaker, on his ability as a thinker or his artfulness, on the familiarity or the pleasantness of the topic (DL IX 94, tr. Hicks).[15]

Now this talk of persuasion and persuasiveness has an identifiable historical resonance. In a context (*M* VIII 51) closely parallel to the passage just quoted, and not long after a mention of Aenesidemus (*M* VIII 40), Sextus equates what persuades us (*to peithon hēmas*) with the Academic notion of *to pithanon*. '*Pithanon*' is often mistranslated 'probable', but what the word normally means in Greek is 'persuasive' or 'convincing', and Carneades defined a *pithanē* impression as one which appears true (*M* VII 169, 174).[16] The important point for our purposes is that in the sceptic historiography, as in most history books since, Carneades was supposed to have made *to pithanon* the Academic criterion for the conduct of life (*M* VII 166 ff.): a fallible criterion, since he allowed that in some instances we

15. I should explain why, without explicit textual warrant, I attribute the content of this last paragraph also to Aenesidemus. The paragraph is one of two (IX 91–4) which intrude into a sequence of arguments announced earlier at IX 90. Not only is it likely, therefore, to derive from a different source, but the sequence of arguments follows immediately on the account of the Five Modes of Agrippa (IX 88–9), and its argumentation is largely Agrippean in construction, while the intruding paragraphs have a certain affinity of content and expression with the section 78–9 which is definitely associated with the name of Aenesidemus. For example, both passages are dismissive of belief due to something being familiar (σύνηθες) or pleasing (79: τέρποντα, 94: κεχαρισμένον). Perhaps the most telling affinity is in the use of the verb πείθειν to denote the dogmatic belief which the author opposes: the verb does not occur in (what I suppose to be) the Agrippean sequence IX 88–91, 94–101, nor is it usual for Sextus to employ it as part of his own technical vocabulary for the key concept of dogmatic belief. Where he does use it is in discussing Academic fallibilism, as we are about to see. Cp. also *PH* I 226, 229–30.

16. For the correct translation of πιθανός, see Couissin 1929a, 262, Striker 1980, § III. Getting the translation right is a first step towards undoing the myth of Carneades as a proponent of 'probabilism.'

would be persuaded of something which was actually false (*M* VII 175). He also said that our belief is greater—and the Pyrrhonists read him as meaning that it should be greater—when our senses deliver consistent reports (*M* VII 177); this idea, which we saw to be one of Aenesidemus' targets, is the basis for the second and stricter criterion in Carneades' three-level criterial scheme, the impression which is not only *pithanē* but also not 'reversed' by any of the associated impressions. If, then, *to peithon* is the Academic *pithanon,* and if I am right to detect Aenesidemus behind the passages in Diogenes and Sextus where *to peithon* is under fire, then his campaign against persuasion and belief was at the same time a polemic against the Academy from which he had defected.[17] The general purpose of the Ten Modes is to unpersuade us of anything which persuades us that it represents truth and reality. Aenesidemus' more particular target is the idea, which he attributes to the Academy (whether rightly or polemically),[18] that one has a satisfactory enough criterion of action in taking to be true that which is persuasive in the sense that it appears true. In Aenesidemus' view, one should not take anything to be true, and he had arguments to show that, in fact, nothing is true (*M* VIII 40 ff.).

I conclude, then, not only that the life without belief was a fundamental feature of Pyrrhonism from Aenesidemus onwards, but that it was put forward by Aenesidemus in conscious opposition to (what he represented as) the teaching of the New Academy. If the Ten Modes have their intended effect, we will be weaned from the Academic criterion for the conduct of life to Aenesidemus' new Pyrrhonist ideal of a life without belief. It is quite possible, however, that this was not so much a new proposal as the revival of one much older.

The idea that one should live without belief (the word used is *adoxastōs,* as in Sextus) is prominent in the most extended doxographical account we

17. The evidence for Aenesidemus having begun his philosophical career in the Academy is that he dedicated his *Pyrrhonian Discourses* to L. Tubero, described as a fellow associate of the Academy (Phot. *Bibl.* 169 b 33). Zeller, E. *Die Philosophie der Griechen in ihrer geschichtlichen Entwicklung,* iii, Abt. 1 and 2: *Die nacharistotelische Philosophie* (4th edn., Leipzig, 1903–9); English translation of the 2nd section of iii Abt. 1: Alleyne, S. F. Zeller, *A History of Eclecticism in Greek Philosophy* (London, 1883). Abt. 2, p. 23 n. 2, is perhaps right in suggesting that because Photius' report of this work (which is mentioned also at DL IX 106 and 116) says nothing of the Ten Modes, it is to be distinguished from the *Outline Introduction to Pyrrhonism* which Aristocles and Diogenes indicate as the place where the Modes were developed.

18. Both rightly and polemically if his target is Philo of Larissa: see below.

possess of the philosophy of Pyrrho himself: the quotation in Eusebius (*PE* XIV 18, 2–4) from Aristocles, a Peripatetic writer of the second century A.D., which gives what purports to be a summary of the views attributed to Pyrrho by his follower Timon.[19] We should not put any trust in our perceptions or beliefs, says the summary, since they are neither true nor false, and when we are thus neutrally disposed, without belief, tranquillity results. It is possible that Aristocles received this report through Aenesidemus himself,[20] but that need not mean it gives a distorted interpretation of Timon's account of Pyrrho. Quite a few of the fragments of Timon which have come down to us are at least suggestive of later Pyrrhonism.[21] Moreover, various stories relating how Pyrrho's friends had to follow him about to keep him from being run over by carts or walking over precipices (DL IX 62—the precipice fantasy may derive from Aristotle, *Metaph.* Γ4, 1008$^b$ 15–16) are exactly of the type one would expect to grow up around a man known for teaching a life without belief. And these stories are old. They are cited from the biography of Pyrrho written by Antigonus of Carystus in the late third century B.C., well before Aenesidemus; in fact Aenesidemus felt it necessary to combat the idea that a philosophy based on suspending belief would make Pyrrho behave without foresight (DL IX 62). This seems rather clear evidence that for Aenesidemus himself the life without belief was the revival of a much older ideal.

It is not difficult, moreover, to guess something of the philosophical reasons why Aenesidemus should have resorted to Pyrrho for his model. On the one hand, the Academy at the time of Philo of Larissa appeared less sharply sceptical than it had been; in particular, on Philo's controversial interpretation of Carneades (cf. *Acad.* II 78, *ind. Acad. Herc.* XXVI, 4), *to pithanon* could be and was offered as a positive criterion of life.[22] On the

19. Timon, frag. 2 in Diels, H. *Poetarum Philosophorum Fragmenta* (Berlin, 1901); translation and discussion in Stough 1969, Chap. 2.

20. The ground for this suspicion is a somewhat odd, textually disputed, reference to Aenesidemus tacked on at the end of the summary. See Dumont, J.-P. *Le Scepticisme et le phénomène* (Paris, 1972), 140–7.

21. For discussion, see Burnyeat 1980. The question of the historical accuracy of Timon's account of Pyrrho is a further matter which need not concern us here.

22. For the controversy about Carneades, see Striker 1980. That Aenesidemus' target was the Academy of Philo is indicated above all by Photius' report (*Bibl.* 170 a 21–2) that he characterized his Academic opponents as determining many things with assurance and claiming to contest only the cataleptic impression. This

other hand, the great difficulty for Academic scepticism had always been the objection—Hume's objection—that total *epochē* makes it impossible to live.[23] The tradition concerning Pyrrho offered a solution to both problems at once. The way to live without belief, without softening the sceptical *epochē*, is by keeping to appearances. This was the plan or criterion for living that Aenesidemus adopted (DL IX 106), again not without some support in the fragments of Timon,[24] and we shall find it elaborated in Sextus Empiricus. It is a pleasing thought that not only does Sextus anticipate Hume's objection, but also, if I am right about the philosophical context which prompted Aenesidemus to his revival of Pyrrhonism, it was in part precisely to meet that objection more effectively than had been done hitherto that Aenesidemus left the Academy and aligned himself to Pyrrho.

## Living By Appearances

A sceptical restructuring of thought, a life without belief, tranquillity—these are not ideas that we would nowadays associate with philosophical scepticism, which has become a largely dialectical exercise in problem-setting, focused, as I noted earlier, on knowledge rather than belief. Even

---

corresponds not to Carneades' sceptical outlook but to the distinctive innovation of Philo, according to whom it is not that in their own nature things cannot be grasped but that they cannot be grasped by the Stoics' cataleptic impression (*PH* I 235). The alternative target would be Antiochus, but he does not fit Aenesidemus' scornful description of contemporary Academics as Stoics *fighting* Stoics (Phot. *Bibl.* 170 a 14–17). It would appear that Aenesidemus was also provoked by Philo's claim (*Acad.* I 13) that there were not two Academies, but a single unified tradition reaching right back to Plato. This amounted to the assertion that Plato stood for scepticism as Philo understood it, and Aenesidemus was at pains to deny that Plato could rightly be regarded as a sceptic (*PH* I 222, reading κατὰ τούς with Natorp and noting the disjunctive form of the argument: Plato is not sceptical if either he assents to certain things as true *or* he accepts them as merely persuasive. For a decisive defence of Natorp's reading against the alternative κατὰ τῶν, which would mean that Aenesidemus thought Plato was sceptical, see Burkhard, U. *Die angebliche Heraklit-Nachfolge des Skeptikers Aenesidem* (Bonn, 1973), 21–7).

23. Above, p. 27 n. 4.

24. Esp. frags. 69: 'But the phenomenon prevails on every side, wherever it may go'; and 74: 'I do not assert that honey (really) is sweet, but that it appears (sweet) I grant' (tr. Stough).

Peter Unger, who has recently propounded a programme for a sceptical restructuring of thought,[25] does not really try to dislodge belief. Having assiduously rediscovered that scepticism involves a denial of reason, and the connection between scepticism and the emotions, as well as much else that was familiar to Sextus Empiricus, he agrees that all belief is unreasonable, and he even has an argument that in fact no one does believe anything—belief itself is impossible. But he does not really believe this last refinement, since his programme envisages that concepts like *knowledge* and *reason* be replaced by less demanding assessments of our cognitive relation to reality, rather in the spirit of Academic fallibilism; thus it seems clear that, while a great number of our present beliefs would go (for a start, all those beliefs having to do with what is known and what is reasonable), believing as such would remain firmly entrenched at the centre of our mental life. The ancient Greek Pyrrhonist would not let it rest there. He is sceptical about knowledge, to be sure: that is the burden of all the arguments against the Stoics' cataleptic impression—the impression which, being clear and distinct (DL VII 46), affords a grasp of its object and serves as a foundation for secure knowledge. But his chief enemy, as we have seen, is belief. So the question arises, What then remains for a man who is converted by the sceptic arguments to a life without belief, where this means, as always, without belief as to real existence? This is the question we have to ask if we want to probe the secret of sceptic tranquillity.

The sceptic's answer, in brief, is that he follows appearances (*PH* I 21). The criterion by which he lives his life is appearance. In more detail, he has a fourfold scheme of life (*PH* I 23–4), allowing him to be active under four main heads, as follows. First, there is the guidance of nature: the sceptic is guided by the natural human capacity for percipience and thought, he uses his senses and exercises his mental faculties—to what result we shall see in due course. Second comes the constraint of bodily drives (*pathōn anankē*): hunger leads him to food, thirst to drink, and Sextus agrees with Hume that you cannot dispel by argument attitudes the casual origin of which has nothing to do with reason and belief (*M* XI 148). In this respect, indeed, perfect *ataraxia* is unattainable for a human being, physical creature that he is, and the sceptic settles for *metriopatheia* (*PH* I 30, III 235–6): the disturbance will be greatly moderated if he is free of the additional element of belief (*to prosdoxazein*) that it *matters* whether he secures food and drink. Third, there is the tradition of laws and customs: the sceptic keeps the rules

25. Peter Unger, *Ignorance—A Case for Scepticism* (Oxford, 1975).

and observes in the conduct of life the pieties of his society.[26] Finally, the fourth element is instruction in the arts: he practises an art or profession, in Sextus' own case medicine, so that he has something to do. All of this falls under the criterion of appearance, but Sextus does not really aim to develop the scheme in practical detail. Once he has pointed us in these four directions, his main concern, and therefore ours here, is with the general criterion of appearance.

In the section of the *Outlines of Pyrrhonism* where it is formally stated that the criterion by which the sceptic lives his life is appearance (*PH* I 21–4), not only does appearance contrast with reality but living by appearances contrasts with the life of belief. Evidently, the mental resources left to the sceptic when he eschews belief will be commensurate with whatever falls on the side of appearance when the line is drawn between appearance and real existence. So it becomes important to ask, as I have not so far asked, just what the sceptic is contrasting when he sets appearance against real existence. By the same token, if appearance is identified with some one type of appearance—and the most likely candidate for this is sense-appearance— that will have restrictive implications for the mental content of the life without belief.

Let us go back briefly to the passage where Sextus gave his definition of scepticism as a capacity for bringing into opposition things that appear and things that are thought etc. When Sextus comes to elucidate the terms of his definition, he says that by 'things that appear' (*phainomena*) we *now* mean sensibles (*aisthēta*) in contrast to things thought (*nooumena* or *noēta*) (*PH* I 8–9). This surely implies that he does not always or even usually mean sensibles alone when he speaks of what appears (cp. *M* VIII 216). Some scholars, most recently Charlotte Stough, have taken the sceptic criterion to be sense-appearance, in the narrow meaning,

26. I have done a little interpretation here, taking τὸ μὲν εὐσεβεῖν παρα-λαμβάνομεν βιωτικῶς ὡς ἀγαθὸν τὸ δὲ ἀσεβεῖν ὡς φαῦλον in the light of such passages as *PH* I 226, II 246, III 12, *M* IX 49. Note the verb forms τὸ εὐσεβεῖν, ἀσεβεῖν: not attitudes but practices (which were in any case the main content of Greek piety and impiety) are what the sceptic accepts. To say that it is βιωτικῶς, not as a matter of belief, that he accepts the one as good and the other as bad comes to little more than that he pursues the one and avoids the other; in short, he tries to observe the pieties of his society. If custom demands it, he will even declare that gods exist, but he will not believe it (*PH* III 2) or mean it *in propria persona* as do both the dogmatists and the ordinary man (*M* IX 49–50): on the existence of the gods, as on any question of real existence, the sceptic suspends judgement (*PH* III 6, 9, 11; *M* IX 59, 191).

because when Sextus says the criterion is what appears (*to phainomenon*), he adds that the sceptics mean by this the impression (*phantasia*) of the thing that appears (*PH* I 22).[27] But the point here is simply to explain that what the sceptic goes by in his daily life is not, strictly, the thing itself that appears, but the impression it makes on him, and in Sextus' vocabulary (as in Stoic usage—cf. DL VII 51) there are impressions (*phantasiai*) which are not and could not possibly be thought to be sense-impressions. I need only cite the impression, shared by all opponents of Protagoras, that not every impression is true (*M* VII 390). As for *to phainomenon*, what appears may, so far as I can see, be anything whatever. Sextus is prepared to include under things appearing both objects of sense and objects of thought (*M* VIII 362), and sometimes he goes so far as to speak of things appearing to reason (*logos*) or thought (*dianoia*) (ambiguously so *PH* II 10, *M* VIII 70, unambiguously *M* VII 25, VIII 141). Finally, there is a most important set of appearances annexed to the sceptic's own philosophical utterances; as Michael Frede has emphasized,[28] these are hardly to be classed as appearances of sense.

Time and again Sextus warns that sceptic formulae such as 'I determine nothing' and 'No more this than that' (*PH* I 15), or the conclusions of sceptic arguments like 'Everything is relative' (*PH* I 135), or indeed the entire contents of his treatise (*PH* I 4), are to be taken as mere records of appearance. Like a chronicle (*PH* I 4), they record how each thing appears to the sceptic, announcing or narrating how it affects him (his *pathos*) without committing him to the belief or assertion that anything really and truly is as it appears to him to be (cp. also *PH* I 197). Clearly it would be impossible to regard all these appearances as impressions of sense.[29] But the practice of argumentative enquiry is so considerable a portion of the sceptic's way of life that they must certainly be included

---

27. Stough 1969, 119 ff. Stough's initial mistake (as I think it) is to treat the statement as a contribution to a theory of experience. She then elicits the consequence that one perceives only one's own impressions, not the external object, since that which appears *is* (according to Stough's reading of the present passage) our impression. This goes flatly against the innumerable passages where that which appears is the very thing whose real properties cannot be determined, e.g. the honey at *PH* I 20. A further undesirable and unwarranted feature of Stough's interpretation is the divergence it leads her to postulate between Aenesidemus and Sextus (p. 124–5).

28. Frede 1973.

29. *Contra* Stough 1969, 146 n. 83.

under the sceptic criterion. They are one outcome, surely, and a most important outcome, of his natural capacity for percipience *and thought*. Sense-appearance cannot be all that is involved when the sceptic says he follows appearances.

It may be granted that the conclusion of a sceptic argument is typically that the real nature of something cannot be determined and that we must content ourselves with saying how it appears, where this frequently does mean: how it appears to the senses. But essentially the same formulae are used when the subject of enquiry is, say, the existence of species and genera (*PH* I 138–40), the rightness or wrongness of certain customs and practices (*PH* I 148 ff.), or, quite generally, objects of thought (*noēta*) as contrasted with sensible things (*PH* I 177). Further, the conclusion of a sceptic argument may be also that a certain concept cannot be formed: for example, the concept of man (*PH* II 27). In this connection Sextus contrasts asserting dogmatically that man really is e.g. a featherless two-footed animal with broad nails and a capacity for political science and putting forward this same definition as something merely persuasive (*pithanon*); the former is the illegitimate thing which is the target of his argument, the latter what he thinks Plato would do (*PH* II 28). I think it would be wholly in keeping with the spirit, if not the letter, of this text to add the properly Pyrrhonist alternative of saying what man appears to one to be. For Sextus insists[30] that the sceptic is not prohibited from *noēsis*, the forming of conceptions. He can form his own conceptions just so long as the basis for this is that things he experiences appear clearly to reason itself and he is not led into any commitment to the reality of the things conceived (*PH* II 10).

I suggest, therefore, that the sceptic contrast between appearance and real existence is a purely formal one, entirely independent of subject matter. The sceptic does not divide the world into appearances and realities so that one could ask of this or that whether it belongs to the category of appearance or to the category of reality. He divides questions into questions about how something appears and questions about how it really and truly is, and both types of question may be asked about anything whatever.

In his chapter on the sceptic criterion Sextus says: 'No one, I suppose, disputes about the underlying subject's appearing thus or thus; what he enquires about is whether it is such as it appears' (*PH* I 22). The point is one familiar in modern philosophy, that how a thing appears or seems is authoritatively answered by each individual. When Sextus says that a

30. *Contra* Naess 1968, 51.

man's impression is *azētētos*, not subject to enquiry (*PH* I 22), the claim is that his report that this is how it appears to him cannot be challenged and he cannot properly be required to give reason, evidence or proof for it. It is only when he ventures a claim about how something really is that he can be asked for the appropriate justification. It follows that the sceptic who adheres strictly to appearance is withdrawing to the safety of a position not open to challenge or enquiry. He may talk about anything under the sun—but only to note how it appears to him, not to say how it really is. He withdraws to this detached stance as the result of repeatedly satisfying himself that enquiry as to the real nature of a thing leads to unresolvable disagreement. We can understand, now, why the only use the sceptic has for reason is polemical. Quite simply, nothing he wants to say in his own person is such as to require a reasoned justification.[31] Reason is one more important notion which is tied to truth and real existence.

It turns out, then, that the life without belief is not the mental blank one might at first imagine it to be. It is not even limited as to the subject matter over which the sceptic's thoughts may range. Its secret is rather an attitude of mind manifest in his thoughts. He notes the impression things make on him and the contrary impressions they make on other people, and his own impressions seem to him no stronger, no more plausible, than anyone else's.[32] To the extent that he has achieved *ataraxia*, he is no longer concerned to enquire which is right. When a thing appears in a certain light to him, that no more inclines him to believe it is as it appears than would the fact of its so appearing to someone else. It is merely one more impression or appearance to be noted. Thus the withdrawal from truth and real existence becomes, in a certain sense, a detachment from oneself.

31. In keeping with this Sextus does not claim knowledge or (*pace* Hossenfelder, M. Sextus Empiricus, *Grundriss der pyrrhonischen Skepsis* (Frankfurt am Main, 1968), 60–1) certainty about how things appear to him. If pressed, the radical Pyrrhonist will actually deny that he knows such things (Galen, *De diff. puls.* VIII 711, 1–3 K = Deichgräber op. cit, frag. 75, p. 135, 28–30). See further Burnyeat 1982.

32. It is of the essence of scepticism, as defined *PH* I 8 and as practised throughout the sceptic literature, to set one person's impressions against those of another. Questions could be raised about the sceptic's entitlement to talk of other people's impressions, and suitable answers could be devised. But on the whole such questions are not raised, any more than the sceptic inquires into the basis for his extensive historical surveys of the views of other philosophers. The radically first-person stance of the scepticisms we are familiar with is a distinctively modern development (cp. n. 8 above).

## Assent and Constraint

With this conclusion we reach, I think, the real point of scepticism as a philosophy of life. So thoroughgoing a detachment from oneself is not easy to understand—indeed, it is here that I would locate the ultimate incoherence of the sceptic philosophy—but the attempt must be made if we are to appreciate the kind of restructuring which the sceptic arguments aim to produce in a man's thought, and thereby in his practical life. To this end I must now broach the difficult topic of assent and the will.

I have already explained that assent is a wider notion than belief. The sceptic's non-belief, his *epochē*, is his withholding assent to anything not given in appearance (*PH* I 13). But there are things he assents to: *ta phainomena*, anything that appears. This doctrine is stated in full generality at *PH* I 19–20, with no restriction to any specific class of appearances; although the example to hand is a sensible appearance, the taste of honey, I hold, as before, that Sextus means any kind of appearance and hence that the important further characterization he gives in this connection is to be applied to all appearances without exception.

The further characterization is as follows: things that appear lead us to assent (sc. to them) *aboulētōs*, without our willing it, in accordance with the impression they affect us with (*kata phantasian pathētikēn*). Much the same is said on numerous occasions elsewhere. When the sceptic assents, it is because he experiences two kinds of constraint. First, what he assents to are *kata phantasian katēnankasmena pathē*, states with which we are forcibly affected in accordance with an impression (*PH* I 13). He can assent to an impression, or, as Sextus also puts it (*PH* II 10), he can assent to what is presented in accordance with an impression he is affected with in so far as it appears, because the impression itself, the way the thing appears, is a passive affection not willed by the person who experiences it and as such is not open to enquiry or dispute (*en peisei kai aboulētōi pathei keimenē azētētos estin*) (*PH* I 22); in other words, it is merely what is happening to him now. But second, besides having the impression forced upon us, we are also constrained in these cases to assent. The sceptic yields to things which move us affectively (*tois kinousin hēmas pathētikōs*) and lead us by compulsion to assent (*kai anankastikōs agousin eis sunkatathesin*) (*PH* I 193).

What, then, is the content of the sceptic's assent? Assent is described as assent to something in so far as it appears, or to the state/impression which is its appearing to us, but the expression of this assent is propositional: e.g. 'Honey appears sweet' (*PH* I 20). In another place (*PH* I 13) Sextus puts the point in a negative way: when the sceptic is warmed or chilled, he would not say 'I think I am not warmed/chilled.'[33] Arne Naess takes the negative formulation to be an attempt to articulate the idea that the sceptic does not accept or reject 'It now seems cold to me' as a proposition.[34] I do not find in Sextus any evidence of a contrast between assenting to a state or to the impression of a thing and assenting to a proposition about how something appears to one. We concede, says Sextus (*PH* I 20), that honey appears sweet because we are sweetened perceptually (*glukazometha aisthētikōs*), which I take to mean: we have a perceptual experience featuring the character of sweetness. The sceptic's assent is simply the acknowledging of what is happening to him, and the compulsion to assent, to acknowledge what is happening to him, is equally simple. It is not that there is resistance to overcome, but that there can be no dispute about what the impression is; it is *azētētos*, not open to enquiry. The impression is just the way something appears to one, and assent to it is just acknowledging that this is indeed how the thing appears to one at the moment.

So far, I have illustrated these points, as Sextus does, by reference to impressions of sense. As it happens, however, at least one of the statements cited occurs in a context describing the attitude of mind which the sceptic brings to the practice of argumentative enquiry. This is the statement (*PH* II 10) that the sceptic assents to things presented to him in accordance with an impression which they affect him with (*kata phantasian pathētikēn*), in so far as they appear to him. Given the context, it is natural to refer the remark to the appearances annexed to the sceptic's various philosophical pronouncements. That the *phantasia*, the impression, is characterized as *pathētikē*, something one is affected with, is no hindrance to this; we have already seen that an impression need not be an impression of sense, and to call it *pathētikē* simply means it is a passivity (*peisis*) or *pathos*, as at *PH* I 22. Sextus is perfectly prepared to speak of a *pathos*, affection, annexed to the sceptic formula 'I determine nothing' (*PH* I 197; cp. I 203). As he explains, when the sceptic says 'I determine nothing', what he is saying is, 'I am now affected (*egō houtō pepontha nun*) in such a way as not to affirm or deny dogmatically any of the matters under enquiry.' At *PH* I 193 this is generalized to all expressions of sceptical non-assertion (*aphasia*) and linked with the topic of compulsory assent to states of appearance. Clearly, 'I

---

33. On the translation of θερμαίνεσθαι and ψύχεσθαι, see below.
34. Naess 1968, 8. Naess, however, has a rather special theory about what it is to accept or reject something as a proposition, a theory which is claimed to rescue Pyrrhonism from Hume's critique: see Alistair Hannay, 'Giving the Sceptic a Good Name', *Inquiry* 18 (1975), 409–36.

determine nothing', as an expression of the sceptic's non-assertion, does not indicate a sense-impression. But it does indicate a *pathos*, a passive affection. It would seem, therefore, that this *pathos*, and assent to it, is forced upon the sceptic as the outcome of his arguments just as much as a sense-impression is forced upon him by an encounter with some sensible object and then forcibly engages his assent.

I think this is right. Look through a sample of sceptic arguments and you will find that a great number of them end by saying that one is forced to suspend judgement, the word most commonly used being *anankazō*, the same word as describes our passive relationship to an impression of sense and the assent it engages. The sceptic assents only when his assent is constrained, and equally when he withholds assent, suspends judgement, this is because he finds himself constrained to do so. A marked passivity in the face of both his sensations and his own thought-processes is an important aspect of the sceptic's detachment from himself. But, once again, there is neither mystery nor effort involved in the constraint.

We are all familiar with the way in which an argument or overwhelming evidence may compel assent. In just this way, the sceptic's arguments are designed to check assent (*epechein* has a transitive use = 'to check', as well as the standard intransitive meaning 'to suspend judgement'). Imagine a man so placed that he really can see no reason at all to believe *p* rather than not-*p*; the considerations for and against seem absolutely equal no matter how hard he tries to resolve the question. Then, as Sextus puts it, he will be checked (*epischethēsetai*—*PH* I 186; cp. I 180, *M* VII 337). If it was a matter of acting where he could see no reason to choose this rather than that, he could toss a coin or simply do whatever one has been brought up to do in the circumstances. In effect, that is what the sceptic does do when he adheres to the conventions of whatever society he lives in without himself believing in them or having any personal attachment to their values. But believing is not like that. Of course, it is a good philosophical question whether it is not possible in some circumstances to decide or will to believe something, but these will have to be circumstances more auspicious than those I have described, where one can literally see nothing to choose between *p* and not-*p*. To quote Epictetus (*Diss.* I 28.3), just try to believe, or positively disbelieve, that the number of the stars is even.[35]

---

35. The example is traditional, i.e. much older than Epictetus. It is a standard Stoic example of something altogether non-evident, which can be discerned neither from itself nor through a sign (*PH* II 97, *M* VII 393, VIII 147, 317; cp. VII 243, XI 59). It occurs also in Cicero's reference (*Acad.* II 32) to certain *quasi desperatos* who say that

I repeat: try it. Make yourself vividly aware of your helpless inability to mind either way. *That* is how the sceptic wants you to feel about everything, including whether what I am saying is true or false (you are not to be convinced by the reputation or the artfulness of the speaker). That is *ataraxia*. If a tyrant sends a message that you and your family are to perish at dawn unless you commit some unspeakable deed, the true sceptic will be undisturbed both about whether the message is true or false and about whether it would be a good thing or a bad thing to comply with the command. You will be undisturbed not because your will has subjugated the tendency to believe and to be emotionally disturbed, but because you have been rendered unable to find any reason to think anything is true rather than false or good rather than bad. This is not to say that you will do nothing— Hume's charge of total lethargy. Sextus meets this old complaint, first by acknowledging the role of bodily drives like hunger and thirst and by the rest of the fourfold scheme of activity, and in the case of the tyrant (*M* XI 162–6) by saying that of course the sceptic will have his preconceptions, the result of being brought up in certain forms of life (cf. *PH* II 246), and these will prompt him to act one way or the other. But the point is that he does not identify with the values involved. He notes that they have left him with inclinations to pursue some things and avoid others, but he does not believe there is any reason to prefer the things he pursues over those that he avoids.[36]

The assumptions at work here are reminiscent of Socrates, as is much else in Hellenistic moral psychology. The emotions depend on belief, especially beliefs about what is good and bad. Remove belief and the emotions will disappear; as fear, for example, fades when one is dissuaded of one's belief that the thing one was afraid of is dangerous. At least, to the extent that emotions derive from reason and thought, they must disappear when judgement is suspended on every question of fact and value. This will not eliminate bodily disturbances such as hunger and thirst, nor the tendencies to action which result from the endowments of nature and from an upbringing in human society (cf. *PH* I 230–1). For they

---

everything is as uncertain as whether the number of the stars is odd or even, a reference which is sometimes taken to point to Aenesidemus: so Brochard, 1923[2], 245, Striker 1980, 64.

36. Compare, perhaps, Feyerabend's reply to the question why his 'epistemological anarchist' does not jump out of the window: Paul Feyerabend, *Against Method* (London, 1975), 221–2. He notes his fear, and its effect on his behaviour, but he does not endorse any reasons for the fear. See further n. 37 below.

do not depend on reason and thought. But they will be less disturbing without the added element of belief about good and bad, truth and falsity (above, p. 37). One may feel that this added element of belief is the very thing that gives meaning and sense to a life, even if it is also the source of trouble and disturbance. Without it, the sceptic's life will be a hollow shell of the existence he enjoyed, and was troubled by, prior to his sceptical enlightenment. Such is the price of peace and tranquillity, however, and the sceptic is willing to pay it to the full. Or rather, he is constrained by argument to suspend judgement and belief, and then finds that this just happens to bring tranquillity (*PH* I 28–30; above, p. 29). He exercises no deliberated choice in the matter, any more than when hunger leads him to get food.[37] So far from relying on the will to control assent, the sceptic panacea, beginning with the Ten Modes of Aenesidemus, is to use reason to check all the sources of belief and destroy all trust in reason itself, thereby eliminating the very inclination to believe. The life without belief is not an achievement of the will but a paralysis of reason by itself.[38]

37. According to Timon, frag. 72, quoted *M* XI 164, the follower of Pyrrho is ἀφυγὴς καὶ ἀναίρετος. According to Sextus (*PH* I 28) he does not pursue or avoid anything eagerly (συντόνως), i.e. he does not mind how it turns out. This detachment in action is interestingly discussed by Hossenfelder op. cit., esp. 66–74. On Socratic assumptions, it is the logical outcome of the sceptical conclusion that nothing is by nature good or bad, i.e. nothing is really *worth* pursuit or avoidance (Timon, frag. 70 = *M* XI 140, discussed in Burnyeat 1980; *PH* I 27, III 235–8, *M* XI 69 ff.).

38. The passivity of the sceptic's *epochē* has not, I think, been appreciated in the modern scholarly literature, Hossenfelder op. cit. excepted. One reason for this is the tendency to read appearance as sense-appearance wherever possible, with the consequence that Sextus' remarks about compulsion are taken to extend no further than bodily and perceptual sensation. That I have already taken issue with. The other reason is that it has been widely held to be common ground to philosophers of different persuasions in the period we are concerned with that 'assent is free' (so e.g. Brochard 1923[2], 138, 391). If that is so, it is easy to assume that, except when the sceptic is compelled to assent, he is free to give his assent or withhold it, and always he chooses—chooses of his own volition—to withhold it.

The idea that assent is free is Stoic doctrine in the first place, and there are indeed plenty of Stoic texts which say that assent is voluntary or in our power. But there are also texts which say that at least some impressions compel assent. The cataleptic impression lays hold of us almost by the hairs, they say, and drags us to assent (*M* VII 257; cp. 405); in another image, the mind yields to what is clear as a

# Controversial Interlude

It is time to take stock. A life has been described, and we want to know whether it is a possible life for man. But there is a prior question of some moment to face first: is the life described a life without belief, as Sextus so often claims (*adoxastōs bioumen* etc., *PH* I 23, 226, 231, II 246, 254, 258, III 235)?[39] The sceptic is supposed to content himself with appearances in lieu of beliefs, but it may be objected that, whatever Sextus may say, at least some of these appearances are beliefs in disguise. 'Honey tastes sweet' may pass muster as the record of a perceptual or bodily experience, but when it comes to 'All things appear relative' (*PH* I 135) or 'Let it be granted that the premisses of the proof appear' (*M* VIII 368) or 'Some things appear good, others evil' (*M* XI 19), we can hardly take 'appear' (*phainesthai*) other than in its epistemic sense. That is, when the sceptic offers a report of the form 'It appears to me now that *p*', at least sometimes he is chronicling the fact that he believes or finds himself inclined to believe that something is the case.

This epistemic reading of the sceptic's talk of appearances may be presented in either of two forms: as an objection to Sextus or as an objection

---

scale yields to the weights (*Acad.* II 38; cf. Epict. *Diss.* II 26.7). Assent in such cases is still voluntary because, it would seem, all that is meant by saying it is voluntary is that it depends on my judgement, hence on me, whether I assent or not. At any rate, that is all there is to Sextus' account of the Stoic view in a passage (*M* VIII 397) which explicitly contrasts voluntary assent with involuntary impression. The impression is involuntary (ἀκούσιος), not willed (ἀβούλητος), because whether or not I am affected by an impression does not depend on me but on something else, namely, the thing which appears to me; the impression once received, however, it does depend on me whether I assent to it, for it depends on my judgement. This leaves it quite open what factors influence my judgement, and how, and therefore leaves it open whether the influence could be regarded as in any sense a type of compulsion. In fact, recent studies on the Stoic side have pursued with illuminating results a line of interpretation according to which assent is determined internally, by a man's character and the education of his mind, and is voluntary just because and in the sense that it is internally determined in this way: see Long, A. A. 'Freedom and Determinism in the Stoic Theory of Human Action', in Long [82], 173–99, Voelke, A.-J. *L'Idée de volonté dans le stoicisme* (Paris, 1973), and cp. Epict. *Diss.* I 28 1–5. If that is the content of the doctrine that assent is free, it fits perfectly well with the emphasis I have placed on the passivity of the sceptic's *epochē*. He does not and could not choose *epochē* for the sake of *ataraxia*.

39. Cp. the talk of stating or assenting to something ἀδοξάστως at *PH* I 24, 240, II 13, 102, III 2, 151.

to my interpretation of Sextus. In the second version, which I take up first, the claim will be that the sceptic's assent to appearance, as Sextus describes it, is not the assertion of the existence of a certain impression or experience but the expression of a non-dogmatic belief about what is the case in the world. It will then follow that what the sceptic eschews, when he suspends judgement about everything, is not any and every kind of belief about things, but belief of a more ambitious type, which we may call (pending further elucidation) dogmatic belief.[40]

I do not doubt that a good number of the appearance-statements in Sextus Empiricus *can* be read epistemically. But if this fact is to yield an objection not to Sextus but to my interpretation of him, it needs to be shown that the epistemic reading has the approval of Sextus himself. The passage which comes closest to showing it is *PH* I 13. There Sextus says that some people define a broad sense of '*dogma*' meaning to accept something or not contradict it,[41] and with this he contrasts a narrower sense explained by some (? the same) people as assent to one of the non-evident things investigated by the sciences. The point of this distinction is to clarify the sense in which the sceptic does not dogmatize: he will have nothing to do with *dogma* in the second and narrower sense, 'for the Pyrrhonist does not assent to anything that is non-evident'. But he does assent to states with which he is forcibly affected in accordance with an impression, and such assent (we are given to understand) is or involves *dogma* in the broader sense to which the Pyrrhonist has no objection. For example (an example we have met before), 'He would not say, when he is warmed or chilled, "I think I am not warmed or chilled." ' Two questions now arise. First, does Sextus' tolerance of the broad sense signify approval of an epistemic reading for appearance-statements generally? Second, does his account of the narrower sense restrict his disapproval to what we have provisionally called dogmatic belief?

(1) What the sceptic accepts or does not contradict is 'I am warmed/ chilled'. This is a *dogma* (in the broad sense) inasmuch as the sceptic thinks, or it seems to him, that he is warmed/chilled.[42] But it does not follow that it

---

40. For the challenge to try to meet this objection I am indebted to the conference and to discussions with Michael Frede. In the space available I cannot hope to do justice to the subtlety with which Frede, ch. 1, expounds a very different interpretation of Sextus from that advocated here.

41. εὐδοκεῖν, on which see Frede, chap. 1.

42. Sextus evidently intends to bring out the semantic connection between δόγμα and δοκεῖν.

is an epistemic seeming, in the sense relevant to our discussion, unless its content 'I am warmed/chilled' is a proposition about what is the case in the world rather than a proposition about the sceptic's experience.

We must be careful here. The Greek verbs *thermainesthai* and *psuchesthai* do not normally *mean* 'I feel hot/cold', although translators (Bury, Hossenfelder) have a tendency to render them in such terms here, just because Sextus is illustrating an affection (*pathos*). They normally mean 'be warmed/chilled'.[43] On the other hand, neither does 'I am warmed/chilled' necessarily refer to an objective process of acquiring or losing heat. And my own view is that to insist that Sextus' illustrative *pathos* must be either a subjective feeling or an objective happening is to impose a Cartesian choice which is foreign to his way of thinking.

Sextus' terminology here is probably Cyrenaic. *Thermainesthai* and *psuchesthai* appear (by a well-motivated editorial insertion) on a list of Cyrenaic terms for *pathē* of perception in Plutarch, *Col.* 1120 e, along with *glukainesthai*, 'to be sweetened', which Sextus uses at *M* VIII 211 (cp. *glukazesthai PH* I 20, 211, II 51, 72, *M* VIII 54, IX 139); *leukainesthai*, 'to be whitened', and the like, applied by Sextus to the activity of the senses, look to be of similar provenance (*M* VII 293 with 190–8). As Plutarch describes the Cyrenaic doctrine which was the original home of this peculiar terminology,[44] it is that I can say *thermainomai*, 'I am warmed', but not *thermos ho akratos*, where this does not mean 'Neat wine is warm' but 'Neat wine is warming' (*thermos = thermantikos, Col.* 1109 f.). The case is exactly comparable to one we find in Aristocles (*apud* Eus. *PE* XIV 19, 2–3): according to the Cyrenaics, when I am being cut or burned I know I am undergoing something (*paschein ti*), but whether it is fire that is burning or iron that is cutting me, I cannot say. Do they mean, when they talk of undergoing something, the physical event or the way it feels? To that question *there is no clear answer*, and the terminology makes it impossible to decide. It is the same with Sextus. The reference of these funny verbs is plainly to a perceptual process rather than to the transmission of heat (cf. the case of the neat wine: conversely, the warming of a man so chilled that he could not feel a thing when you rubbed his hands would not illustrate Sextus' point at all), but we should keep the translation 'be warmed/chilled'. The man is being affected perceptually (cf. 'We are sweetened perceptually', *glukazometha aisthētikōs*, at *PH* I 20 and the uses of *thermainein* at *PH* I 110,

43. See Frede, chap. 1.

44. Plutarch's report shows that the Cyrenaic terminology was caricatured as peculiar.

II 56, *M* I 147, VII 368, IX 69), but we cannot 'split' the affection (*pathos*) into separate mental (subjective) and physical (objective) components. The moral to draw is not that the Pyrrhonist allows himself some beliefs about what is the case, but that scepticism is not yet associated with a Cartesian conception of the self.[45]

If this is correct, *PH* I 13 offers no justification for an epistemic reading of the sceptic's appearance-statements. The broader sense of '*dogma*' is simply the accepting of a perceptual experience as the experience it is, in the manner we have found amply attested already (above, pp. 42–3).[46] Sextus is not going out of his way to leave room for a non-dogmatic type of belief about matters of real existence. On the contrary, he says that when as a sceptic he makes statements with the verb 'to be', he is to be understood as meaning 'to appear' (*PH* I 135, 198, 200), and he glosses this use of 'to be' at *M* XI 18 in terms which are unmistakably non-epistemic:

> The word 'is' has two meanings: (a) 'is actually (*huparchei*)', as we say at the present moment 'It is day' in place of 'It is actually day', (b) 'appears', as some of the mathematicians are accustomed to say often that the distance between two stars 'is' a cubit's length, meaning this as equivalent to 'It appears so and doubtless is not actually so'; for perhaps it is actually one hundred stades, but appears a cubit because of the height and distance from the eye.

He then applies this elucidation to one of the statements that troubled us earlier, 'Some things appear good, others evil' (*M* XI 19).

(2) Moving on to the narrower sense of '*dogma*', the point to observe is that *any* thing which is non-evident is something for the sciences to investigate, the non-evident being by definition that which can only be known by the mediation of inference.[47] The scope for investigation or enquiry will be determined by the extent of things non-evident, 'for', as Sextus says, 'the Pyrrhonist does not assent to anything that is non-evident.' But the Pyrrhonist attack on the criterion of truth abolishes the evidence of everything that the dogmatists consider evident (*PH* II 95, *M* VIII 141–2). Take one of the dogmatists' favourite examples of things too patently obvious to be doubted, 'It is day', which turns up both in connec-

---

45. This is a topic that has come up before: see n. 8 above and Burnyeat 1982.

46. δοκῶ θερμαίνεσθαι is thus parallel to φαίνεται ἡμῖν γλυκάζειν τὸ μέλι at *PH* I 20.

47. See n. 9 above.

tion with the criterion (*M* VIII 144) and in the passage just quoted: the sceptic denies it is evident and, as we have seen, he accepts it only as a non-epistemic statement of appearance, 'It appears to be day [sc. but may not actually be so]'. *Anything* which goes beyond (non-epistemic) appearances is subject to enquiry (*PH* I 19; above, pp. 40–1; cp. *M* VIII 344–5).

In sum, I do not think that one solitary reference to the sciences (for it is not repeated elsewhere in Sextus) in a definition borrowed from someone else[48] is sufficient basis to credit Sextus with a distinction between dogmatic and non-dogmatic belief. It is not sufficient even when we add to the scales that Sextus frequently restricts what he suspends judgement about to the question how things are 'in nature' (*pros tēn phusin* etc., *PH* I 59, 78, 87, *et al.*) or how things are 'so far as concerns what the dogmatists say about them' (*PH* II 26, 104, III 13, 29, 135, *M* VIII 3) or, ambiguously, how things are 'so far as this is a matter for *logos* (statement, definition, reason)' (*PH* I 20, 215).[49] Just how restrictive these qualifications are depends on what they are contrasted with, and in every case the contrast is with how things appear, where this, as we have seen, is to be taken non-epistemically. All we are left with, then, is a passive impression (*phantasia*) or experience (*pathos*), expressed in a statement which makes no truth-claim about what is the case. As Sextus sums up the sceptic's avoidance of dogmatism, at the end of the passage which has detained us so long, it is simply this: 'He states what appears to himself and announces his own experience without belief, making no assertion about external things' (*PH* I 15).

48. That the two definitions of '*dogma*' are borrowed from some previous sceptic writer is evidenced not only by Sextus' saying so, but by the structurally parallel *PH* I 16–17. Here too we have a contrasting pair of 'someone's' definitions, this time of the term αἵρεσις ('philosophical system'), to one of which the sceptic objects and one he does not, and the first definition, couched (it would appear) in terms of the narrower sense of '*dogma*', can be found almost verbatim in an unfortunately truncated passage of Clement (*SVF* II, p. 37, 8–10), where it is again attributed to 'some people'.

49. ὅσον ἐπὶ τῷ λόγῳ: it is a nice question for interpretation how to take λόγος here. Bury translates 'in its essence' at *PH* I 20, while *PH* III 65, *M* X 49, XI 165 ὅσον ἐπὶ τῷ φιλοσόφῳ λόγῳ may seem to favour 'reason', but Sextus' own elucidation at *PH* I 20 (what honey is ὅσον ἐπὶ τῷ λόγῳ is what is said about the thing that appears) has decided several scholars for 'statement': Janáček, K. *Sextus Empiricus' Sceptical Methods* (Prague, 1972), Ch. 2, Hossenfelder op. cit., 64 n. 124. Perhaps 'theory' would do justice to the resonances of ambiguity (cp. e.g. *PH* III 167, *M* VII 283, VIII 3), provided we remember that what counts as theory and what as evidence is itself part of the dispute between Sextus and his opponents.

To which we may add that if the sceptic did allow himself some belief, opponents of Pyrrhonism would be guilty of serious *ignoratio elenchi* when they bring up the simple instinctive beliefs which, they claim, are inseparable from the use of the senses and from everyday actions (see the arguments from Aristocles and Galen cited n. 4 above). Aristocles repeatedly takes his target to be a philosophy which pretends to eschew all judgement and belief whatever, so that he can say that it is inconsistent for the Pyrrhonist to advance any assertion or argument (*apud* Eus. *PE* XIV 18, 8–9; 15; 16–17; 24). Sextus, as we have seen, connects dogmatism with claims that something is (simply) true, and he needs to do so if he is to undercut the ordinary man's hopes and fears. For clearly, hope and fear can come from any type of belief about what is or will be the case; it need not be dogmatic belief in some more stringent sense. What is at issue here is the ordinary man's ordinary belief that it is good and desirable to have money, say, or fame or pleasure, and bad to be without them (*M* XI 120–4, 144–6; cp. *PH* I 27–8). Belief, in the sense Sextus is attacking, is responsible for *all* the things men pursue and avoid by their own judgement (*M* XI 142, using *doxa*). The internal logic of Pyrrhonism requires that *dogma* and *doxa*—Sextus does not differentiate between these two terms—really do mean: belief.[50]

---

50. The same is implied by the original sense of several key words in the sceptical vocabulary. προσδοξάζειν is the Epicurean term for the judgement or belief which is added to perception, where perception is ἄλογος, involving no judgemental element at all (see Taylor, C.C.W., " 'All Perceptions Are True' ", in *Doubt and Dogmatism: Essays in Hellenistic Epistemology*, edited by Malcolm Schofield, Myles Burnyeat, and Jonathan Barnes (Clarendon Press 1980), 105–124. ἀδόξαστος credits the Stoic sage with the capacity to avoid *all* belief falling short of certainty (DL VII 162). δογματίζειν may again be Epicurean, as at DL X 120 (the earliest occurrence I can find), where it appears to mean nothing more stringent than not being in a state of puzzlement (ἀπορεῖν). The first instance I can find of δογματικός is attributed to Aenesidemus, who calls the *Academics* δογματικοί because they affirm some things without hesitation and deny others unambiguously, whereas Pyrrhonists are aporeutic (N.B.) and free of all belief (παντὸς ἀπολελυμένοι δόγματος) and do not say that things are such rather than such (Phot. *Bibl.* 169 b 36–170 a 2; on the general accuracy of the relevant sections of Photius' report, see Janáček op. cit. Equally, it is Aenesidemus' contention, as it is Sextus', that one dogmatizes if one gives credence to what is *pithanon* (*Bibl.* 170 a 18–20, *PH* I 222, 230).

δόγμα itself may look harder since, although it originally means just 'belief' (above, p. 31), some contrast with δόξα is indicated by Cicero's translating the terms *decretum* and *opinio* respectively. But the reason for this contrast would seem

Behind this issue of interpretation lies a philosophical question of considerable interest, the question whether and in what terms a distinction between non-dogmatic and dogmatic belief can be made out. One promising line to start might be to distinguish a belief that honey is sweet and a belief that honey is *really* sweet in the sense that sweetness exists in the honey, as part of its objective nature. Such talk has a familiar philosophical ring where the sensible qualities are concerned, but it would need to be explained what it amounted to when applied to such examples as 'It is day', 'I am conversing' (*M* VIII 144), or 'This is a man' (*M* VIII 316). Again, one may suggest that non-dogmatic belief is belief not grounded in or responsive to reasons and reasoning—but that will bring with it a breaking of the connection between belief and truth. What Sextus objects to is the accepting of anything as true. Any such acceptance he will count as dogmatizing (*PH* I 14–15; above, pp. 30–1). I do not myself think there is a notion of belief which lacks this connection with truth and, in a more complicated way, with reason.[51] Nor, at bottom, did Hume: else he would not have found it paradoxical that the sceptical arguments fail to dislodge belief. But all I have contended here is that Sextus has no other notion of belief than the accepting of something as true.

## Detachment and Philosophical Belief

It remains to consider whether it is an objection to Sextus that many of his appearance-statements seem to demand the epistemic reading which he refuses. One instance out of many would be the following: 'To every

---

to be that the Stoics contrast δόξα (mere opinion, defined as assent to something uncertain or to something false—*Acad.* II 59, 68, 77, *M* VII 151) with κατάληψις and ἐπιστήμη. They therefore need another word than δόξα for the wise man's belief. The wise man avoids δόξα (opinion as opposed to knowledge) but he has δόγματα, every one of them unwavering and true (*Acad.* II 27, 29; cp. *SVF* II, p. 37, 10–11). Notice that in Cicero's account it is not part of the meaning of δόγμα that it should be firmly held, but rather the consequence of its being the wise man who holds it: for the Academics say that all their *decreta* are 'probabilia non percepta' (*Acad.* II 109–10). Readers of Plato are often perplexed by the way δόξα sometimes means 'opinion' in contrast to knowledge and sometimes 'belief' or 'judgement' in the broad sense in which it is a component of knowledge: my suggestion is that δόγμα in Hellenistic usage conveniently takes over the latter role. It is a broader and more nearly neutral term than δόξα, not a term for a more stringently defined type of belief.

51. For a contrary view, see Striker, 1980, pp. 80–1.

dogmatic claim I have examined there appears to me to be opposed a rival dogmatic claim which is equally worthy and equally unworthy of belief' (freely rendered from *PH* I 203). Sextus insists that this utterance is not dogmatic, i.e. not expressive of belief. It is an announcement of a human state or affection (*anthrōpeiou pathous apangelia*), which is something that appears or is apparent to the person who undergoes it (*ho esti phainomenon tōi paschonti*). And this would be all right if 'It appears to me to be so' meant here 'I have some inclination to believe it is so'. Perhaps there could be an experience it was appropriate to record in those terms. But an inclination to believe is the last thing the sceptic wants to enter in his chronicle. The verb 'appears' in the above statement, and dozens like it, is to be taken non-epistemically, as we have seen. At times, no doubt, the non-epistemic reading is sheer bluff on Sextus' part, but the objector's opposition will itself be no better than bare counter-assertion unless he can muster more to say. I think there is more to say about the appearances annexed to the sceptic's philosophical pronouncements. They form a class of appearances which lie at the centre of the sceptic's conception of himself and his life.

Remember that we know perfectly well *why* it appears to the sceptic that any dogmatic claim has a contrary equally worthy or unworthy of acceptance. It is the result of a set of arguments designed to show, compellingly, that this is in fact the case. Such arguments can compel him to suspend judgement because they compel him to accept their conclusion—to accept, that is, that in each and every case dogmatic claims are indeed equally balanced and hence that one ought to suspend judgement. (Which is often enough, of course, the way Sextus does conclude his arguments.) But accepting the conclusion that *p* on the basis of a certain argument is hardly to be distinguished from coming to *believe* that *p* is *true* with that argument as one's *reason*. In being shown that there is as much, or as little, reason to believe the first-level proposition that honey is bitter as that it is sweet, the sceptic has been given reason to believe the second-level proposition that the reasons for and against are equally balanced. In being shown, both on general grounds and by the accumulation of instances, that no claim about real existence is to be preferred to its denial, he has, again, been given reason to believe that generalization true. Certainly it appears to him that dogmatic claims are equally balanced, but this appearance, so called, being the effect of argument, is only to be made sense of in terms of reason, belief and truth—the very notions the sceptic is most anxious to avoid.[52] He

52. Notice that it is for these higher-level generalizations that Sextus invokes the defence of cheerful self-refutation (*PH* I 14–15 and other passages discussed in

wants to say something of the form 'It appears to me that $p$ but I do not believe that $p$', with a non-epistemic use of 'appears', but it looks to be intelligible only if 'appears' is in fact epistemic, yielding a contradiction: 'I (am inclined to) believe that $p$ but I do not believe that $p$.' How is this result to be avoided?

The difficulty is not to be overcome by suggesting that the sceptic emerges from his arguments in a state of bafflement rather than belief. Bafflement could be the effect of arguments for and against; you are pulled now this way, now that, until you just do not know what to say (cf. *M* VII 243). The problem is to see why this should produce tranquillity rather than acute anxiety.[53]

Nor should we allow Sextus to deny that the sceptic's philosophical appearances are the effect of argument. He does on occasion claim that the sceptical arguments do not give demonstrative disproof of the dogmatists' views but mere reminders or suggestions of what can be said against them, and through this of the apparently equal strength of opposed positions (*PH* II 103, 130, 177, *M* VIII 289). In the technical terms of the period the arguments are not indicative but commemorative signs. I need not enlarge on the technicalities because (to be blunt) Sextus offers no elucidation whatever of the crucial notion of something's being said *against* a doctrine or belief but not by way of reasons or evidence against it. If the sceptic works through reasoned argument to the point where the reasons on either side balance and reason stultifies itself, if his arguments are (in the now famous phrase) a ladder to be thrown over when you have climbed up (*M* VIII 481), then we must insist that they make their impact through the normal operations of our reason. *Epochē* is not a blind, mechanical effect but, supposedly, the natural and intelligible outcome of following with our human capacity for thought along the paths marked out by the sceptical arguments.

Another suggestion might be that what the sceptic records as the outcome of his arguments is an interrogative rather than an assertive frame of mind: 'Is it the case, then, that contrary claims are equally balanced?' This

---

Burnyeat 1976. Self-refutation presupposes that the propositions do make a truth-claim. Sextus would not need (and could not use) the defence if the generalizations were really the expressions of appearance which he simultaneously claims them to be.

53. Cp. Hume's marvellous description of the despair of sceptical doubt, *A Treatise of Human Nature*, Bk I, Pt IV, § VII, p. 268–9 in Selby-Bigge's edition (Oxford, 1888).

would fit the sceptic's characterization of himself as *zētētikos,* one who goes on seeking (*PH* I 2–3, 7, II 11), and Sextus does at one point say that some sceptics prefer to take the formula 'No more this than that' as a question, 'Why this rather than that?' (*PH* I 189; cp. *M* I 315). But again we must be careful about *ataraxia.* The sceptic goes on seeking not in the sense that he has an active programme of research but in the sense that he continues to regard it as an open question whether *p* or not-*p* is the case, at least for any first-level proposition concerning real existence. But this should not mean he is left in a state of actually *wondering* whether *p* or not-*p* is the case, for that might induce anxiety. Still less should he be wondering whether, in general, contrary claims are equally balanced. For if it is a real possibility for him that they are not, that means it is a real possibility that there are answers to be found; and it will be an immense worry to him, as it was at the very beginning of his sceptical education, that he does not know what these answers are.

In other words, if tranquillity is to be achieved, at some stage the sceptic's questing thoughts must come to a state of rest or equilibrium.[54] There need be no finality to this achievement, the sceptic may hold himself ready to be persuaded that there are after all answers to be had. He is not a negative dogmatist furnished with *a priori* objections that rule out the possibility of answers as a matter of general principle once and for all (cf. *PH* I 1–3). But *ataraxia* is hardly to be attained if he is not in some sense satisfied— so far—that no answers are forthcoming, that contrary claims are indeed equal. And my question is: How can Sextus then deny that this is something he believes?

I do not think he can. Both the causes (reasoned arguments) of the state which Sextus calls appearance and its effects (tranquillity and the cessation of emotional disturbance) are such as to justify us in calling it a state of belief. And this objection to Sextus' claim to have described a life without belief leads on to an answer to our original question about the possibility, in human terms, of the life Sextus describes.

The source of the objection we have been urging is that the sceptic wants to treat 'It appears to me that *p* but I do not believe that *p*', where *p* is some philosophical proposition such as 'Contrary claims have equal strength', on a par with perceptual instances of that form such as 'It appears (looks) to me that the stick in the water is bent but I do not believe it is'. The latter is acceptable because its first conjunct describes a genuine experience—in Greek terms, a *pathos,* a *phantasia,* which awaits my assent. And it is

54. στάσις διανοίας *PH* I 10; ἀρρεψία, *PH* I 190, *M* VIII 159, 332 a, DL IX 74. Hossenfelder op. cit., 54 ff., is excellent on this, but I do not think we need go along with him in detecting an ambiguity in the term *epochē.*

important here that assent and impression are logically independent. For they are not independent in the philosophical case. In the philosophical case, the impression, when all is said and done, simply *is* my assent to the conclusion of an argument, assent to it as true. That is the danger of allowing talk about appearances or impressions of thought: it comes to seem legitimate to treat states which are in fact states of belief, presupposing assent, as if they were independent of assent in the way that sense-impressions can be. For if, beneath its disguise as a mere passive affection, the philosophical impression includes assent, it ought to make no sense for the sceptic to insist that he does not assent to it as true. That would be to contemplate a further act of assent to the assent already given. If the sceptic does insist, if he refuses to identify with his assent, he is as it were detaching himself from the person (namely, himself) who was convinced by the argument, and he is treating his own thought as if it were the thought of someone else, someone thinking thoughts within him. He is saying, in effect, 'It is thought within me that *p*, but *I* do not believe it.' In the right circumstances, that could be said. But not all the time, for every appearance/thought one has.[55] Yet that is what it will come to if absolutely every appearance, higher-level as well as lower-level, is construed non-epistemically.

One of the more memorable sayings attributed to Pyrrho is a remark regretting that it is difficult to divest oneself entirely of one's humanity.[56] (As the story goes, this was his reply to a charge of failing to practise what he preached when once he was frightened of a dog.) Sextus makes out that the sceptic ideal preserves all that is worth preserving in human nature. But it seems to me that Hume and the ancient critics were right. When one has seen how radically the sceptic must detach himself from himself, one will agree that the supposed life without belief is not, after all, a possible life for man.[57]

---

55. It is instructive in this connection to read through § II x of Wittgenstein's *Philosophical Investigations*, which discusses among other things Moore's paradox '*p* but I do not believe that *p*'.

56. DL IX 66, Aristocles *apud* Eus. *PE* XIV 18, 26: ὡς χαλεπὸν εἴη ὁλοσχερῶς ἐκδῦναι τὸν ἄνθρωπον. The source is Antigonus of Carystus, which means, as Long has shown, that the remark probably derives from something in Timon.

57. This paper has benefited greatly, especially in its last two sections, from helpful criticism at the Conference and at various universities where earlier drafts were read (Amsterdam, Berkeley, Essex, Oxford, Pittsburgh, Rutgers, SMU Dallas, and UBC Vancouver). Among the many individuals to whom thanks is due, I should like to mention Jonathan Barnes, David Sedley, Gisela Striker, and, above all, Michael Frede.

# 3

# The Beliefs of a Pyrrhonist[1]

## Jonathan Barnes

### I

A Pyrrhonist's researches do not end in discovery; nor yet do they conclude that discovery is impossible. For they do not terminate at all: the researches continue (*PH* I 1,4), and the researcher finds himself in a condition of ἐποχή (*PH* I 7). Ἐποχή is defined as 'a standstill of the intellect, as a result of which we neither deny nor affirm anything' (*PH* I 10). The Sceptical investigator[2] neither asserts nor denies, neither believes nor disbelieves.[3]

Ἐποχή is characteristically produced by argument—indeed, one of the most refreshing features of the Pyrrhonist tracts of Sextus Empiricus is that they are stuffed full of argumentation. When a philosopher offers us an argument, he normally implies that, if we accept the premises, we ought to accept the conclusion. It is thus natural to suppose that a Pyrrhonist's arguments similarly imply an intellectual *ought:* 'Consider these premises', the Sceptic urges, 'and you will see that you should suspend judgement'. A few Pyrrhonian passages do indeed contain such an intellectual *ought;*[4] But those passages are, I think, misleading. Sextus usually says, not 'you *should*

---

1. Drafts of this paper have been read at Cambridge, Rome and Milan: I am indebted to my three audiences for numerous suggestions and improvements.

2. I shall use 'Sceptic' and 'Pyrrhonist' interchangeably; I have nothing to say about the Academic Sceptics.

3. Modern sceptics customarily reject *knowledge* and they may allow themselves a full measure of *belief.* Ancient Sceptics reject *belief:* they also, of course, reject knowledge, but that is only a trivial consequence of their rejection of belief.

4. E.g. *PH* I 34 (οὐδέπω χρῆ συγκατατίθεσθαι); DL IX 81 (ἐφεκτέον); Timon, *apud* Aristocles, *apud* Eusebius, *P.E.* 14.18.3 (μηδὲ πιστεύειν δεῖ).

suspend judgement', But 'you *will* (or: *must*) suspend judgement'.[5] 'Εποχή
is 'an affection (πάθος) that comes about (γίγνεται) in the inquirer after
the investigation' (*PH* I 7). The onset of ἐποχή is something which simply
*happens* to us.

More specifically, Scepticism is a δύναμις ἀντιθετική, 'a capacity
for opposing what appears and what is thought in any way at all, from which,
because of the equipollence in the opposed objects and statements, we
reach first ἐποχή and then ἀταραξία' (*PH* 1.8). The sequence for the
Sceptic is: investigation—opposition—equipollence—ἐποχή—ἀταραξία.
That sequence is causal: famously, ἀταραξία follows ἐποχή 'by chance'
(*PH* I 26) or 'like a shadow' (*PH* I 29; DL IX 107); and ἐποχή follows
ἰσοσθένεια in just the same fashion. The Pyrrhonist's arguments lie
before you: read them, and you will find yourself in a state of ἐποχή.[6]

Any investigation attacks some specific subject-matter and poses some
particular question. The state of ἐποχή resulting from any investigation will
therefore itself be directed towards some specific subject-matter and some
particular question. A Pyrrhonist asks: 'Is it the case that *P*?' ('Do there exist
gods?', 'Can we discern true from false appearances?', 'Is the world a
structure of atoms and void?'). He then assembles arguments in favour of an
affirmative answer, and arguments in favour of a negative answer. The two
sets of arguments exactly balance one another. 'Εποχή supervenes—ἐποχή
directed towards the proposition that *P*.

Pyrrhonism thus works piecemeal. The δύναμις ἀντιθετική is a
general capacity, but it can only be exercised on particular issues. 'Εποχή is
not a global state—a state of total intellectual paralysis; rather, it is a
particular attitude, essentially directed towards some specific issue. 'Εποχή
on one issue does not imply ἐποχή on any other issue.[7] Hence if you ascribe
ἐποχή to a man you must indicate the object of his ἐποχή: towards what
issue is his ἐποχή directed? and if a Pyrrhonist claims that ἐποχή is the
route to ἀταραξία we must equally ask him to specify the object of that
ἐποχή: over what range of issues is his ἐποχή extended?

It is pointless to ask a Pyrrhonist whether we ought to suspend judgement
on this or that specified topic: ἐποχή is not something to be adopted

5. E.g. *PH* I 59 (ἐφέξομεν); I 78 (ἐπέχειν ἀναγκασθήσομαι); I 89 (εἰσάγεσθαι
τήν ἐποχήν).

6. The point needs stressing: unless it is firmly grasped we cannot begin to understand the Pyrrhonist's bizarre attitude to his own arguments (*PH* III 280–1).

7. Hence the Stoics may consistently indulge in selective ἐποχή: Cic. *Acad.* 2.29.94;
*PH* II 253; cf. DL III 52 (on Plato).

or rejected at will. But it is wholly appropriate to ask where—over what range of topics—a Pyrrhonist will exercise his δύναμις ἀντιθετική, and hence to ask what is the scope of his Scepticism.

## II

We may wonder what is the extent of a Pyrrhonist's Scepticism; and we may ask, equivalently, what a Pyrrhonist believes. (The questions are equivalent since a man may have beliefs on a topic just in case he does not find himself in a state of ἐποχή towards it.) The question, 'What may a Pyrrhonist believe?', or 'What is the scope of Pyrrhonian ἐποχή?', is of the last importance for an understanding of ancient Scepticism; and it has been the subject of scholarly controversy.[8]

But the question, generally posed, has no general answer. Different Pyrrhonists underwent ἐποχή to different degrees and exercised their δύναμις ἀντιθετική over different areas. Whether or not we can detect a line of development running through the long history of ancient Pyrrhonism and see ἐποχή becoming gradually more moderate in its claims,[9] there can be no doubt that there was no single Pyrrhonian orthodoxy: Galen, for example, was able to distinguish extreme and moderate Sceptics among the Pyrrhonists of his own day.[10] The unanswerable general question must thus be replaced by a series of specific questions. Here I shall limit my attention to Sextus Empiricus (who is, after all, the chief representative of Pyrrhonism for us today); moreover, to avoid any problems raised by the possibility of change and development in Sextus' own views,[11] I shall restrict myself to one of Sextus' works. My question is this: What is the

---

8. See esp. Myles Burnyeat, 'Can the Sceptic Live His Scepticism?' (= chap. 2), in *Doubt and Dogmatism*, edd. M. Schofield, M. F. Burnyeat, J. Barnes (1980), and Michael Frede, 'Des Skeptikers Meinungen' (= chap. 1), *Neue Hefte für Philosophie* 15/16 (1979) 102–29. (Cf. Burnyeat 1982, esp. pp. 23–32.) My paper is indebted on every page to the work of those two scholars and friends.

9. See esp. Brochard 1923[2].

10. Galen, *diff. puls.* 7.711K; *praenot.* 14.628K.

11. Sextus' extant writings were probably composed in the order: *PH—M* 7–9—*M* 1–6 (see esp. K. Janácek, 'Die Hauptschrift des Sextus Empiricus als Torso Erhalten?', *Philologus* 107 (1963) 271–7). Janácek's various philological studies have shown in detail how Sextus' *style* altered in the course of his career. I think it plausible to suppose developments in his *thought* too—but the topic awaits detailed investigation.

scope of ἐποχή in Sextus' *Outlines of Pyrrhonism?* what, if anything, may the Pyrrhonist of the *Outlines* believe?[12]

Two rival answers to that question define two types of Scepticism. The first type I shall call, following Galen,[13] *rustic Pyrrhonism.* The rustic Pyrrhonist has no beliefs whatsoever: he directs ἐποχή towards every issue that may arise. The second type of Scepticism I shall call *urbane Pyrrhonism.*[14] The urbane Pyrrhonist is happy to believe most of the things that ordinary people assent to in the ordinary course of events: he directs

12. There may, of course, be no determinate answer to *that* question either—*PH* may, in the end, turn out to offer no coherent view on the extent of ἐποχή.

13. ἀγροικοπυρρωνεῖοι: see the passages cited above, n. 10.

14. Myles Burnyeat has called this the country gentleman's Scepticism, in honour of Montaigne. (I take this from an unpublished paper on 'The Sceptic in his Place and Time' ( = chap. 4), which he has kindly allowed me to read.) Burnyeat suggests that urbane Pyrrhonists 'insulate' their philosophy from the rest of their life, and that only a rustic treats his Scepticism as a philosophy to live by. But 'insulation' may be taken in either of two ways. *(a)* Some modern Sceptics claim that their doubts are 'philosophical' doubts, not ordinary doubts. 'Philosophical' doubt is allegedly compatible with ordinary belief: a man may believe, with everyone else, that roses are red and violets blue—and at the same time he may doubt, philosophically, that violets are blue and roses red. A Scepticism which limits itself to philosophical doubt 'insulates' itself from real life, inasmuch as a Sceptic may share in all the beliefs—and hence join in the normal activities—of his fellow men. The distinction between philosophical doubt and ordinary doubt is scarcely to be found in ancient Scepticism. (But some scholars find it at *M* XI 165; and Michael Frede has in effect suggested that it underlies the theorising of the Methodical School of medicine: see his 'The Method of the so-called Methodical School of Medicine', in *Science and speculation*, edd. J. Barnes, J. Brunschwig, M. F. Burnyeat, M. Schofield (1982).) The 'insulation' which 'philosophical' doubt introduces was no part of normal Pyrrhonism. *(b)* The urbane Pyrrhonist directs his ἐποχή to philosophico-scientific matters; although he never doubts and believes the *same* things, his doubts are still, in a sense, 'insulated' from ordinary life—for they touch only on the concerns of professionals. But that is not to say that his doubts have no *practical* manifestations. For, first, in some cases at least he may well part company with ordinary beliefs and practices. And secondly, his professional doubts may have a profound effect on his professional practices. One ancient example may illustrate that point. The Empirical doctors were urbane Sceptics; and their Scepticism had a notable effect upon their approach to medicine—it affected their research, their classification of diseases, their diagnoses and prognoses, their therapy. See, most strikingly, the remarks on anatomy and vivisection at Celsus, *prooem.* 40–3 (with 23–4).

ἐποχή towards a specific target—roughly speaking, towards philosophical and scientific matters. Thus the rustics hotly reject everything, while the urbane coolly dismiss the rash claims of the *soi-disant* savants.

An interpreter who finds rustic Pyrrhonism in *PH* will appeal primarily to two features of Sextus' work. First, many of the arguments in *PH* appear to demolish *all* beliefs on a given topic if they demolish any beliefs: the attacks on causation or on time or on truth, say, do not appear to restrict their target to scientific or philosophical positions in those areas; and the Five Tropes of Agrippa, in terms of which much of the argumentation of *PH* is conducted, seem wholly indifferent to any distinction between scientific theory and everyday opinion. Secondly, *PH* makes it plain that the opponents of Pyrrhonism regularly construed Pyrrhonism in a rustic fashion—the notorious argument that Sceptics cannot act evidently presupposes that Pyrrhonists have no beliefs at all.

The rustic interpreter takes his motto from Timon: 'That honey is sweet, I do not affirm; that it appears so I allow'.[15]

An interpreter who finds urbane Pyrrhonism in *PH* will also appeal primarily to two features of Sextus' work. First, Sextus frequently characterizes Pyrrhonism by reference to its opponents, the 'Dogmatists': 'the Sceptic, being a philanthropic sort, wishes to cure by argument, to the best of his ability, the pretension and temerity of the Dogmatists' (*PH* III 280). Pyrrhonism is a therapy, a cure for the mental illnesses induced by scientists, philosophers, and other learned charlatans: it is not concerned with the ordinary beliefs of ordinary men. Secondly, Sextus frequently presents himself as the champion of βίος, of Ordinary Life or Common Sense. Like Berkeley, he is eternally attacking Metaphysics and reducing men to Common Sense. He is a defender, not an opponent, of ordinary beliefs.

The urbane interpreter takes his motto from Diogenes' summary of Scepticism: 'That fire burns we perceive; as to whether it has a caustic nature, we suspend judgement'.[16]

Is *PH* rustic or urbane? A full discussion of the question would demand an investigation of a major part of Sextus' text. Here I shall consider only three issues raised by the question—the three which seem to me the most significant, both historically and philosophically, of the many which the question suggests. I shall look first at *PH*'s commitment to τὰ φαινόμενα; then at the notion of δόγμα and *PH*'s opposition to οἱ δογματικοί; and thirdly at *PH*'s attitude to βίος and the Meaning of

15. Timon, frag. 74 Diels = DL IX 105.

16. DL IX 104; cf. *M* VII 197–9; Galen, *simp. med.* 11.380K.

Life. As an epilogue I shall briefly suggest that the question itself may be ill-conceived.[17]

<h1 style="text-align:center">III</h1>

The major part of Book I of *PH* presents the Ten Tropes of ἐποχή. The characteristic conclusion of the Tropes is this: 'how each of the external objects appears (φαίνεται) we can perhaps say; but how it is in its nature we cannot assert' (*PH* I 87). The Pyrrhonist of *PH* is undeniably committed to τὰ φαινόμενα: he is prepared to say how things appear. Surely that in itself is enough to show that he is no rustic? surely in saying how things appear he is exhibiting some beliefs?

The point is not that the phrase 'it appears to me' *means* 'I believe': φαίνεται in Greek, like 'appears' or 'seems' in English, may indeed carry such an epistemic sense; but the word does not do so in *PH* I. There the appearing is 'phenomenological'—φαίνεται reports the way things *look*.[18] (Not necessarily the way they look to perception. Although perceptual appearings predominate in the Ten Tropes, there are also numerous

---

17. Two troublesome side-issues should be mentioned. *(a)* Very many sentences in the text of *PH* appear to commit the Pyrrhonist to beliefs of various sorts: Sextus says that men's eyes are differently structured from those of cats (*PH* I 47), and his account of the Ten Tropes is largely composed of such observations; he says that Plato was not a Sceptic (*PH* I 222), and his writings are full of such doxographical remarks. Surely all that indicates a mass of ordinary beliefs? (So already the ancient critics of Pyrrhonism: see Aristocles, *apud* Eusebius, *P.E.* XN 18.11.) It does not, and the passages will bear no weight: sometimes we should plainly understand a καθάπερ φασίν (cf. *PH* I 80, 85)—Sextus is not speaking *in propria persona;* sometimes an εἶναι must be read 'catachrestically' as φαίνεσθαι (cf. *PH* I 135, 195, 202; cf. *M* XI 18–19)—Sextus is not saying how things *are;* sometimes, no doubt, we should simply suppose an understandable carelessness on Sextus' part. If *PH* is urbane, then (some of) those passages may be taken to express Pyrrhonian beliefs; but the passages cannot be adduced as evidence for urbanity. *(b)* Sextus is a Pyrrhonist attempting to describe Pyrrhonism: the attempt, as Sextus is acutely aware, is always close to incoherence—how can someone who purports to have no philosophical beliefs describe his own philosophical position? I am not here concerned with that problem, or with Sextus' efforts to surmount it. For it is a problem independent of the dispute between rustic and urbane interpreters (it arises for the urbane no less than for the rustic). My question is this: how should *we*, who are probably not Pyrrhonists, describe the philosophy which Sextus advocates in *PH?*

18. Burnyeat, chap. 2, 7–50 is convincing on this point.

examples of non-perceptual appearings. The phenomenological sense Of 'seem' or φαίνεται is not in any way tied to perception. I may say, phenomenologically, 'That argument *looks* sound—but don't be taken in by it'.)[19]

Rather, the point is that the utterance of phenomenological φαίνεται sentences itself seems to commit the utterer to various beliefs. Sextus' Pyrrhonist will say things like: 'The honey tastes sweet to me now'; 'The tower looks round to me from here'; 'Incest strikes me as wrong in Alexandria'.[20] Such utterances appear to imply beliefs in at least four different ways. First, the utterer appears to refer to himself, and hence to presuppose his own existence (and perhaps also certain facts about his own nature, e.g. that he is a being capable of perception and thought). Secondly, the utterer appears to refer to the present time, and hence to presuppose that there is such a thing as time. Thirdly—and more strikingly—the utterer appears to refer to external objects, and hence to assume their existence; for if I say 'That tower looks round', I may be in doubt about the 'real nature' of the tower, but I can hardly doubt that there *is* a tower there of some sort or other. Finally—and most obviously—the utterer appears to be expressing a belief by his very utterance, namely the belief that the honey tastes sweet to him, etc. For the utterance of an indicative sentence functions characteristically as a manifestation of belief in the proposition expressed by the sentence.

His use of the Ten Tropes, then, commits the Pyrrhonist of *PH* to at least a limited number of beliefs; and that is enough to show that he is not a rustic.

That argument supposes that the Sceptic's utterances are to be construed as statements or affirmations. And the supposition must not be allowed to go unquestioned. Not every utterance is a statement: modern philosophers are familiar with the notion of a 'speech act' and with the idea that there are many things other than stating which an utterer may do in making an utterance; nor do we suppose that every utterance of an indicative sentence must be construed as the making of a statement. Those

19. See further J. Barnes, 'Aristotle's Methods of Ethics', *Revue Internationale de Philosophie* 133/4 (1980) 490–511, at 491 n. 1.

20. The canonical form of the Pyrrhonist's φαίνεται sentences is: 'x appears F to me now' (see e.g. *PH* I 196 τὸ δὲ φαινόμενον ἡμῖν περὶ αὐτῶν ὅτε ἡμῖν ὑποπίπτει λέγομεν; cf. e.g. I 4, 193, 197). Sextus says little about what appears *to others* or to us *at other times;* but I assume that the conclusions of the Ten Tropes, at least, are implicitly limited to what appears *to me now*.

notions are not modern: Greek philosophers had recognized, centuries before Sextus, that statements were only one among many speech acts. We must ask—and we may do so without anachronism—what speech act the Pyrrhonist is performing when he utters φαίνεται sentences.[21]

Diogenes says that the Pyrrhonist's utterances are ἐξομολογήσεις, 'confessions' (IX 104). Sextus does not himself use that term;[22] But he does say that the Sceptic's utterances 'show' or 'reveal' his mental state (πάθος),[23] and his term for the utterances is ἀπαγγελίαι, 'avowals'.[24] It is plain that avowals and confessions were supposed by the Pyrrhonists to be speech acts of a different kind from statements or affirmations: Sextus in effect compares them to questions (and to admissions of ignorance)[25] and contrasts them with assertions.

The term 'avowal' has recently attained currency in Wittgensteinian circles. In a celebrated passage Wittgenstein wrote: 'Words are connected with the original and natural expression of feeling [Empfindung = πάθος], and are put in their place. A child hurts itself and cries: adults then talk to

21. Burnyeat, chap. 2, 30–31, takes a different line. He argues, in effect, that φαίνεται sentences were not regarded by the Pyrrhonists—or, in general, by the Greeks—as being *true* (or false); for truth was, for them, a matter of correspondence with external reality, and φαίνεται sentences say nothing about external reality. Now since belief is tied to truth (believing something is believing it true), φαίνεται sentences do not express beliefs at all. I am not happy with that argument; but I have no room to examine it here. The argument I produce in the text may be regarded either as an alternative or as a complement to Burnyeat's.

22. At *M* I 269, 272, ἐξομολογεῖν is merely a synonym for ὁμολογεῖν. Note that ἐξομολογεῖν is the technical term in Christian writings for 'confess' (e.g. Tertullian, *paen.* 9.2, and see Lampe, *Patristic Lexicon*, s.v.). Ἐξαγορεύειν also has the sense of 'confess' (e.g. Bion F 30 Kindestrand = Plutarch, *superst.* 168D; Ptolemy, *tetrab.* 154); but I have found no occurrences of the word in a Pyrrhonian context.

23. *PH* I 187 (μηνυτικός); 197, 201 (δηλωτικός).

24. See *PH* I 4, 15, 197, 200, 203. (At *M* I 255, 258, ἀπαγγέλλειν means no more than λέγειν.) I have not found any clear parallels to this usage outside Sextus. But there is something close in Plotinus, who frequently uses ἀπαγγέλλειν for the 'reports' made by, or on the testimony of, the senses (e.g. *Enn.* 4.4.18.35, 19.6, 23.28; 5.4.24)—i.e. for reports of πάθη.

25. See *PH* I 88–91: some Sceptics construed οὐδὲν μᾶλλον as a *question;* Sextus himself says that 'although the phrase οὐδὲν μᾶλλον has the form of an assertion or denial, we do not use it in this way; rather, we employ it ἀδιαφόρως καὶ καταχρηστικῶς, either in lieu of a question or instead of saying "I do not know whether . . ." ' (I 191).

him and teach him exclamations and later sentences—they teach the child a new pain-behaviour.—"Then you're saying that the word 'pain' really means crying?"—Quite the opposite: the verbal expression of pain replaces crying and does not describe it' (*Philosophical Investigations* I §244). Elsewhere Wittgenstein calls such 'expressions of feelings' *Äusserungen* or avowal; and he explicitly says that 'to call the avowals of a feeling a statement is misleading' (*Zettel*, §549).[26]

Children cry when they are in pain: they thereby *express* their pain, but they do not *state that* they are in pain (they state nothing at all). Adults, when they are in pain, may utter the sentence 'I am in pain' (or some vulgar equivalent): they thereby *express* their pain, but they do not (according to Wittgenstein) *state that* they are in pain (they state nothing at all). The Pyrrhonist of *PH*, when he is mentally affected, may utter the sentence 'The tower seems round': he thereby *expresses* his πάθος, but he does not *state that* he is experiencing a certain πάθος (he does not state anything at all).

The child's cry is not a statement, and it does not manifest a belief. The adult's avowal expresses his pain, not his *belief* that he is in pain. Avowals are not statements; and they by-pass belief. The avowals of a Pyrrhonist may similarly bypass belief.[27] The Pyrrhonist of *PH* is committed to τὰ φαινόμενα, and he readily assents to φαίνεται sentences.[28] But his utterances are avowals, not statements;[29] they express πάθη and do not evince beliefs. Thus

26. For details and discussion see e.g. P. M. S. Hacker, *Insight and Illusion* (1972) ch. 9.

27. Do they also by-pass *truth?* There is no need to suppose so, *pace* Wittgenstein. When I say 'It hurts' it may be *true* that it hurts, even if I am not *stating* that it hurts. (If I say 'Suppose it's raining in London' it may be *true* that it's raining in London, though I am not *stating* that it's raining in London.) A Pyrrhonist who is committed to avowals does not require a metaphysically loaded concept of truth (see above, n. 21).

28. *(a)* Why does he limit his verbal repertoire to φαίνεται sentences? Instead of uttering '*x* is *F*' to make a statement he utters '*x* appears *F*' to make an avowal—why not retain '*x* is *F*' but use it to make an avowal? Not everything can be avowed: an avowal is an expression of your πάθη, and sentences of the form '*x* appears *F*' were taken by the Pyrrhonists as canonical formulae for expressing πάθη. *(b)* Does the Pyrrhonist hold that '*x* appears *F*' is *always* used to make avowals? He need not: *he* uses it to make avowals, but he need not claim that other men do or must use it so, nor that the formula characteristically functions in ordinary speech as an expression of πάθη.

29. The Cyrenaics held that μόνα τὰ πάθη καταληπτά (e.g. *PH* 1.215; *M* 7.191; Anon. *in Tht.* 65.30). Like the Pyrrhonist of *PH*, they assent only to sentences of the form '*x* appears *F*' (for their curious neologisms—λευκαίνομαι, γλυκάζομαι—are merely verbal variants on φαίνεταί μοι); unlike the Pyrrhonist, they apparently used such sentences to make statements and express beliefs. (Hence, incidentally,

if we are prepared to take seriously Sextus' talk of avowals,[30] the Pyrrhonist may support τὰ φαινόμενα volubly while remaining an exemplary rustic.

## IV

The *PH* Pyrrhonist is not only a supporter of τὰ φαινόμενα: he is also a devoted opponent of οἱ δογματικοί and of their δόγματα. Now according to the urbane interpreter of *PH*, δόγματα are beliefs of a special sort: they are, roughly speaking, philosophico-scientific opinions—doctrines, principles, tenets.[31] In rejecting δόγματα, then, the Pyrrhonist rejects not beliefs but doctrines; and insofar as the Pyrrhonist is defined as a non-dogmatist, he is apparently able to admit and to profess all ordinary beliefs.

To assess the force of that urbane contention, we must determine the sense and the colour of the word δόγμα. I shall first survey the use of the word outside *PH*,[32] and then consider Sextus' own usage. The survey is, I fear, tedious; but it is an indispensable preliminary to an understanding of Sextus' attitude to Dogmatism.

---

*their* notion of truth was not the one mentioned in n. 21 above.)—Galen says of certain people influenced by the Pyrrhonians that ἴσως οὐδ' ὅτι φαίνεταί τις αὐτοῖς κίνησις ἀποφήνασθαι τολμήσουσιν, εἰ τὰ πάντα πείθοιντο τοῖς ἀπορητικοῖς· ἐκείνων γοῦν ἔνιοί φασιν οὐδὲ τὰ σφῶν αὐτῶν πάθη βεβαίως γινώσκειν, οὓς καλοῦσιν εἰκότως ἀγροικοπυρρωνείους (*diff. puls.* 7.711K). Galen does not mean that rustics do not assent to φαίνεται sentences: he means that they do not use such sentences to make *assertions* (ἀποφήνασθαι) or to express *knowledge* (βεβαίως γινώσκειν) of their own πάθη.

30. These remarks are an elucidation, not a defence, of Sextus. Sextus *means* the Pyrrhonist's utterances to be construed as avowals; and that shows that, *in his view*, the Pyrrhonist is not thereby committed to belief, i.e. it shows that the *PH* Pyrrhonist is rustic so far as his φαίνεται sentences go. In order to *defend* Sextus' account from a philosophical point of view, we should require a decent analysis of avowing. *One* element in that analysis would presumably be the claim that the Pyrrhonist's utterances are produced as a direct and natural response to external stimuli—just as a child's cry is a direct and natural response to the stimulus of pain.

31. This is vague—intentionally and harmlessly so. For a more rigorous definition see below, n. 86.

32. The survey is impressionistic: I have not conned every occurrence of δόγμα and its cognates in Greek. In addition to the authors mentioned in the text, I have consulted concordances or indexes to all the major prose-writers from 400 B.C. to A.D. 250: the general conclusions I reach in this section would doubtless be refined by further study, but I hardly think that they would be overthrown.

The noun δόγμα first appears in extant Greek at the turn of the fifth century. Its syntax and its sense are not obscure. Syntactically, δόγμα derives from the verb δοκεῖν.[33] (Δογματίζειν[34] and δογματικός are later formed from δόγμα.) Semantically, δόγμα takes its sense from its parent verb: as a πρᾶγμα is ὃ πράττει τις or a τάγμα ὃ τάττει τις, so a δόγμα is ὃ δοκεῖ τινι.

The verb δοκεῖν presented itself to fifth century Athenians, with monotonous frequency, in public documents: ἔδοξε τῇ βουλῇ καὶ τῷ δήμῳ. And δόγμα, in its earliest surviving occurrences, has a political colouring: a δόγμα is what δοκεῖ to an official or to an authoritative body; it is a decree or a resolution.[35] The word is found in Plato with the same political tone;[36] and throughout its history it appears frequently in political or semi-political contexts.[37] I shall return to the fact later.

Plato was perhaps the first philosopher to use the word δόγμα.[38] In the maieutic section of the *Theaetetus* Socrates states that his task will be to bring Theaetetus' δόγματα into the light (157 D 2). As the context shows, the δόγματα of Theaetetus are simply ἃ δοκεῖ τῷ Θεαιτήτῳ (157 C 2,5).[39] Since the things which δοκεῖ to Theaetetus are his beliefs or opin-

---

33. For verbal nouns in -μα see C. D. Buck and W. Petersen, *A reverse index of Greek nouns and adjectives* (1944) 221: they suggest that the -μα termination was an intellectual's favourite. See also Pollux, *onom.* 6.180.

34. See DL 3.51 αὐτὸ τοίνυν τὸ δογματίζειν ἐστὶ δόγματα τίθεναι ὡς τὸ νομοθετεῖν νόμους τίθεναι [= Suda, s.v. δογματίζει]. δόγματα δὲ ἑκατέρως καλεῖται, τό τε δοξαζόμενον καὶ ἡ δόξα αὐτή [i.e. a man's δόγματα are either the things he believes or his believings].

35. E.g. Lysias, 6.43 (399 B.C.); Andocides, 4.6 (c. 395); Xenophon, *Anab.* 3.3.5 (c. 375); *IG* II² 96 (375/4), 103 (369/8), 123 (357/6).

36. E.g. *Laws* 644D3, 797C9, 926D2; *Rep.* 403A2, 506B9, 538C6; cf. *Minos* 314BE; *Def.* 415B8, 11, C2.

37. See g. Mauersberger's Lexicon to Polybius or Rengstorf's concordance to Josephus; cf. δογματίζειν = to decree (e.g. Josephus, *Ant.* 14.249; LXX, 2 *Mac.* 10.8, 15.36).

38. At Heraclitus, B 50 DK ( = 26 M, from Hippolytus (?), *ref. haer.* 9.9.1), the MSS read δόγματος: editors generally accept Bernays's λόγου (see M. Marcovich, *Heraclitus* (1967) 113), but δόγματος has recently been defended by D. Holwerda, *Sprünge in die Tiefe Heraklits* (1979) 9–10.

39. Cf. *Rep.* 506B8, τὰ τῶν ἄλλων . . . δόγματα, picking up B6, τὸ τοῖς ἄλλοις δοκοῦν. Δόγμα occurs some 30 times in the Platonic *corpus*, usually in political contexts (see Brandwood's concordance).

ions, we should surely translate δόγμα as 'belief'.[40] In the six centuries that separate Plato from Sextus, words had time to change their senses; but I find no evidence that the word δόγμα underwent any semantic change, and I suppose that, outside political contexts, 'belief' generally conveys the sense of δόγμα.

But the sense of a word is only one component of its meaning. Another equally important component is tone or colour: if the English 'belief' conveys the sense of δόγμα, it may still be false to its colour.[41] To discover the colour of δόγμα we must learn the contexts in which it was customarily used and the types of belief which it standardly designated.

The beliefs which Plato denotes by δόγμα are usually philosophical opinions.[42] Aristotle uses the word once or twice, again of philosophical tenets;[43] so too does Epicurus (who may have been the first philosopher to use the verb δογματίζειν).[44] But the word only comes into its own some centuries later: Philo of Alexandria is the first author we know to have made frequent use of δόγμα; δόγματα pervade his writings, and the δόγματα he adverts to are almost invariably philosophical tenets or religious beliefs—the δόγμα that the soul is immortal, the δόγμα that the world was created by God, the δόγματα of Moses.[45] Δόγματα are weighty, substantial beliefs—tenets, doctrines, principles. It is significant that Philo

---

40. LSJ s.v. offer 'notion' for δόγμα at *Tht.* 158D3; and the *Supplement* s.v. discovers a new sense for the word, viz. 'thought, intention', for which *Tim.* 90B and *Laws* 854B are cited. But at *Tht.* 158D and *Tim.* 90B the word is used in the same way as in *Tht.* 157C; and at *Laws* 854B the δόγμα is a decree or resolution.

41. The distinction between sense and colour *(Färbung)* is due to Frege: see M. Dummett, *Frege—Philosophy of language* (1973) 83–9.

42. E.g. *Laws* 791D5, 798E2, 900B4; *Phlb.* 41B5; *Tim.* 48D6, 55D1; *Soph.* 265C5.

43. See *Phys.* 209b15 (Plato's ἄγραφα δόγματα); *Met.* 992a21, 1076a14. (But at *Top.* 101a31–2 the word appears to have a broader denotation.) See also *Met.* 1062b25; *M.X.G.* 974b12; *Rhet. ad Alex.* 1430b1, 1443a25 (and Bonitz's *Index*).

44. For δογματίζειν see frag. 562 Us = DL 10.121 (cf. Burnyeat, chap. 2, n. 50). For δόγμα see esp. frag. 29 Arr., at 28.5, 6, 10, 12 (with Arrighetti's note, 602–3); cf. frags. 30 (31.1), 31 (2, 4, 6), 36 (10.3), and Arrighetti's index. Note also the title of Colotes' pamphlet: περὶ τοῦ ὅτι κατὰ τὰ τῶν ἄλλων φιλοσόφων δόγματα οὐδὲ ζῆν ἔστιν (Plutarch, *adv. Col.* 1107E). For δόγμα in later Epicurean texts see the index to Philodemus by Vooys; and cf. Diogenes of Oenoanda, frag. 27 Ch, 1.8.

45. See Leisegang's index (vol. VII of the Cohn-Wendland edition of Philo).—I say 'almost invariably' only because Philo occasionally uses δόγμα of decrees.

uses the adjective δογματικός in a commendatory sense to mean 'full of import'.[46]

Philo's usage is typical. In Plutarch's *Moralia*, for example, the word δόγμα is not infrequent: outside a few political contexts, Plutarch's δόγματα are philosophical doctrines—I have found no text in which Plutarch uses δόγμα to denote a common or garden belief.[47] Again, Alexander of Aphrodisias uses δόγμα to refer to the philosophical beliefs of the Peripatetics and of their rivals: δόγματα, in Alexander, are beliefs of weight and substance.[48]

The theological writers, as we might expect, love δόγμα. Early patristic Greek is crammed with references to δόγματα.[49] Lampe, in his *Lexicon*, gives the main sense of δόγμα as 'fixed belief, tenet'. He indicates that the word is used to denote philosophical principles, the tenets of pagan religion, the teachings of Moses, and—above all—the doctrines of Christianity. The Fathers use δογματίζειν, in the sense of 'lay down as doctrine'; and we also find δογματικός, δογματισμός, δογματιστής, δογματοθεσία, δογματοποιΐα. The writings of Clement and Hippolytus and Origen are rich in evidence: the δόγματα they allude to are always philosophical, religious, or scientific beliefs.[50]

Not every belief is appropriately called a δόγμα. I believe that Rome is north of Naples and that Oxford is west of Cambridge; but no Greek would call such beliefs δόγματα. The Suda has a brief entry running thus: δογματίζει, θεολογεῖ, φυσιοῦται—'he dogmatizes—he theologizes, he is puffed up'.[51] Its hostility apart, the notice is just.

And recall Galen's standard nomenclature for the medical schools of the day. The Logical Doctors are also called δογματικοί: they propound and rely upon δόγματα—theories about the internal structure of the body or the typology of diseases, doctrines about the nature of causation or the

---

46. *Leg. alleg.* 2.25.100; *migr. Abr.* 21.119.

47. See Wyttenbach's index.

48. See the indexes to the relevant volumes in *CIAG;* e.g. *de fato* 164.16; 165.1; 177.6; 187.9, 12, 27; 188.17, 22; 190.6, 12; 192.21; 199.23; 205.23; 212.2; *in Met.* 40.31; 78.2, 24; 197.1, 8; 652.33. See also, e.g., Atticus, frags 2 (83, 113, 149), 4 (33, 60), 7 (10, 12, 35) des Places; Lucian, *vit. auct.* 17, *bis acc.* 21.

49. The way was prepared by the LXX (e.g. 3 *Macc.* 1.3; 4 *Macc.* 10.2) and the NT (e.g. *Col.* 2.14, 20). See further G. Kittel (ed.), *Theologisches Wörterbuch zum neuen Testament* II (1933–5) 233–5.

50. See e.g. Stählin's index to Clement, Wendland's to Hippolytus, *ref. haer.*, Koetschau's to Origen, *c. Cels.*

51. For φυσιόω in this metaphorical sense see Lampe's *Lexicon* s.v., sense A.

relation of perception to knowledge. The Dogmatists are opposed by the ἐμπειρικοί. These Empirics abjure δόγματα; they are against theory and for observation. But in abjuring δόγματα they do not, of course, abjure belief. On the contrary, they rely wholly on the rich store of beliefs which experience—their own and other men's—has amassed for them.[52] Galen's use of the term δόγμα is not idiosyncratic, and Galen is especially close, both in date and in interests, to Sextus. His works show clearly that a man may reject all δόγματα and yet retain innumerable beliefs.[53]

That conclusion is apparently controverted by one important set of texts— I mean the writings of the Stoic philosophers. The word δόγμα rarely occurs in the surviving fragments of the Old Stoa;[54] but it is very common in the works of the imperial Stoics, in Epictetus and Marcus Aurelius.[55] There its range of application is not limited to philosophico-scientific tenets; and if Sextus' chief opponents were the Stoics, it might be thought that Stoic usage of the term δόγμα was peculiarly relevant to the interpretation of *PH*.

At first sight, Epictetus seems prepared to call any belief a δόγμα. At all events, he offers the sentences 'οὗτος τέκτων ἐστι', 'οὗτος μουσικός, 'οὗτος φιλόσοφος', as paradigm expressions of δόγματα (*diss.* 4.8.4.); and he says, quite generally, that ἑκάστου δόγματος ὅταν ἡ χρεία παρῇ πρόχειρον αὐτὸ ἔχειν δεῖ· ἐπ' ἀρίστῳ τὰ περὶ ἀρίστου, ἐν βαλανείῳ τὰ περὶ βλανείου, ἐν κοίτῃ τὰ περὶ κοίτης (*diss.* 3.10.1)— δόγματα about breakfast, bath, and bed are unlikely to be philosophical tenets. If such beliefs are δόγματα, then surely any beliefs are δόγματα.

52. See, e.g. Galen, *in Hipp. vict. acut.* 15.728K (those who construe Hippocrates as a δογματικός think he is referring to τόποι, διαθέσεις and αἰτίαι; those who make him an ἐμπειρικός hold that he is talking about ὧραι, χῶραι, etc.); *in Hipp. art.* 18A.735K (Heraclides advances his views οὔθ' ἕνεκα δόγματος κατασκευῆς ψευσάμενος ὡς ἂν οἱ πολλοὶ τῶν δογματικῶν ἐποίησαν . . . ). cf. *opt. sect.* 1.146K (the ἐμπειρικοί say that when ὁ ἱστορῶν ἱστορῇ μὴ διὰ δόγματος προσπαθῶς . . . , τότε ἀληθὲς εἶναί φαμεν ἡμεῖς τὸ ἱστορούμενον). —Note that Galen may supply a new term from the δόγμα family, viz. ἀδογματικός or ἀδογματιστκός (see *subfig. emp.* 65.15: the Latin has *in dogmatibus*, emended by Schöne to *indogmaticus*).

53. Compare also the use of δόγμα in the stock definition of a αἵρεσις: *PH* 1.16; DL 1.20; Clement, *strom.* 8.5.16.2 (p. 89.24 St); [Galen], *hist. phil.* 7; *def. med.* 13, 19.352K; Suda, s.v. αἵρεσις.

54. See DL 7.199 (a title of a work on ethics by Chrysippus: πιθανὰ λήμματα εἰς τὰ δόγματα πρὸς Φιλομαθῆ); Origen, *c. Cels.* 8.51 (from Chrysippus' περὶ παθῶν θεραπευτικόν); Stobaeus, *ecl.* 2.62, 112; Philo, *om. prob. lib.* 97 (6.28.5–9).

55. Compare also Seneca's frequent use of *decretum* (see below, n. 58).

Yet it would be hasty to conclude that, in Stoic usage, every belief may be called a δόγμα. Epictetus' δόγματα fall, almost all of them, into one of two classes. First, δόγματα are often philosophical tenets[56]—here Epictetus is not departing from normal Greek usage. Secondly, δόγματα are far more often practical or evaluative judgements—judgements which, by grounding προαιρέσεις, lead to action.[57] Typically, such δόγματα are judgements about what is good or bad, just or unjust, right or wrong. Those are the δόγματα to which Epictetus refers in his monotonous injunctions to maintain ὀρθὰ δόγματα; for those are the δόγματα over which a man has control and in virtue of which he is the sole determiner of his moral well-being. Such judgements, in Epictetus' view, run through our whole lives: we need them at breakfast, in the bath, in bed.

Epictetus' usage, narrowly considered, does not suggest that any belief at all may be called a δόγμα. His first class of δόγματα is familiar. His second class reflects what I earlier called the political colour of the word δόγμα: in public life, a δόγμα is an official decree; in the Stoic's private life, a δόγμα is a practical resolution. The use of δόγμα for evaluative judgements, which seems to be peculiar to the Stoics, is a natural extension of the original public use.

From the fact that Epictetus uses δόγμα to refer to two different types of judgement, we should not infer that the word is ambiguous. Consider Cicero. He determined to translate δόγμα, in its philosophical applications, by the Latin *decretum*.[58] Why? He could, after all, have called upon *credo* or *opinor* had he wanted a general word for 'belief'; he could have used *doctrina* or *perceptum* had he wanted a specific term for 'tenet'. Instead, he appealed to *decerno*, a word primarily at home in the language of politics and the law. Cicero was a conscientious and sensitive translator.[59] His choice of *decretum*

---

56. E.g. *diss.* 2.22.37; 3.7.20–29, 16.7.

57. The same is true for Marcus—see Dalfen's index. For Epictetus see the index to Schenkl's edition.

58. See *Acad.* 2.9.27 . . . *de suis decretis, quae philosophi vocant* δόγματα (cf. 29; 34.109; *Tusc.* 2.11; *fin.* 2.28, 99). Seneca uses *decretum* frequently in this sense (see the Concordance of Busa and Zampolli). See esp. *Ep.* 95.12 *decreta sunt quae muniant, quae securitatem nostram tranquillitatemque tueantur, quae totam vitam totamque rerum simul contineant;* cf. *ib* 45 *persuasio ad totam pertinens vitam—hoc est quod decretum voco.* See further *TLL* s.v.—the word *dogma* was itself used by Cicero (it had already been Latinised by the poet Laberius), and it is common in later authors, always with reference to principles or tenets: see *TLL* s.v.

59. See, e.g., his worries over the translation of ἐποχή, where he is explicitly concerned to get the colour right: *ad Att.* 13.21.3.

shows that he perceived a political colouring to δόγμα even in its philosophical applications; and if Cicero perceived it, so, I suppose, did the Greeks.

There are two striking things about official δόγματα, about what ἔδοξε τῇ βουλῇ καὶ τῷ δήμῳ. First, they are weighty, formal things. Secondly, they are practical, aimed at action. I suggest that those two features colour the word δόγμα throughout its life, and explain its range of application. In some cases, where the δόγμα is a tenet or principle, the notion of weight is uppermost. (But even abstract tenets may have an influence upon action: Hellenistic philosophy was, above all else, an Art of Living.) In other cases, where the δόγμα is an evaluative judgement, the notion of practicality is uppermost. (But practice and theory must not be divorced: in Epictetus, philosophical principles are never far from the surface of the practical texts.)

Δόγμα, in sum, has a single *sense:* a man's δόγματα are what δοκεῖ to him, the things which seem good or right. But the word has a distinctive colouring, derived from its public use: the colouring is that of weight and practicality.[60]

It is time to return to Sextus. First, some rough statistics.[61] Sextus uses δόγμα some 25 times, δογματίζειν 30 times, δογματικός 200 times, δογματικῶς 20 times.[62] About 150 of those passages are texts where Sextus uses οἱ δογματικοί to refer to the Pyrrhonist's opponents. By my count, in 45 of those 275 places, δόγμα (or one of its cognates) indubitably refers to a philosophico-scientific tenet. As far as I can see, in only two texts does δόγμα certainly *not* refer to such a tenet (*M* 11.150, 166); and in each of those passages the δόγμα in question is a practical or evaluative judgement—a δόγμα falling into the second Epictetan class. Although the remaining passages are, strictly speaking, neutral, it would, I think, be wholly perverse to suppose that in them δόγμα usually or even often referred to ordinary beliefs. It is really plain that when Sextus uses a term from the δόγμα family he is designating a philosophical principle or a scientific theory. In short, Sextus' use of δόγμα is entirely comparable to the usage of Galen or of Clement or of any other Greek of that era.

---

60. That conclusion may seem pretty unexciting. But it is not uncontroversial. Burnyeat, chap. 2, n. 50, concludes that δόγμα in Hellenistic usage 'is a broader and more nearly neutral term than δόξα, not a term for a more stringently defined type of belief; it means ' "belief" or "judgement" in the broad sense in which it is a component of knowledge.'

61. See Janácek's index.

62. Note that over half (*c.* 140) of those occurrences are in *PH*, though *M* is three times the length of *PH*. I detect no difference in Sextus' use of δόγμα between *PH* and *M*.

Sextus also has some explicit remarks to make about the sense of the word δόγμα. When he considers the question 'Do Pyrrhonists dogmatise?',[63] he begins by distinguishing two senses of δόγμα:

> We say that Sceptics do not dogmatise not in the sense [i] in which some people say, fairly broadly, that dogma is τὸ εὐδοκεῖν τινι πράγματι . . . ; rather, we say that they do not dogmatise in the sense [ii] in which some people say that dogma is an assenting to some object from among the unclear things being investigated by the sciences. (*PH* 1.13)

There are two senses of δόγμα: in the narrow sense, sense [ii], Pyrrhonists have no δόγματα; in the broad sense, sense [i], Pyrrhonists do have δόγματα.

The narrow sense, as Sextus characterizes it, corresponds closely enough to the colour of the word δόγμα in the vast majority of its occurrences: δόγματα in sense [ii] are, roughly speaking, philosophico-scientific tenets. Of course no Pyrrhonist accepts such δόγματα. But a Pyrrhonist *does* accept δόγματα in sense [i]—and surely that is an explicit recognition on Sextus' part that a Pyrrhonist will have some *beliefs?*

Sense [i] requires scrutiny.[64] Sextus explains it by the phrase τὸ εὐδοκεῖν τινι πράγματι. The verb εὐδοκεῖν is not classical, but it is common in prose from Polybius onward, and its meaning emerges clearly from the texts it appears in:[65] εὐδοκεῖν τινι means 'be content with something'. Often the contentment is minimal, and 'acquiesce in' is an appropriate English translation; sometimes—particularly in Christian texts—the contentment is maximal, and 'rejoice in' is required.[66]

Pyrrhonists, then, 'are content with' certain things—why does Sextus say that?

> . . . τὸ εὐδοκεῖν τινι πράγματι. For the Sceptic assents to the affections [πάθη] which are forced upon him κατὰ φαντασίαν [cf. *PH* 2.10]—e.g. when he is warmed or cooled he will not say, 'I believe (δοκῶ) that I am not warmed (or: cooled)'. (*PH* 1.13)

63. Cf. DL 9.102–4 (see below, n. 70).

64. With what follows compare Frede, chap. 1, 16–21.

65. See Lampe's *Lexicon* s.v.; Kittel's *Theol. Wört*, II 736–48; Mauersberger's Lexicon to Polybius. Typical texts: Polybius, 2.38.7; 3.8.7; 4.22.7; 8.14.8; cf. Suda, s.vv. εὐδοκεῖν, etc.

66. So at NT, *Mark* 1.11 ('Thou art my only begotten son: in thee I am well pleased'), the Greek is ἐν σοὶ εὐδόκησα.

If a Pyrrhonist experiences a feeling of warmth he will *not* say 'I think I'm not being warmed'; and that is what τὸ εὐδοκεῖν is for him.

It is clear that τὸ εὐδοκεῖν is being used to convey a minimal notion of contentment—a Pyrrhonist *acquiesces* in his πάθη, he does not speak out against them or deny them.[67] It is clear, too, that his acquiescence, as Sextus describes it, does not involve any *beliefs*. For Sextus' language is scrupulously careful. He says that a Pyrrhonist will *not* say 'I believe I'm *not* warmed'. From that it does not follow that a Pyrrhonist *will* say 'I believe I *am* being warmed': his εὐδοκία is a matter of *refraining* from belief (he will not say 'I believe . . .'), and not a matter of believing anything at all. If a Pyrrhonist dogmatises in sense [i], he may do so while preserving his rusticity; for a δόγμα in sense [i] is not a belief of any sort.[68]

Thus from *PH* 1.13 we learn two things: that a Pyrrhonist will not accept any scientific or philosophical theories; and that he will acquiesce in his πάθη.[69] And that information is peculiarly unsatisfying. A Pyrrhonist rejects science and avows his πάθη; but what attitude does he take to ordinary beliefs? The sentences of breakfast-time, bath-time, and bed-time—'The

---

67. See Bekker, *Anec. Gr.* II 260 εὐδοκούμενος· ὁ συγκατατιθέμενος καὶ μὴ ἀντιλέγων, where I take καί to be epexegetic. Note that συγκατατίθεσθαι, outside its Stoic use to mean 'assent', regularly means 'accept', 'acquiesce in'; see e.g. Polybius, 21.30.8, where εὐδοκεῖν and συγκατατίθευθαι appear in the same sentence as synonyms.

68. Why does Sextus think that τὸ εὐδοκεῖν gives a sense of δογματίζειν? I have found no texts outside *PH* 1.13 where δόγμα or its cognates are used in that weak way. I can only suppose that the 'broad' sense of δόγμα is a dialectical concession by the Pyrrhonists (who do not indulge in φωνομαχία: *PH* 1.195, 297). An opponent urges: 'Of course you Pyrrhonists dogmatise—after all, you avow your πάθη'. The Pyrrhonist retorts: 'If you like to use "dogmatise" in *that* sense, we do indeed dogmatise—but that does not imply that we also dogmatise in the normal, narrow sense'.

69. [Galen], *def. med.* 14, 19.352–3K, should be quoted: δόγμα ἐστι τὸ μὲν ἰδίως τὸ δὲ κοινῶς λεγόμενον· κοινῶς μὲν ἡ ἐνεργείᾳ πράγματος συγκατάθεσις, ἰδίως δὲ πράγματος συγκατάθεσις· διὸ δὴ μᾶλλον ἡ λογικὴ αἵρεσις δογματικὴ κέκληται. The text is hardly sound. Ἐναργοῦς for ἐνεργείᾳ is easy enough; but I suspect the corruption is more extensive. E.g. κοινῶς μὲν ἡ [ἐνεργείᾳ] πράγματος συγκατάθεσις, ἰδίως δὲ πράγματος <ἀδήλου> συγκατάθεσις. If something like that is right, then [Galen] may be recognizing 'belief' as the general sense of δόγμα (i.e. he may be allowing that, in one sense, *any* belief may be called a δόγμα). Then [Galen] is close to DL 9.102–4 (see below, n. 70) and his distinction of senses is not the same as the one in *PH* 1.13.

butter's hard', 'The water's cold', 'The springs are protruding'—do not express scientific δόγματα, nor yet do they serve in avowals. If we are concerned to discover the scope of ἐποχή in *PH*, it is precisely such humdrum sentences which will most exercise us; yet of them Sextus says nothing.

It might be suggested that, since ordinary beliefs patently do not fall under the heading of δόγματα, they must somehow be accommodated under the heading of εὐδοκία.[70] Alternatively, it might be thought that ordinary beliefs, evidently escaping the net of εὐδοκία, must somehow be caught in the snares of δόγμα. I shall end my remarks on δόγμα by pursuing that second suggestion.

Δόγμα in sense [ii] is ἡ τινι πράγματι τῶν κατὰ τὰς ἐπιστήμας ζητουμένων ἀδήλων συγκατάθεσις. The phrase κατὰ τὰς ἐπιστήμας ζητούμενα does not function as a restrictive qualification on τὰ ἄδηλα. Sextus is not insinuating a distinction between those ἄδηλα which are subject to scientific investigation and those which are not: when he later adverts to δόγματα in sense [ii] he drops the reference to the sciences—a 'dogmatic supposition' is defined simply as 'assent to something unclear' (*PH* 1.197), and that is Sextus' normal way of identifying δόγματα.[71] Τὰ κατὰ τὰς ἐπιστήμας ζητούμενα ἄδηλα are simply τὰ ἄδηλα.

And τὰ ἄδηλα here are what Sextus later distinguishes as τὰ φύσει ἄδηλα, i.e. 'those things which do not have a nature of the sort to fall under our direct perception (e.g. imperceptible pores)' (*PH* 2.98). Τὰ ἄδηλα contrast with τὰ πρόδηλα (or, equivalently, with τὰ ἐναργῆ or τὰ φαινόμενα[72]). Paradigm sentences which involve only πρόδηλα are 'It is

70. That urbane suggestion may appear appropriate to DL 9.102–4. Replying to the charge that they dogmatise, the Pyrrhonists there are made to concede that ὅτι ἡμέρα ἐστὶ καὶ ὅτι ζῶμεν καὶ ἄλλα πολλὰ τῶν ἐν τῷ βίῳ διαγιγνώσκομεν. In other words, they allow that, if δόγμα may cover ordinary beliefs, then they do dogmatise. Of course, if that is the meaning of DL's Pyrrhonists, it does not follow that the same is true of *PH*. And in any event, the meaning of DL's Pyrrhonists is by no means clear-cut. For the sentence I have just quoted is introduced by the remark that περὶ ὧν ὡς ἄνθρωποι πάσχομεν ὁμολογοῦμεν, and followed by the assertion that μόνα τὰ πάθη γιγνώσκομεν. Thus ἡμέρα ἐστί and the like are apparently to be constructed as expressions of πάθη. DL's Pyrrhonists accept ordinary beliefs— but only because they reconstrue them as beliefs about their own πάθη. Hence they are not exactly urbane (though they are not rustic either, if we insist on the claim that they *know*—γιγνώσκομεν—their πάθη). It must be said, however, that the text of this passage in DL is very confused, and it would be unwise to rely upon it for the interpretation of any piece of Pyrrhonism.

71. E.g. *PH* 1.16, 193, 198, 200, 202, 208, 210, 219, 223; 2.9; cf. 1.18, 201.

72. See Janáček's index, s.v. ἐναργής; cf. [Galen], *opt. sect.* 1.175–6 K.

day', 'I am conversing' (*PH* 2.97; *M* 8.144). Now those sentences, being explicitly said to involve πρόδηλα, cannot be taken to express δόγματα. On the other hand, they surely do express ordinary beliefs. And an easy generalisation is to hand: all or most sentences expressing ordinary beliefs will involve only πρόδηλα; hence all or most ordinary beliefs will fail to be δόγματα.

That simple argument might seem quite enough to scotch the suggestion that ordinary beliefs should be somehow subsumed under the heading of δόγματα. But there is, in fact, an equally simple counterargument available.

The Pyrrhonian attack on 'logic' is rehearsed twice by Sextus, in *PH* 2 and in *M* 7–8. In each case the strategy is the same.[73] The Dogmatists claim knowledge in two areas: since they possess a 'criterion of truth', they have knowledge of τὰ ἐναργῆ or τὰ πρόδηλα; since they can employ 'signs' and 'proofs', they have knowledge of τὰ ἄδηλα. Now the Pyrrhonists dispute *both* parts of that dual claim. They produce reasons for doubting the existence of a criterion (*PH* 2.14–96; *M* 7.24–8.140); and they argue against signs and proofs (*PH* 2.97–192; *M* 8.141–481). By the end of the attack on 'logic' it seems that the Pyrrhonist will entertain beliefs neither about τὰ ἄδηλα nor about τὰ πρόδηλα. Both parts of the Pyrrhonian attack are directed against the Dogmatists. Sextus' presentation makes it appear that τὰ πρόδηλα, no less than τὰ ἄδηλα, are the subject-matter for δόγματα. But τὰ πρόδηλα are the subject-matter for ordinary beliefs. Hence ordinary beliefs are, after all, to be classified as δόγματα.

Thus there seems to be an inconsistency within *PH* over the status of ordinary beliefs,[74] and that inconsistency makes it unclear what the Pyrrhonist's attitude to such beliefs is supposed to be. But in fact the inconsistency is only apparent.

Consider the ordinary bath-time belief that the water is tepid. That belief makes no reference to τὰ ἄδηλα, nor is it a δόγμα. For all that, we cannot *affirm* that the water is tepid unless we have a criterion of truth—a way of judging that the πάθος with which the water affects us corresponds to the actual state of the water. The criterion is needed not to *infer* that the water is tepid (there is nothing to infer it from) but rather to *judge* that the water is tepid; we

73. See esp. *PH* 2.95; *M* 7.25; 8.140–1.

74. There is another connected inconsistency in the same stretch of argument. Sextus plainly states that the Pyrrhonist attack on κριτήρια undermines belief in τὰ ἐναργῆ (*PH* 2.95; *M* 7.25); he also expressly defines a κριτήριον as μέτρον ἀδήλου πράγματος (*PH* 2.15; *M* 7.33). I see no escape from that inconsistency— except the appeal to a systematic and unexpressed ambiguity in such terms as ἄδηλος, πρόδηλος, ἐναργής.

require not reasons for an inference but grounds for a judgement—and unless we have such grounds we are not warranted in making the judgement.

A Pyrrhonist will only believe that the water is tepid if he judges it to be so; and he can only judge it to be so if he possesses a criterion of truth by which to judge it. But the thesis that there is a criterion of truth is itself a δόγμα—indeed it is a perfect specimen of those philosophico-scientific tenets which the Greeks called δόγματα. Now the Pyrrhonist of *PH* rejects all δόγματα. Hence he will not have—or rather, will not believe that he has—a criterion of truth. Hence he will not be able to judge, or to believe, that the water is tepid.

In general, the Pyrrhonist of *PH* will have no ordinary beliefs at all. Ordinary beliefs are not δόγματα,[75] nor do they advert to ἄδηλα. Nonetheless, in rejecting δόγματα the Pyrrhonist must reject ordinary beliefs; for the possession of ordinary beliefs presupposes the possession of at least one δόγμα—the δόγμα that there is a criterion of truth.

In that way, the apparent inconsistency within *PH* is dissolved,[76] and the *PH* Pyrrhonist emerges as a rustic. In rejecting δόγματα he explicitly rejects any scientifico-philosophical theory; but he implicitly rejects all other beliefs as well.[77]

75. Myles Burnyeat has suggested to me that anything which depends on a δόγμα must itself be a δόγμα. Hence ordinary beliefs *are* δὸγματα in the Pyrrhonists' eyes.

76. Again (see above, n. 30), I am concerned to explain Sextus, not to defend him. Against the argument advanced in the text it might be objected that, although in order to judge that *p* I must possess a criterion, it is not true that in order to judge that *p* I must *believe* that I possess a criterion. Thus the Pyrrhonian may *possess* a criterion even if he himself does not *believe* that he does; and in that case he *is* in a position to judge that *p*. That is perhaps true; but could a Pyrrhonist judge that *p after reflecting on* the existence of a criterion and reaching ἐποχή on the matter? Sextus might plausibly argue that, having reached ἐποχή on the δόγμα of the criterion, a Pyrrhonist will naturally find himself in a state of ἐποχή *vis-à-vis* ordinary judgements.

77. Something must be said about the word ἀδόξαστος, which occurs 16 times in *PH*, all but once in its adverbial form. The word is rare outside *PH* (it does not appear in *M*). It is found in a fragment of Sophocles (fr. 223, where it means 'unexpected'), at *Phaedo* 84A (where τὸ ἀδόξαστον is joined with τὸ ἀληθές and τὸ θεῖον to characterize the objects of the soul's proper study), at DL 7.162 (Ariston μάλιστα προσεῖχε τῷ Στωϊκῷ δόγματι τῷ τὸν σοφὸν ἀδόξαστον [Scaliger: δοξαστόν codd.] εἶναι), at Aristocles, *apud* Eusebius, *P.E.* 14.18.3 (according to Timon we should be ἀδοξάστους καὶ ἀκλινεῖς καὶ ἀκραδάντους: cf. *ib* 16—πῶς ἀσυγκατάθετοι καὶ ἀδόξαστοι γενοίμεθ᾽ ;). In *PH* the adverb ἀδοξάστως usually qualifies either a verb describing the Pyrrhonist's way of life (βιοῦν: 1.23, 231, 2.246, 258; ἔπεσθαι τῷ βίῳ: 1.226, 3.235; etc.) or a verb describing the Pyrrhonist's utterances (ἀπαγγέλλει: 1.15; φαμέν: 1.24, 3.151;

# V

Sextus frequently characterises his Pyrrhonist negatively, as an opponent of Dogmatism. But he also sometimes characterizes him positively, as a champion of Life. Βίος in classical Greek usually means 'way of life', 'life style'. Sextus employs the word in a somewhat different way: βίος contrasts with φιλοσοφία,[78] βιωτικός with δογματικός.[79] The contrast is

---

συγκατατιθέμενοι: 2.102). The word *may* be part of the Pyrrhonist vocabulary adopted by Sextus; but it is not clear to what extent Aristocles is citing Timon's own words, and ἀδοξάστους could well be his own gloss on ἀκλινεῖς καὶ ἀκραδάντους (which are presumably genuine Timon). What does ἀδόξαστος mean in *PH?* Plainly, it means 'having no δόξα'; but that is capable of three importantly different glosses, according to the colour we see in δόξα here. [α] 'Having no mere opinions': that is the word's meaning in DL 7.162 (and in the *Phaedo*—'not an object of mere opinion'). *If* the word was used by Timon, then it might well bear that meaning in his sentence: 'having no mere opinions', i.e. 'fixed', 'firm' (cf. ἀκλινεῖς καὶ ἀκραδάντους). In many—but not all—the passages in *PH* a sense like 'fixedly', 'unwaveringly', fits perfectly well. [β] 'Having no δόγματα': that meaning is hardly suggested by the word's etymology or by its history; but ἀδοξάστως is frequently contrasted with δογματικῶς *vel sim*, and such a contrast could well give the word that particular colouring. (And some might see a neat polemical point: the Stoic Sage lives ἀδοξάστως, with δόγμα but without δόξα, and so in tranquillity; the Pyrrhonian lives ἀδοξάστως, without δόγμα, and so in tranquillity.) All the *PH* passages will readily accept that meaning. [γ] 'Having no belief of any sort': that is surely how Aristocles intends the word at 14.18.16—and therefore how he intends us to understand it in Timon. That sense is, I think, compatible with most of the occurrences in *PH*, if not with all. (The coupling ἐμπείρως τε καὶ ἀδοξάστως at 2.246 does not sit easily with [γ] inasmuch as ἐμπειρία normally is supposed to involve beliefs; and [γ] does not have any obvious intelligibility at 1.239 and 240, where Sextus talks of using technical terms ἀδοξάστως.)

*If* sense [γ] is correct for *PH,* then there are two corollaries of immediate relevance to my theme. First, we have Sextus *explicitly* stating that the Pyrrhonist's avowals do not involve him in any beliefs: τὸ πάθος ἀπαγγέλλει τὸ ἑαυτοῦ ἀδοξάστως (1.15). Secondly, we have Sextus *explicitly* claiming that the βιωτικὴ τήρησις (below, pp. 13–18) does not require belief in the Pyrrhonist who follows it: ἔπεται ἀδοξάστως τῇ βιωτικῇ τηρήσει (3.235). (See further, below nn. 96, 98). Indeed, if [γ] is right, then that alone virtually makes *PH* rustic. Unfortunately, I can see no way of determining the sense of ἀδόξαστος without presupposing the rustic/urbane dispute solved; hence I have relegated ἀδόξαστος to a footnote and shall not rest any argument upon its interpretation.

78. E.g. *PH* 1.165; *M* 7.322, 8.355, 9.138; 1.232.

79. E.g. *PH* 2.105, 258, 3.235; *M* 9.50.

roughly that between the layman and the professional, between real life and theory. Βίος means something like 'ordinary life', 'everyday life'. Thus οἱ ἀπὸ τοῦ βίου (*M* 11.49) are ordinary men, non-professionals; τὰ βιωτικὰ κριτήρια are the standards used in everyday judgements, as opposed to the technical or 'logical' standards invented by the philosophers (*PH* 2.15; *M* 7.33);[80] βίος itself is often used to mean 'Everyman' (e.g. *M* 2.18; 9.50).

Sometimes βίος is connected with language: βίος denotes ordinary language as opposed to technical usage (*M* 1.232; 8.129). Here Sextus is following the terminology of the grammarians.[81] Indeed, the Sextan use of βίος is not peculiar to him: in later Greek the word frequently marks off the lay from the professional;[82] in the patristic writers βίος invokes the affairs of the world as opposed to the affairs of heaven, and οἱ βιωτικοί are laymen as opposed to clerics and monks.[83]

Sextus is not unreservedly favourable to βίος. In a few passages the views of Everyman are subjected to the δύναμις ἀντιθετική along with the δόγματα of the professionals;[84] and the First Trope of Agrippa—the ubiquitous trope of διαφωνία—makes explicit reference to βίος: 'we discover that there has arisen an undecidable dissension both among ordinary men (παρὰ τῷ βίῳ) and among the philosophers' (*PH* 1.165).[85]

But an urbane interpreter of *PH* should not be discountenanced by such references. Laymen and professionals do sometimes make pronouncements on the same subjects. If a Pyrrhonist directs ἐποχή towards all δόγματα,

80. Cf. τὰ βιωτικὰ κριτήρια at NT, 1 *Cor.* 6.3–4.

81. E.g. Apollonius Dyscolus, *adv.* 130.6; *conj.* 245.21, 246.10; *synt.* 40.1; Galen, *meth.med.* 10.269 K. For the various locutions for 'ordinary usage' see Schneider's note in *Grammatici Graeci* II i 2, 45.

82. E.g. Plutarch, *mor.* 25C, 1033A, 1116C; Epictetus, *diss.* 1.15.2, 26.1, 3, 7, 17; 2.3.3, 5; frags 1, 2; Galen, *subf. emp.* 68.7; *diag. puls.* 8.78K; Soranus, *gyn.* 1.4.1; 3.3.1. See Epictetus, frag 16 εἰδέναι χρὴ ὅτι οὐ ῥᾴδιον δόγμα παραγενέσθαι ἀνθρώπῳ εἰ μὴ καθ' ἑκάστην ἡμέραν τὰ αὐτὰ καὶ λέγοι τις καὶ ἀκούοι καὶ ἅμα χρῷτο πρὸς τὸν βίον.

83. See Lampe's *Lexicon* s.vv. βίος (6), βιωτικός (cf. e.g. NT, *Luke* 21.34; 2 *Tim.* 2.4). In Christian writers βίος is often contrasted with δόγμα (e.g. Eusebius, *P.E.* 7.8.41); but that is only verbally comparable to what we find in Sextus: the Christian contrast is between deeds and words, between works and doctrine.

84. See *M* 9.50, 138.

85. Cf. DL 9.88 ὁ μὲν οὖν ἀπὸ τῆς διαφωνίας [sc. τρόπος] ὃ ἂν προτεθῇ ζήτημα παρὰ τοῖς φιλοσόφοις ἢ τῇ συνηθείᾳ πλείστης μάχης καὶ ταραχῆς πλῆρες ἀποδεικνύει. Here συνήθεια, as often, is synonymous with βίος.

he will in consequence direct ἐποχή toward some beliefs of Everyman. (Most obviously, there will be an overlap between δόγμα and βίος in the area of religion; and it is just there that we find Sextus being sceptical about βίος.) That does not commit a Pyrrhonist to a uniformly hostile attitude to βίος.[86]

Moreover, Sextus frequently expresses a friendly attitude toward Everyman. 'It is enough, I think, to live by experience and ἀδοξάστως, in accordance with the common observations and preconceptions, suspending judgement about what is said out of dogmatic embellishment and far beyond the needs of ordinary life (ἔξω τῆς βιωτικῆς χρείας)' (*PH* 2.246; cf. 254; 3.235).[87] Such passages seem to imply a limited ἐποχή: a Pyrrhonist will suspend judgement on δόγματα, but he will not allow his ἐποχή to spill over into 'common observations' and the beliefs of 'ordinary life'.

The crucial passage on βίος occurs near the beginning of *PH*. It requires detailed analysis.

Attending to the appearances, we live ἀδοξάστως in accordance with ordinary observation (κατὰ τὴν βιωτικὴν τήρησιν), since we cannot be altogether inactive. And this ordinary observation seems to consist of four parts and to depend first upon instruction of nature, then upon necessity of affections, then upon tradition of laws and customs, and finally upon teaching of arts: on natural instruction, in virtue of which we are capable of perception and of thought; on necessity of affections, in virtue of which hunger guides us to food and thirst to drink; on tradition of customs and laws, in virtue of which we accept in accordance with

---

86. The contrast between βίος and δόγμα, like the term δόγμα itself, is vague. I do not think the vagueness is harmful (see above, n. 31), but a little precision can readily be supplied. For Sextus' remarks enable us to define δόγμα as follows: A sentence expresses a δόγμα iff i) it expresses a proposition and (ii) it contains at least one term which denotes something ἄδηλον. Most ordinary beliefs will not be δόγματα; most philosophico-scientific tenets will be δόγματα. But βίος will include *some* δόγματα, notably *(a)* involving reference to the Gods, and *(b)* those involving moral concepts (for, in the Pyrrhonist's eyes, terms like ἀγαθόν and κακόν denote ἄδηλα). If an urbane Pyrrhonist defends the beliefs of βίος, he does so only for the most part.

87. See also *M* 9.165. A similar respect for βίος was ascribed to Pyrrho himself by Galen (*subf. emp.* 62.20), by Aenesidemus (DL 9.62), and perhaps by Timon (frag 81 Diels = DL 9.105—but see Fernanda Decleva Caizzi, *Pirrone—Testimonianze* (1981) 236–41). It was a commonplace among the Empirical doctors: e.g. Galen, *diff. puls.* 8.783K; *Med. Exp.* 18.5 Walzer.

ordinary life (βιωτικῶς) pious action as good and impious action as wicked; on teaching of arts, in virtue of which we are not inactive in the arts we accept. (*PH* 1.23–4; cf. 226, 237)

That paragraph details the Pyrrhonist's allegiance to βίος, and the context in which it does so is of some importance.

Dogmatists had charged Pyrrhonians with inactivity: if a Pyrrhonist is consistent, he will never *do* anything; for, having no beliefs, he will have no motive for doing anything.[88] In *PH* 1.23–4 Sextus gives his reply to that charge: the four-part 'ordinary observation' is meant to explain how it is that a Pyrrhonist can *act* despite his Scepticism. Thus we must construe the elements of the βιωτικὴ τήρησις as types of explanation of action: the Pyrrhonian *does* act; the four-part τήρησις categorises the possible explanations of *how* he can act.

Here I am not concerned with the adequacy or the plausibility of Sextus' explanatory scheme. My sole question is this: does the βιωτικὴ τήρησις commit the Sceptic to any *beliefs* at all? The *PH* Pyrrhonian supports βίος just insofar as his actions are explicable by appeal to the βιωτικὴ τήρησις: if that appeal does not invoke beliefs, then the Pyrrhonist may support βίος while remaining rustic; if the appeal does invoke belief, then his support for βίος makes the *PH* Sceptic urbane.

I shall consider each part of the τήρησις[89] in turn—though for dramatic reasons I shall not follow Sextus' order.

[1]’ Ἀνάγκη παθῶν, the necessity of affections, causes little trouble. Pyrrhonians eat and drink. How is that to be explained?—By the fact that they are hungry and thirsty. There is no need to advert to anything else: his πάθη alone suffice to drive the Sceptic—like any other man or animal—to food and drink. Sextus does not explicitly say that ἀνάγκη παθῶν invokes no beliefs; but he will surely have thought that it does not.[90] That part of the τήρησις seems compatible with rusticity.

88. The argument had a long history and went through different forms; see e.g. Burnyeat, chap. 2, n. 4; Gisela Striker (1980).

89. The word τήρησις has the same ambiguity as the English 'observation'— observation of rules etc. (i.e. obedience), or observation of objects and events (i.e. perception etc.). Sextus generally uses the word in the latter sense (see Janáček's index), but the former is more appropriate at *PH* 1.13.

90. 'But surely "Because he was hungry" will not by itself explain why men eat? We need, in addition, some reference to *beliefs*. "Why did he eat that tough steak?"—"Because he was hungry, and thought that the steak was the only food available". The πάθη by themselves are not sufficient to explain even our sim-

[2]Διδασκαλία τεχνῶν, teaching of arts, is needed to explain the professional activities of a Pyrrhonist. Some Sceptics, like Sextus himself, were doctors,[91] and other trades were Pyrrhonianly permissible.[92] The Sceptic's professional actions will be explained, in part at least, by reference to what his master taught him.

Now it might seem that teaching ineluctably involves beliefs. Tradesmen believe things; doctors have professional opinions; 'teaching of arts'—in Medical School, Agricultural College, or Naval Academy—will surely consist in the transmission of facts and the inculcation of beliefs. But I do not think that a Pyrrhonian is obliged so to understand the activity of teaching.[93] Why may he not construe teaching as the instilling of know-how, of skills and capacities? Teaching a man medicine, on that view, is like training him to ride: you are attempting to impart a *power* or skill to him; you are not trying to give him any *beliefs*. A Pyrrhonian doctor's professional activities can thus be explained by reference to his professional training, without supposing that the explanation involves belief.

That view of teaching is not found in any Sextan text; but it is strongly suggested by a curious passage from the end of *PH* 1. At *PH* 1.236–41 Sextus the Empiric argues that Pyrrhonism is incompatible with medical Empiricism, and he assimilates Scepticism rather to medical Methodism. The first of two points of association which Sextus finds between Pyrrhonists and

---

plest actions'. But that objection misses the point: Sextus is *not* implying that 'Because he is hungry' explains, in general, why a man eats; he may properly allow that in all normal cases an explanation will invoke beliefs as well as πάθη. His point rather is that such actions *can* be explained *even if* the agent has no beliefs: strike a man on the knee and his foot will kick, by a sort of natural necessity; similarly, if a Pyrrhonian is thirsty he will drink, by a sort of natural necessity. Non-Pyrrhonian drinking is no doubt only explicable *via* beliefs: but, according to Sextus, drinking *can* be explained even in the absence of belief—and that is all a Pyrrhonian requires.

91. See the list of Pyrrhonists at DL 9.115–6 (Menodotus, Sextus, Saturninus); add, e.g., Cassius (Galen, *subf. emp.* 40.15), Dionysius of Aegae (Photius, *bibl.* codd. 185 = codd. 211).

92. *M* 5.1–2 accepts farming, seamanship and astronomy as legitimate professions.

93. There is in any case a tension within *PH;* for Sextus argues at *PH* 3.252–73 (cf. *M* 11.216–56; 1.9–18) that διδασκαλία is impossible, and his argument does not appear to make any exceptions for the διδασκαλία τεχνῶν which *PH* 1.23 accepts. (Nor will the distinction between transmitting beliefs and inculcating skills help: many of the arguments against διδασκαλία are equally applicable to each sort of teaching.)

Methodists leads him to say that 'everything said by the Methodists can be subsumed under the necessity of affections' (239).

For 'just as the Sceptic, in virtue of the necessity of his affections, is guided by thirst to drink and by hunger to food, so the Methodical doctor is guided by the affections to their corresponding treatments—by contraction to dilatation . . . , by fluxion to its staunching . . .' (238). A Methodical doctor will observe his patient's condition, and that condition will guide him—by a kind of natural necessity—to the appropriate therapy. That must seem fantastical as an account of medical practice; but I suppose it is to be taken seriously. And Sextus explicitly connects his account of professional medical practice to his description of the βιωτικὴ τήρησις.[94]

Presumably that account of medical practice will be extended by the Pyrrhonist to cover all the professions. Thus professional expertise is not a matter of factual—still less of theoretical—knowledge and belief: it is a matter of capacity or skill; a professional is a man who responds in the appropriate way to the relevant stimuli. If that is so, then teaching an art is simply the inculcation of a capacity. Sextus' account of medical practice indicates that medical τέχνη is to be conceived of as skill or know-how. It is plausible to generalize that account, and to construe all τέχναι as skills or know-hows. If a τέχνη is a skill, then διδασκαλία τεχνῶν is the instillation of a skill. And thus—finally—a Pyrrhonist may explain his actions by reference to διδασκαλία τεχνῶν without thereby admitting to any beliefs. So far, the βιωτικὴ τήρησις is compatible with rusticity.

[3]Παράδοσις ἐθῶν καὶ νόμων, the tradition of customs and rules, will explain certain conventional acts which the Pyrrhonist performs. Why does Sextus wear trousers, spell his name with a sigma, take off his hat in churches, drive on the right?—'Because that is the custom, that is the law'. Sextus' primary point is doubtless this: a Pyrrhonian does not have to believe that *it is a good thing* to wear trousers or drive on the right—having abandoned beliefs about goodness and badness, he may still act as other men do, and he acts 'because that is the done thing'.

But it is plausible to go further. A Pyrrhonist need not believe that it is good to drive on the right; nor need he believe that it is the custom to drive on the right; nor, indeed, need he believe anything at all about driving on the right. He drives on the right because that is the custom—not because he believes that it is the custom (nor because he

94. *PH* 1.237 (ἐλέγομεν ἐν τοῖς ἔμπροσθεν) refers back explicitly to 1.23–4.

believes anything else).[95] Thus the tradition of laws and customs is also compatible with rusticity.

It is, I said, plausible to go further in that way; but is it faithful to Sextus' intentions? The answer might seem to be No. For Sextus' illustration of custom and law appears to invoke beliefs of some sort: he says 'we accept (παραλαμβάνομεν) . . . pious action as good'—and does not that mean 'we believe that pious action is good'? Moreover, at *PH* 3.2, prefacing his remarks on dogmatic theology, Sextus expressly states that 'following ordinary life ἀδοξάστως, we say that there are gods and we revere the gods and we say that they care for us.'[96] The ordinary customs which the Pyrrhonist of *PH* accepts include religious beliefs as well as religious practices.

That might be right, but it is not actually forced upon us by the texts. At *PH* 1.24, the phrase 'we accept . . . pious action as good' may mean, not 'we *believe* pious action *to be* good', but rather 'we *adopt* pious action *as though* it were good.'[97] So construed, the phrase does not imply any beliefs on the part of the Pyrrhonist. As for 3.2, it must be allowed that the Pyrrhonist will *say* 'The gods exist', 'The gods care for us' and the like; but Sextus asserts only that he will *say* such things, not that he will *believe* them.[98] A Pyrrhonist who goes to church will do the customary things—he will bare his head, genuflect, cross himself, and so on; and he will also *say* certain things. Those utterances are parts of the ritual: they do not betoken belief any more than the Sceptic's other ritual gestures do.[99]

95. Again (see above, n. 90), Sextus does not imply that other men's conventional actions are explicable without invoking beliefs: his point is simply that a *Pyrrhonian* may act conventionally, 'because it's the custom', without subscribing to any beliefs.

96. τῷ . . βίῳ κατακολουθοῦντες ἀδοξάστως φαμὲν εἶναι θεοὺς καὶ σέβομεν [cf. εὐσεβεῖν, 1.24] θεοὺς καὶ προνοεῖν αὐτοὺς φαμέν. I incline to construe ἀδοξάστως with κατακολουθοῦντες rather than with the three finite verbs. See below n. 98.

97. παραλαμβάνειν may certainly indicate adoption without any implication of belief (see e.g. *PH* 1.191, 195, 240). But ὡς ἀγαθόν is more difficult to construe in a belief-neutral way. (See e.g. *M* 1.201, where τὴν συνήθειαν . . . ὡς πιστὴν παραλαμβάνειν means 'to accept ordinary usage as reliable', i.e. to *believe that* it is reliable.)

98. If ἀδοξάστως is construed with φαμέν (see n. 96) and if the adverb means 'without belief' (see n. 77), then *PH* 3.2 actually *asserts* this; for Sextus then expressly argues that the Pyrrhonist will *say* 'There are gods' but will not *believe* that there are gods.

99. Again, Wittgenstein might be invoked: see, e.g. his *Lectures and Conversations on . . . Religious Belief,* esp. 53–9. (But according to Wittgenstein, *all* churchgoers are playing the language game which in the text I prescribe for the Pyrrhonian.)

Thus a rustic interpretation of the 'tradition of laws and customs' can be produced. But I confess that I find the interpretation forced; for although Sextus' abstract description of 'tradition' is perfectly compatible with rusticity, his illustration of the Pyrrhonist's traditionalism strongly suggests belief—if Sextus intends *PH* 1.24 (and 3.2) to be understood in a rustic fashion then his language is misleading and perhaps disingenuous.

[4] Ὑφήγησις φυσική, natural instruction,[100] seems, from its name, a probable source of belief; and when Sextus glosses the phrase by reference to perception and thought, that probability increases—for perception and thought are surely prime originators of belief. But what exactly has Sextus got in mind when he refers to 'natural instruction'? A part of the answer to that question comes from Book 2 of *PH*.

In *PH* 2, as I have already remarked, Sextus argues against the Dogmatists' use of signs and proofs. But his rejection of signs is not wholesale; on the contrary, he carefully records a distinction between two types of sign, and explicitly states that he is arguing against only one of those types. 'Indicative' signs allegedly enable us to learn about naturally unclear objects (τὰ φύσει ἄδηλα): Sextus will have nothing to do with them. But in addition to indicative signs there are 'recollective' signs; and for them Sextus has more respect.

'They call a recollective sign something which has been directly observed together with the thing signified and which, at the same time as it strikes us, while the latter is unclear, leads us to a recollection of the thing which was observed together with it and is now not striking us directly—as in the case of smoke and fire' (*PH* 2.100). Smoke is a recollective sign of fire because *(a)* we have often directly observed smoke and fire together, and *(b)* when we directly observe smoke and do not directly observe fire, the smoke leads us to think of fire.[101]

Sextus admits such signs. 'Recollective signs are relied upon in ordinary life. When a man sees smoke he infers (σημειοῦται) fire, and when he has noticed a scar he says that a wound has been received. Thus not only do we not fight against ordinary life, but we actually struggle at its side, assenting

---

100. For ὑφήγησις with the sense 'instruction' (not 'guidance') see *PH* 1.6, 2.120; *M* 7.22, 8.300, 11.47; 1.35, 172, 258, 3.18, 5.3.

101. This is a rough characterisation; for a detailed and subtle treatment see now M. F. Burnyeat, 'The origins of non-deductive inference', in *Science and Speculation*. J. Barnes, J. Brunschwig, M. Burnyeat, M. Schofield edd., *Science and Speculation: Studies in Hellenistic Theory and Practice* (Cambridge/Paris 1982), 93–238.

ἀδοξάστως to what it relies upon and opposing the private fictions of the Dogmatists' (*PH* 2.102).[102]

The ordinary man sees smoke rising from the hillside or a speck of blood on your chin (there he relies on αἴσθησις). He then infers (σημειοῦται) that there is a brush-fire or that you cut yourself shaving (there he exercises νόησις). He starts from one belief, based upon perception; and his deduction leads him to another belief. The Pyrrhonist accepts recollective signs and fights on the side of βίος. It is natural to infer that the Pyrrhonist is thereby committed to those beliefs which Everyman employs when engaged in sign-inference; and it is plausible to regard that as a particularly good illustration of ὑφήγησις φυσική. In that case, the Pyrrhonist of *PH*, siding with βίος and relying on recollective signs, is urbane and not rustic.

A rustic interpreter must explain three things if his interpretation is to survive the acceptance of recollective signs. He must explain (i) how the Pyrrhonist can *embark upon* the inference—how he can rely on αἴσθησις and report the smoke; (ii) how he can *end* the inference—how he can come to report the fire; and (iii) how he can *make* the inference—how he can infer from the smoke to the fire. For all three of those things apparently involve beliefs, and the rustic interpreter does not allow beliefs to his Pyrrhonist.

Now it is easy to see how the rustic interpreter will proceed. On (i) and (ii) he will suggest that, in uttering the initial and the final stages of the sign-inference, the Pyrrhonist is not stating beliefs but simply avowing his πάθη: 'It looks like smoke over there', 'It looks like fire over there',[103] he

---

102. Cf. *M* 8.156–8, which makes the same point in similarly forthright terms.

103. 'But it does *not* look like fire over there. The whole point of the sign is that it allows us to grasp that there *is* fire there even when we *cannot* see or otherwise perceive the fire: the fire is ἄδηλον-ἄδηλον πρὸς καιρόν, not φύσει ἄδηλον—and if it were not, we should have no need of a sign'. The rustic may say, in reply, that when he experiences the πάθος normally reported by 'It looks like smoke', he *also* experiences the πάθος normally reported by 'It looks like fire'—i.e. he experiences the πάθος which he normally experiences when (as a nonPyrrhonist would put it) he is actually looking at the fire itself. Naturally, he reports the second πάθος in the standard way, saying 'It looks like fire'—there is no reason why all cases of its looking like fire should be qualitatively indistinguishable. (But is that really coherent? Suppose a rustic looks at an oar in water; why shouldn't he say 'It looks *straight*'? For there is no reason why all cases of oars looking straight should be qualitatively indistinguishable. Maybe a Pyrrhonist *will* sometimes say 'It looks straight': he is, after all, simply reporting his πάθη, and there is nothing in Pyrrhonism which demands that the πάθος caused (as a non-Pyrrhonist would put it) by a submerged oar should always be the πάθος normally reported by 'It

will say; and those utterances, employing typical φαίνεται sentences, will
commit him to no beliefs. As for (iii), the inference, that may be interpreted,
analogously to the ἀνάγκη παθῶν, as a piece of natural necessity: having
the πάθος reported by 'It looks like smoke', the Pyrrhonist finds that he also
has the πάθος reported by 'It looks like fire'—he makes no inference at all,
strictly speaking; rather, as Sextus says, nature 'leads him' to the second πάθος.
A Pyrrhonist, like Everyman, uses recollective signs; and he therefore produces
utterances of the form '*p*—so *q*'. But in those utterances neither '*p*' nor '*q*'
expresses a belief (they merely avow πάθη); and the word 'so' does not signify
an inference (it marks a psychological compulsion). The whole affair takes
place without any beliefs being invoked.

That is, I hope, a moderately coherent account of the way in which a
'sign-inference' might work; and it shows that a rustic Pyrrhonist could give
a coherent explanation of his use of recollective signs.[104] But that is not
enough. I am not asking whether a rustic *could* give such an explanation: I
am asking whether the account in *PH* 2 is rustic. And it is, I fear, hard to read
the account I have just given into the text of *PH*. Everyman surely has
beliefs and makes inferences when he employs recollective signs. Sextus
says that his Pyrrhonist sides here with Everyman: he does not say that the
Pyrrhonist transmutes Everyman's statements of belief into avowals of
πάθη; he does not say that the Pyrrhonist replaces Everyman's inference by
a psychological event. Had Sextus wanted to indicate that the Pyrrhonist's
use of recollective signs involves no beliefs he could have done so quite
easily. He does not do so. If, nevertheless, he intends a rustic reading of
recollective signs we must suppose, again, that his language is misleading
and perhaps disingenuous.

---

looks bent'.)—The second example of a recollective sign at *PH* 2.102 introduces an
important point which Sextus nowhere develops. For the 'conclusion' of the second
sign is 'He looks as though he has been wounded', and that contains a reference to *the past*.
The Pyrrhonist's φαίνεται sentences are always present-tensed: he reports his *present*
πάθη (see above, n. 20). But the *contents* of those πάθη may themselves advert to past—or to
future—times. A Pyrrhonist may say—to make the point fully explicit—'The man *now*
appears to me as *having been* wounded', 'The clouds *now* appear to me as *being about to*
produce rain'. In that way a rustic Pyrrhonist may have some purchase on the past and the
future; and plainly some purchase on the future is necessary if his actions are to be given any
adequate explanations.

104. My standard of coherence is pretty low: I mean only that this account of
recollective signs is at least as plausible as, say, Sextus' account of Methodical
medicine.

What, in sum, are we to make of Sextus' account of the βιωτικὴ τήρησις? Three general conclusions seem to me to emerge from an analysis of the texts. First, it is possible to construct an interpretation of the τήρησις which is compatible with a rustic view of *PH*—adherence to the τήρησις does not positively demand a commitment to belief. Or rather, a rustic Pyrrhonist might argue, with some show of plausibility, that his beliefless state is consistent with his following the τήρησις. Secondly, if we insist upon a rustic construal of the τήρησις, then we must dismiss Sextus' claim that his Pyrrhonist sides with βίος: Everyman has everyday beliefs; a rustic Pyrrhonist has no beliefs; it is merely disingenuous for a rustic to pretend that he is on the side of Everyman. (Just as it was disingenuous of Berkeley to pretend to be vindicating Common Sense.) A rustic may with more plausibility suggest that his own style of life need not differ markedly in its external form from the life of Everyman, and to that extent he may reasonably claim an affinity to Everyman. But exactly the same claim could be made—with more propriety—by any Dogmatist; and the claim does not constitute a justification for enrolling the rustic Pyrrhonist as an ally of βίος in its alleged battle against δόγμα. Thirdly, and most importantly, I fear that we must conclude either that *PH* is not uniformly rustic or else that *PH* is culpably disingenuous: if we take Sextus' remarks about βίος at their face value we shall adopt the former conclusion, if we take them with a large pinch of salt we shall adopt the latter conclusion.

And there, for the moment, I rest the case. The general tenor of *PH* is, I think, indubitably rustic. But *PH* also contains important intrusions of urbanity.

# VI

The problem I have been discussing concerns the range or scope of Pyrrhonian ἐποχή. It was granted that different Pyrrhonists may well have set different limits to their ἐποχή—that some may have permitted themselves to believe more than others. But it is a presupposition of the problem, as it has been posed, that any particular Pyrrhonist must, if he is to have a coherent philosophy, define the scope of ἐποχή within his own version of Scepticism. I shall end this paper by questioning that presupposition, and hence by suggesting that the problem of the scope of ἐποχή is in a certain sense unreal.

The goal of Pyrrhonism is ἀταραξία, and the original cause of Sceptical investigations is 'the anomaly in things' and the disquiet which such anomaly arouses (*PH* 1.12). We become aware of an 'anomaly' in, say, the alleged facts about death: do we survive our deaths, as some hold, or do we rather perish utterly, as others maintain? The anomaly upsets us—we are ταραττόμενοι. We begin an investigation of the subject in the hope, initially, of discovering the truth and so setting our minds at rest. But we possess a δύναμις ἀντιθετική; we find that the arguments pro are equally balanced by the arguments con; we end in ἐποχή over the question—and upon ἐποχή there supervenes the desired ἀταραξία.

Will every Pyrrhonist exhibit ἐποχή towards the possibility of an after life? Surely not. For a Pyrrhonist will only reach ἐποχή if he exercises his δύναμις ἀντιθετική; he will only exercise his δύναμις ἀντιθετική if he finds himself suffering from ταραχή; he will only suffer from ταραχή if he perceives a worrying ἀνωμαλία in things. Nothing obliges us to think that ταραχή over death is a universal phenomenon (still less, ταραχή over the nature of time and place, the possibility of causal interconnexions, the existence of numbers). Some men may never light upon the anomaly in the thing. Others may discover the anomaly and laugh it aside. Untroubled, such men have no motive for exercising their δύναμις ἀντιθετική on the puzzles of dying, and hence no means—and no motive—for achieving ἐποχή.

The point of Pyrrhonism is ἀταραξία. Pyrrhonist strategies are relevant only where ταραχή exists. A man who suffers only mildly from ταραχή may be a perfect Pyrrhonist; for he may achieve complete ἀταραξία by exercising his δύναμις and reaching ἐποχή in a very modest way. Others, who find the whole of life a sea of troubles, will not be set at rest until they have achieved universal ἐποχή.

The medical simile which the Sceptics loved is helpful here. Ταραχή is a disease, ἐποχή the cure. The Pyrrhonist is a doctor—a psychiatrist—who claims the ability to cure ταραχή in most of its forms.[105] How much medicine does a man need to be healthy? How far will a competent doctor apply his plasters and administer his drugs? Plainly, it all depends on the disease. Some conditions require massive doses and major surgery, others are assuaged by an aspirin. It is absurd to imagine that doctors can produce a single formula, applicable to all men in all conditions, or pronounce generally that every patient needs so many pills a day.

How much ἐποχή does a man need for ἀταραξία or mental health? How far will a competent Pyrrhonist apply his Tropes and exercise his δύναμις ἀντιθετική? Plainly, it all depends on the disease. Serious mental conditions require strong remedies, minor maladies are righted by a simple argument or two. It is absurd to suppose that a Pyrrhonist can produce a single formula,

---

105. A certain amount of ταραχή is inseparable from the human condition: there the best the doctor can do is produce μετριοπάθεια (*PH* 1.25; 3.235–6).

applicable to all men in all conditions, or pronounce generally that every patient needs so much ἐποχή and so many Tropes a day.

Yet that absurd supposition lies behind the question I have been discussing. 'What is the extent of ἐποχή recommended by the Pyrrhonist of *PH?*' The question is misconceived, for it rests upon a silly presupposition. Ἐποχή may be broad or narrow. Pyrrhonism may be rustic or urbane. Everything depends on the state of the particular patient.

That, I suggest, is the answer which Sextus *should* have given to the question. I do not claim that Sextus *did* give that answer. But I am inclined to imagine that he *would* have given it had the question been put to him directly. For, first, the answer is an obvious corollary of the general remarks about the nature and goal of Pyrrhonism with which Sextus prefaces *PH*. Secondly, the answer makes sense of the closing paragraphs of *PH:* there, at *PH* 3.280–1, Sextus makes some curious comments on the power of his own arguments and he exploits the medical simile in a self-conscious way. Finally, the answer provides an escape from the dismal conclusion to which the body of this paper has led us: we need not accept that *PH* is inconsistent or incoherent or indefinite in its attitude to the scope of ἐποχή; if the scope of ἐποχή is determined by the patient's condition and not by the doctor's theories, then we should not expect the doctor's theories to contain a coherent thesis—or any thesis at all—about the range and scope of ἐποχή.

# 4

# The Sceptic in His Place and Time

## Myles Burnyeat

Nowadays, if a philosopher finds he cannot answer the philosophical question 'What is time?' or 'Is time real?', he applies for a research grant to work on the problem during next year's sabbatical. He does not suppose that the arrival of next year is actually in doubt. Alternatively, he may agree that any puzzlement about the nature of time, or any argument for doubting the reality of time, is in fact a puzzlement about, or an argument for doubting, the truth of the proposition that next year's sabbatical will come, but contend that this is of course a strictly theoretical or philosophical worry, not a worry that needs to be reckoned with in the ordinary business of life. Either way he *insulates* his ordinary first order judgements from the effects of his philosophizing.

The practice of insulation, as I shall continue to call it, can be conceived in various ways. There are plenty of philosophers for whom Wittgenstein's well-known remark (1953: # 124), that philosophy 'leaves everything as it is', describes not the end-point but the starting-point of their philosophizing. There are many who accept one or another version of the idea that philosophy is the analysis or, more broadly, that it is the meta-study of existing forms of discourse—an idea going naturally with the thought that, while a certain amount of revision may be in order, in general philosophy must respect and be responsive to these forms of discourse in the same way as any theory must, in general, respect and be responsive to the data it is a theory of. Others again have invoked Carnap's (1950) distinction between internal and external questions: ordinary inquiries about when and where things happen are inquiries which go on by recognized procedures within the accepted spatiotemporal framework of science and everyday life, whereas philosophical questions and the doubts that inspire them are external questions, about the framework itself, as to whether it provides the best way of speaking about places and times.[1] But I am not here concerned with the credentials of these and other accounts of the practice of insulation. For I believe that, at least in some central areas of philosophical discussion, the sense of a difference between philosophical and ordinary questions lies deep in most of us: much deeper than any particular articulation of it that you might meet yesterday or today in Harvard, Oxford or California.

Admittedly, there are those who, influenced perhaps by Quine, would be reluctant to accept any of these views or to have anything to do with insulation. For them, as for Quine, philosophical reflection and ordinary thought are to be seen as a single fabric, no part of which is immune from the effects of revisions and puzzlements elsewhere. But it is one thing to say this, another to make sure that you fully believe it. One test is how you react to the following argument: It is true that *yesterday* my body was for some time *nearer to* the mantelpiece than to the bookcase; therefore, it is false that space and time are unreal. In my experience,[2] nearly everybody protests that this argument of Moore's (1925) is the wrong *sort* of argument to settle a philosophical dispute about the reality of space or time. They feel strongly that philosophical scepticism cannot be straightforwardly refuted by common sense. But the corollary of this must be that common sense cannot be refuted by philosophical scepticism. And indeed, when we look at the paper which has contributed more than any other single factor to keeping alive an interest in scepticism during these days of exact philosophy, Thompson Clarke's famous paper 'The Legacy of Scepticism' (1972),[3] we find that his starting-point, the foundation of the whole thing, is the thesis that the judgements and knowledge-claims we make in ordinary life are immune (that is his word) from philosophical doubt. Insulation, it turns out, is a two-way business. It protects ordinary life from philosophy and it protects philosophy from ordinary life and G. E. Moore, and you cannot buy the one protection without the other. Alternatively, if you do want your philosophizing to connect with first order concerns, you had better keep it sober.

1. Carnap, I should emphasize, is no insulator, but a verificationist who denies that external questions have cognitive content. Consequently, he thinks of frameworks as up for acceptance or rejection on pragmatic grounds: whole frameworks could be swept away, if they proved inconvenient. But Stroud 1979, rejecting the verificationism and restoring meaning to philosophical debate, does render the internal-external distinction equivalent to insulation.

2. Compare Stroud 1979: 279.

3. Clarke's influence is acknowledged in Stroud 1979: 297, n. 41, 1983: 434, n. 11, Cavell 1979: xii, xx–xxi, Nagel 1979: 19, 27.

I hope that I have said enough for you to recognize the phenomenon I am pointing to: if not in yourselves, then in others and in the philosophy of our time. My thesis is going to be that it is precisely that, a phenomenon of our time. Ancient philosophers would find it puzzling; so would the philosophers of the Renaissance. This sense of the separateness, sometimes even the strangeness, of philosophical issues is not a timeless thing, instrinsic to the very nature of philosophy. It is a product of the history of philosophy.[4] I shall tell of a time when insulation was not yet invented, when philosophical scepticism did straightforwardly clash with common sense, and people took it seriously precisely because they saw it as a genuine alternative to their ordinary views. If my thesis is correct, there will be historical questions to ask about when, and by whom, and why insulation was invented: questions the answers to which might help to explain the atmosphere of 'belatedness' (if I may borrow a term from literary criticism) that so often surrounds twentieth-century philosophical discussions of scepticism. All that thrashing about to discover a way to take the sceptic seriously, and to insist that he is still very much alive, betrays a feeling that the important dealings with scepticism took place long ago. Which I think is true. But I shall come to the historical questions in due course. First, I must establish that once upon a time scepticism was a serious challenge and no-one thought to insulate it from affecting, or being affected by, the judgements of ordinary life.

## II

The first philosophers to title themselves sceptics, in both the ancient sense (*skeptikos* means 'inquirer') and in the modern sense of 'doubter' (for which their word was *ephektikos*, 'one who suspends judgement'), were the members of the Pyrrhonist movement founded by Aenesidemus in the first century B.C.[5] Their use of these words was designed to distinguish their type of philosophy both from that of the Academics and from that of the dogmatic schools. Pyrrhonist enquiry, we are told, has a unique feature: it does not terminate either in the discovery of the truth, as the dogmatic

4. So also, of course, is the recent corrective reaction which flies the banner of 'applied philosophy': a volume could be written on the presuppositions of that phrase.

5. For the Pyrrhonist titles of allegiance, see S. E. *PH* I 7, DL IX 69–70; on the history of the word *skeptikos*, see Janáček 1979, Striker 1980: 54, n. 1, Sedley 1983: 20–3.

philosophers claim theirs does, or in the denial of its discoverability, which is the conclusion argued for by the Academics.[6] This was more than a theoretical distinction. In the ancient context to appropriate *skeptikos* and *ephektikos* to flag a type or school of philosophy was a dramatic and fundamentally new declaration that from now on scepticism, inquiry and doubt, was to be a philosophy to live by.[7]

Not only were the Pyrrhonists the first self-proclaimed sceptics, it was above all their ideas which represented scepticism to the modern world when the writings of Sextus Empiricus (*circa* 200 A.D.) were rediscovered and published in the sixteenth century.[8] The sixteenth century was in fact the time when Pyrrhonism achieved its greatest impact. As Richard Popkin (1979) has taught us, the rediscovery of Sextus played a major role in shaping modern philosophy's preoccupation, from Descartes onwards, with the task of finding a satisfactory rebuttal of sceptical arguments. For a long

6. S. E. *PH* I 1. 'Argued for' can of course be taken two ways: (a) 'argued for but not necessarily endorsed', (b) 'argued for and endorsed'. The difference between (a) and (b) sums up the difference between the dialectical aims of the Academy under Arcesilaus and Carneades (third to second centuries B.C.) and the dogmatizing Academy of Philo (second to first century B.C.). For the complexities of the historical transition from (a) to (b), see Couissin 1929, Sedley 1983, Frede 1984 (= chap. 5).

7. Sadly, the Pyrrhonists failed to persuade the world to observe the distinction between themselves and the Academics. The Academics came to be called, retrospectively, *skeptikoi* and *ephektikoi* because the distinction was disputed or ignored (Aul. Gell. XI 5, *Anonymi prolegomena philosophiae Platonicae* 21–5 Westerink; cf. S. E. *PH* I 221–2). In the course of time the blanketing nomenclature, combined with insensitivity to the difference adverted to in n. 6, gave modern philosophy, and subsequently modern scholarship (including modern scholarship concerned with the beginnings of modern philosophy), a gravely distorted picture of pre-Pyrrhonist scepticism. I would not deny outright the propriety of referring to Arcesilaus and Carneades as 'Academic sceptics'; it is too late now to undo tradition. But I believe, and will argue at length elsewhere, that there was a real and fundamental difference, not only between Pyrrhonism and the dogmatic scepticism of Philo, but also—and here perhaps I diverge from Frede 1984 (= chap. 5), at least in emphasis—between Pyrrhonism and the dialectical arguments for sceptical conclusions put forward by Arcesilaus and Carneades. That is why I start my consideration of the history of scepticism at the point where the sceptic first got his name.

8. The qualification 'above all' is necessary because a full treatment must reckon with the earlier presence of Cicero's *Academica* as a source for 'Academic scepticism'. But it was Sextus who made scepticism a major issue for the modern world: see Schmitt 1983 for a summary of the results of historical research in this area.

time this meant a rebuttal of the arguments in Sextus Empiricus. Thus the notion of scepticism which we find in Sextus Empiricus can claim to be the original one, both for antiquity and for modern times. And it so happens that as far back as Gassendi and, I think, Montaigne we find an interpretation of Pyrrhonian scepticism according to which the sceptic does practise insulation of a kind—of what kind, we shall shortly see.[9]

This interpretation will provide a useful point of departure, first because Montaigne and Gassendi were two of the thinkers most closely involved in the modern revival of Pyrrhonian scepticism; second because their brand of insulation is still to be met with in modern accounts of ancient scepticism;[10] and third because in the modern literature on ancient scepticism the Montaigne-Gassendi type of insulation competes with another, different notion of insulation which is itself something I would like to situate in a historical perspective designed to highlight changes in the role that scepticism has played at different periods.

So now to business.

## III

The key text for all insulating interpretations is *Outlines of Pyrrhonism* (abbreviated '*PH*') I 13, which draws a contrast between certain things the sceptic assents to, and certain others he does not assent to. The contrast defines the scope of Sextus' scepticism, and our decision as to where the line is drawn will determine our interpretation of the scepticism:

> When we say that the sceptic does not dogmatize, we are not using 'dogma' in the more general sense in which some say it is dogma to accept anything (for the sceptic does assent to the experiences he cannot help having in virtue of this impression or that: for example, he would not say, when warmed or cooled, 'I seem not to be warmed or cooled'). Rather, when we say he does not dogmatize, we mean 'dogma' in the

9.  In their separate and quite different ways both Gassendi (most accessible in Brush 1972) and Montaigne 1580 frustrate the attempt to find in them a single, consistent interpretation of Pyrrhonism: see Walker 1983 on the former, Cave 1970: Pt. II, Ch. 4 on the latter. But the insulation I shall be speaking about stands out more clearly than rival tendencies.

10. E.g. Hallie 1967, Striker 1983, and the standard books, like Brochard 1923, to which scholars of the Renaissance are likely to go for information on ancient scepticism.

sense in which some say that dogma is assent to any of the non-evident matters investigated by the sciences. For the Pyrrhonian assents to nothing that is non-evident. (*PH* I 13)[11]

To begin with, we can ask what Sextus means by saying that the sceptic does assent to experiences (*pathē*), like that of being warmed, which are bound up with the use of the senses and, more generally, with the having of impressions (*phantasiai*), whether of sense *or of thought.* (I italicize these words as a quick warning not to take the quoted paragraph as confining the sceptic's assent to sense-impressions. Although the example here is a sense-impression, in Sextus 'impression', 'experience', 'appearance' are not restricted to the sensory,[12] and readers more familiar with British Empiricist ideas and impressions than with Hellenistic epistemology should beware of importing the former into the latter.) But this assent, which is elsewhere and often called assent to appearances, is itself unclear, or at least has been the subject of dispute.[13] The dispute, in a nutshell, is this: if one gives the sceptic a generous notion of appearance, the area of his assent expands and the scepticism contracts, while conversely scepticism spreads and assent draws back if (as I do) one takes a more restricted view of appearance. Let me explain in a little more detail.

Sextus directs us to understand every statement he makes, however expressed, as a record of his experience (*pathos*) telling us how things appear to him (*PH* I 4, 15, 135, 197, 198–9, 200, *M* XI 18–19). If he means 'appear' in its non-epistemic sense, *PH* I 13 implies that the sceptic's assent is restricted to experiential reports like 'It feels warm to me here', 'This argument strikes me as persuasive'. He may say 'It is warm', 'It is a sound

11. My translation of this key passage is an attempt to put into tolerable English the results of minute analysis, by several hands, of nearly every word and phrase occurring in it (Frede 1979, Burnyeat 1980, Barnes 1982; = chap. 1–3 above). Any nuances that may remain doubtful or in dispute will not, I believe, affect the present discussion.

12. See chap. 2, 38–41.

13. Frede 1979 vs. Burnyeat 1980 (chap. 1 and 2). The present paper began as a further contribution to this debate, and an attempt to outflank my opponent. But he, meanwhile, has moved to a new position (Frede 1984; chap. 5) and some of my earlier arguments relied on a thesis, that 'dogma' just means 'belief', which has been dented by Sedley 1983: nn. 57 and 67 and in correspondence earlier, and smashed by Barnes 1982 (= chap. 3). My revised position, like that of Barnes, should still be regarded as an alternative to Frede 1979 (= chap. 1), but it joins with Frede's current concern to see the whole issue in a broader historical framework extending into modern times. As always, I owe much to discussion of these matters with Michael Frede.

argument', but what he means is 'I have the experience of its appearing so'. If, on the other hand, 'appear' carries its epistemic sense, to talk about how things appear is simply to talk in a non-dogmatic way about how things are in the world. We will no doubt want further elucidation of what it is to talk 'in a non-dogmatic way', but *PH* I 13 now leads us to expect that the sceptic will be content to accept (*eudokein*) a host of propositions like 'It is warm here', 'This is a persuasive argument', just so long as these are understood to make no more strenuous claims than suffice for the purposes of ordinary life.

But we can also ask about the other half of the contrast in *PH* I 13. What does Sextus mean by saying that the sceptic does not assent to any of the non-evident matters investigated by the sciences? It is this side of the issue I propose to discuss here. Perhaps it will contribute some light on the first area of dispute.[14]

What, then, are the non-evident objects of scientific inquiry? The notion of the non-evident is the notion of that which we can only know about, if we can know it at all, by inference from what is evident. If knowledge of the non-evident is possible, as Sextus' dogmatist opponent believes, it is mediate knowledge as contrasted with the immediate, non-inferential knowledge of what is evident (*PH* II 97–9). The dogmatist's favourite example of something evident is the proposition 'It is day'. If you are a normal healthy human being walking about in the daytime, it is perfectly evident to you that it is day. But we need an example which relates smoothly to the sciences on the one hand and to the sceptic's experience of being warmed on the other. I do not think that Sextus' dogmatist would hesitate to claim, when he is sitting on his stove, that it is quite evident that it iswarm. Now, if one takes 'The stove is warm' as an example of something evident, and couples it with the reference to the sciences, it becomes rather natural to suppose—and this is what Montaigne and Gassendi did suppose—that dogma in the sense Sextus wishes to eschew is any scientific pronouncement about, for example, the underlying physical structure which makes warm things warm, any theory about the real nature of heat, perhaps even the assertion or the belief that there is such a thing as the real nature of heat about which a theory could in principle be given.

14. Meanwhile, I have found an ancient ally in *Anonymi commentarius in Platonis Theaetetum* 61, 1–46 Diels-Schubart. The author distinguishes between the epistemic and the non-epistemic uses of 'appear' and assigns the latter to Pyrrho. This evidence may be significantly closer in time to Aenesidemus than has generally been thought: see Tarrant 1983.

On this type of interpretation—in honour of Montaigne I should like to call it the country gentleman's interpretation—Pyrrhonian scepticism is scepticism about the realm of theory, which at this period will include both what we would consider philosophical or metaphysical theory and much that we can recognize as science. The non-theoretical judgements of ordinary life are insulated from the scepticism and the scepticism is insulated from them, not because Sextus, like Thompson Clarke, assigns a special status to philosophical doubt, but because he assigns it a special subject matter, different from the subject matters with which the ordinary man is concerned in the ordinary business of life. This is insulation by subject matter or content, a disengagement of life from theory. 'Socrates thought that a man knows enough geometry if he is able to measure out the land he gives or receives' (Montaigne 1580: I 535–6).

Here, for example, is Gassendi defending ordinary life against Descartes' method of doubt:

> But if the tower seen from close up appeared to have no corners and to be quite rounded, then I cannot see why any desire to restrain our belief in appearances or any doubt whether it is round and smooth rather than square would occur to anyone except those you call 'not of sound mind'. (Gassendi 1644 in Brush 1972: 168)

And here he is expounding ancient Pyrrhonism:

> Nor is there enough solidity in the customary objection to those who say that nothing is certain or can be comprehended, namely that they do not really doubt that it is daylight when the sun is shining, that fire is hot, snow white, honey sweet, and other things of that sort; and that therefore they must at least accept the criterion by which those things are determined, namely the senses. For these men, as we observed above, say that the appearances of things, or what things appear to be *on the outside,* is one thing and the truth, or the *inner* nature of things, namely what the things are in themselves, is another matter, and that when they say that nothing can be known certainly and that there is no criterion, they are not speaking of what things appear to be and of what is revealed by the senses as if by some special criterion, but of what things are in themselves, which is so hidden that no criterion can disclose it. (Gassendi 1658 in Brush 1972: 294, my emphasis)

These two quotations can serve as Gassendi's version of the contrast in *PH* I 13: on the one side, a casual acceptance of the standards we ordinarily use in judging that the tower is round, on the other side a strong scepticism about the 'inner nature' of things.

Notice how Gassendi aligns Sextus' contrast with a contrast between the outside of things (what is accessible to everyday observation through the senses) and their inner nature. You will not find Sextus adding the epithet 'inner' on the innumerable occasions when he concludes, 'We can say how things appear, but not what their nature is'. The inner/outer contrast bespeaks a new world, in which the interpretation of ancient Pyrrhonism has been overlaid with the preoccupations of seventeenth-century science.

Now one advantage of the country gentleman's interpretation is that there is no great difficulty in understanding how he can walk about his estate making arrangements for next year's crops while proclaiming himself a sceptic about space and time. There is no difficulty here because what the sceptic suspends judgment about, on this view, is not the spaces and times of ordinary life but the space and time of the natural philosophers. The sceptic is not a man who doubts he is in Cambridge or that he has been talking for at least five minutes. He is a man who is doubtful about the sorts of thing that the natural philosophers say in constructing their theories:

> For some define time as the interval of the motion of the whole (by 'whole' I mean the universe), others as that motion itself; Aristotle (or according to some, Plato) defines it as the number of prior and posterior in motion, Strato (or according to some, Aristotle) as the measure of motion and rest, and Epicurus (as reported by Demetrius Lacon) as the concomitant of concomitants, since it accompanies days and nights and seasons, and the presence and absence of feelings, and motions and rests. (*PH* III 136–7)

The sceptic is doubtful about time both because the dogmatic philosophers disagree with each other and there seems to be no way of resolving the dispute (*PH* III 138–40)—hence the recitation of the different accounts of time—and because he is impressed by certain destructive arguments of the kind promulgated later by Augustine and McTaggart against the reality of time (*PH* III 140–150). Not that the sceptic accepts the negative conclusion of the destructive arguments: that would be dogma too, a negative dogmatism. Rather, just as he cannot find a criterion for deciding which among the competing positive views is correct, so equally he cannot decide whether or not the destructive arguments should be preferred to more positive urgings from the other side. The two dogmas, the affirmation and the denial of the reality of time, balance out and the sceptic suspends judgement on the issue and on all theoretical issues connected with time (*PH* III 140). The same goes for space, as will appear below. The sceptic disengages from the heavy pronouncements of the philosophers and the scientists and gets on with the business of daily life in Cambridge or Montaigne:

> The heavens and the stars have been swinging round for three thousand years, as all the world had believed, until Cleanthes of Samos, or according to Theophrastus, Nicetas of Syracuse, presumed to proclaim that it was the earth that moved, revolving about its axis, through the oblique circle of the zodiac. And, in our days, Copernicus has so well grounded this theory, that he very lawfully uses it for all astronomical conclusions. What can we make of that, except that we need not bother our heads about which of the two theories is right? (Montaigne 1580: II 15)

# IV

So far, then, so good. But how well does the country gentleman's interpretation measure up to the texts (besides *PH* I 13) in which it claims to find evidence of insulation? At first glance it does rather well.

Sextus starts his treatment of *topos* (place) in the *Outlines of Pyrrhonism* with an introductory statement about the scope of his discussion:

> Space, or place, then, is used in two senses, the strict and the loose—loosely of place taken broadly (as 'my city'), and strictly of exactly containing place whereby we are exactly enclosed. Our enquiry, then, is concerned with space of the strict kind. This some have affirmed, others denied; and others have suspended judgement about it. (*PH* III 119, tr. Bury 1933–49)

The parallel passage in Sextus' larger work *adversus Mathematicos* (abbreviated '*M*'), comes not at the beginning but shortly thereafter:

> Now it is agreed that, speaking loosely, we say that a man is in Alexandria or in the gymnasium or in the school; but our investigation is not concerned with place in the broad sense but with that in the circumscribed sense, as to whether this exists or is merely imagined; and if it exists, of what sort it is in its nature, whether corporeal or incorporeal, and whether contained in place or not. (*M* X 15, tr. Bury 1933–49)

These announcements focus the inquiry on a conception of place which is familiar from Aristotle: place as the immediate container of a body. Your place, on this idea of it, is the innermost boundary of the body (of air or other material) surrounding you, the boundary which encloses you and nothing else.[15] We may well think such a conception of place a heavily theoretical one, or at least not an ordinary man's conception of place. Correspondingly, it looks to be a point in favour of the country gentleman's interpretation that Sextus should confine his discussion to the exact or circumscribed sense of 'place'. We could hardly ask for a more explicit statement that his scepticism has no quarrel with ordinary remarks to the effect that someone is in Alexandria.

The country gentleman will be encouraged further by the opening moves in the debate about place. Sextus' usual practice is to set out the arguments in favour of something, match them with the arguments against, and declare a draw: the equal balance of opposing arguments leaves us no choice but to suspend judgement. What the sceptic suspends judgement about is what the dogmatic arguments are for and against. And when we attend to the arguments for affirming that place is real, we find this:

> If, then, there exist upwards and downwards, and rightwards and left-wards, and forwards and backwards, some place exists; for these six

---

15. Ar. *Phys.* 212a 5–6; cf. 109b 1. For the bulk of Sextus' discussion, and therefore for ours, this formulation will suffice. But at *Phys.* 212a 20–1 Aristotle refines it to read: 'the innermost *static* boundary of the surrounding body', which is equivalent (boundaries being what they are) to 'the innermost boundary of the surrounding static body'. The point of the refinement is this: the place of $X$ was to be the boundary of $Y$ enclosing $X$, but if $Y$ is moving, this specifies a carrier or vessel of $X$ rather than $X$'s place (212a 14–18). The solution is to find $Z$ such that $Z$ is static and $Z$ encloses $X$ at the same boundary as $Y$ does. Example: $X =$ a boat, $Y =$ the body of water flowing in the Cayster, $Z =$ the river Cayster as a geographical entity. Thus understood, the refinement does not (*pace* Ross 1936: 57, 575–6) threaten the condition that the place of $X$ is equal to $X$ (211a 28–9) and contains nothing but $X$ (209b 1), and it is wholly unnecessary for Hussey 1983: 117–8 to contemplate treating 212a 20–1 as an interpolation on the grounds that it identifies the boat's place with the river *banks*. Even the circularity with which the refined definition has been charged (Owen 1970: 252, Hussey 1983: 117) becomes a benign regress if 'static boundary' = 'boundary of a static body' and Aristotle's cosmology can provide a terminal place for all bodies to be permanently in (209a 32, 211b 28–9, 212a 21–4, 212b 17–22). Sextus in fact exploits the refinement that places must be fixed and unmoving at $M$ X 25, 26, and at $M$ X 30–5 finds it necessary to make a sally against the Aristotelian cosmology.

directions are parts of place, and it is impossible that, if the parts of a thing exist, the thing of which they are parts should not exist. But upwards and downwards, and rightwards and leftwards, and forwards and backwards, do exist *in the nature of things (en tēi phusei tōn pragmatōn)*; therefore place exists. (*M* X 7, tr. Bury 1933–49; my emphasis)

It sounds Aristotelian, and it is. To say that there are real directions in the nature of things is to say that physical theory must recognize that directionality is an objective feature of nature, not just relative to ourselves, and this is exactly what Aristotle maintained: '. . . the kinds or differences of place are up-down, before-behind, right-left; and these distinctions hold not only in relation to us and by arbitrary agreement, but also in the whole itself' (*Physics* 205b 31–4; cf. 208b 12–22).

We get the same message from *M* X 9, which adduces the (Aristotelian) doctrine of natural places:

Further, if where what is light naturally moves there what is heavy naturally does not move, there exists a place proper (*idios topos*) to the light and to the heavy; but in fact the first <is true>; therefore the second <is true>. For certainly fire, which is naturally light, tends to ascend, and water, which is naturally heavy, presses downwards, and neither does fire move downwards nor water shoot upwards. There exists, therefore, a proper place both for the naturally light and for the naturally heavy. (*M* X 9, tr. Bury 1933–49 with modifications)

That each element tends by virtue of its intrinsic nature to its own proper place in the universe is a central tenet of Aristotle's cosmology and a large part of what he means to be arguing for when he opens his own discussion of place in *Physics* IV 1 (cf. 208b 8 ff.).[16] If this is the positive dogma, the negative dogma set against it will be the denial of these theoretical notions, and the sceptic's suspending judgement will be suspending judgement as to

16. Add *M* X 10 (cf. *PH* III 121), which cryptically claims that three of the factors in the (Aristotelian) causal analysis of something's coming to be require the existence of place, viz. the agent, the matter, and the end or *telos*. Although this argument does not appear in Ar. *Phys.* IV 1, it might have been suggested by 209a 18–22 and the third item confirms that Sextus or his source intended it as an argument using Aristotelian resources (*pace* Bury 1933–49 *ad PH* III 121). The appeal to Hesiod's Chaos at *PH* III 121, *M* X 11 may be compared with Ar. *Phys.* 208b 29–33, the thought-experiment at *M* X 12 with 209b 6–13.

On the relation between natural place and containing place, see Machamer 1978.

theory. Which leaves him free to indulge in as much use as he likes of the ordinary broad sense of 'place'.

## V

But our country gentleman is taking it too easy. To begin with, the arguments just quoted, although Aristotelian in character, do not argue for the existence of place in the narrow as opposed to the broad sense. They argue for the existence of place. Several of the considerations are indeed drawn from natural philosophy, but they make no use of the narrowness of narrow place. Second, we should look more closely at what Sextus says about the broad sense which he is not contesting. And here I must touch briefly on some points of philology.

The key word in *PH* III 119 is *katachrēstikōs*. To say 'My city is the place where I am' is to use 'place' in the broad sense and thereby to speak *katachrēstikōs*. Bury (1933–49) translates 'loosely' but this does not tell you that the adverb derives from a verb meaning 'to misuse'. To use an expression *katachrēstikōs* is to use it improperly (grammarians still say 'catachrestically') and is contrasted here with using it *kuriōs*, in its proper meaning. So the contrast between broad and narrow place is a contrast between an improper and a proper use of the term. Both uses are current *(legetai dichōs)*, but in the proper acceptation of the term 'place' means that by which we are exactly enclosed. Narrow place is not a technical construct of natural philosophy but what 'place' actually means. In his introductory statement about the scope of his discussion Sextus is saying that it will be concerned only with place properly so called, not with anything and everything that gets called 'place' in the sloppy usage exemplified by such remarks as 'My city is the place where I am'.

In the parallel passage *M* X 15 Bury again translates 'loosely' but the word now is *aphelōs*. *Aphelōs* occurs a number of times in Sextus Empiricus and elsewhere, and so far as I can see the best gloss on it would be 'without distinctions', with special reference to technical distinctions by which theory or science purports to represent real distinctions in the nature of things.[17] If you say that someone is in Alexandria, you are simply not

17. At *PH* I 17 (cf. *M* VI 1–2) it is simply the distinction between a narrowly moral and a broader sense of 'correctly'. But at *M* I 153, 177, 179, 232 the context is the efforts of certain grammarians to regiment language so that gender endings, for example, correspond to gender differences in nature, and *aphelēs* expresses the indifference to such distinctions shown by the common speech of ordinary life. As a term of stylistic analysis, the word signifies a period which is simple, not divided

distinguishing between his place and his city, which we would often describe as the place where he is. You are not picking out his *place*, but the surroundings he shares with his fellow citizens. What Sextus is saying, then, is that the dispute will not be about anything and everything that people call place, but about the attempt to identify for each thing its own unique place in the world, distinct from the places of all other things.

We now have two angles on the scope of Sextus' discussion. He will question the existence or reality of place properly so called, and he will question the idea that each thing has its own unique place in the world. The implication is that these are two ways of specifying the same target.[18] If that is so, Aristotle would be the first to recognize that the target is himself. Not only are the arguments in favour of the reality of place, as Sextus sets them out at *M* X 7–12, closely modelled on the corresponding arguments in Aristotle's *Physics* IV 1, but it was Aristotle who invented, in all but name, the distinction between broad and narrow place. The distinction ensues rapidly on the decision to identify that which is called place in its own right (*kath' hauto*) with the *idios topos* unique to each thing. Anything else called something's place will be so called derivatively (*kat' allo*): because and in virtue of the fact that it contains the proper place of the thing in question. Thus we are in the heavens as a place because our place properly so called is in the air and the air is in the heavens (*Phys.* 209a 31–b 1, 211a 23–9).[19] When Aristotle formulates

---

into clauses (*monokōlos*, Ar. *Rhet.* 1409b 16–17), or, more generally, plain unelaborate speech (*M* II 21, 22, 76, 77). Galen, *Meth. med.* X 269, 1–14 Kühn has an extended elucidation, derived from the Methodic school of medicine, the upshot of which is to equate the adverb *aphelōs* with (i) non-dogmatically, (ii) in accordance with the needs of life (*biōtikōs*), (iii) without articulation by distinctions (*mē diērthrōmenōs*) (cf. *M* IX 218, DL VII 84), (iv) not precisely but untechnically and without any special knowledge.

18. Janáček 1948 assembles evidence that Sextus' regular practice was to write the longer *M* treatment of a given topic with the shorter *PH* version before him. The purpose of *M* is to clarify and expand *PH*, filling in the *Outlines*.

19. These two passages show Aristotle noticeably happier to use 'in' than to use 'place' of the broad places intermediate between our proper place and the heavens. I guess that this is because the circumference of the heavens not only provides the ultimate derivative place of everything individually, but *eo ipso* constitutes the place proper of everything collectively. That would explain why the 'common' place of *Phys.* 209a 32–3 is defined as that in which all bodies are and is not equivalent (as Ross 1936 *ad loc.* would wish it to be) to Sextus' 'broad place'. For all that, 'broad place' is nothing but a convenient label for the derivative uses of 'in' which Aristotle does, inevitably, recognize. I know no evidence to justify Sorabji's (1983: 25–6)

his definition of place as the immediate container of a body, he too thinks of this definition as positing for each thing a unique place which is that thing's place in the only strict and proper acceptation of the term.

It is of course beside the point to object that this talk of narrow circumscribed place gives a wrong account of English 'place' or Greek *'topos'*. Nor is it relevant to adduce the scientific superiority of the modern practice of fixing a unique location for something by the method of coordinates. Our concern is with the philosophical presuppositions of an ancient debate, between Sextus and Aristotle, about an older, less abstract method of fixing location by reference to containers and surroundings. My claim has been that both Sextus and Aristotle conceived the debate not as a discussion of a special theoretician's notion of place, but as a discussion of place. They agree that the word 'place' is correctly analyzed as requiring a unique place for each thing. It is not just a contextual synonym of 'city' or 'gymnasium' but has its own proper meaning, its own job in the language: assigning to each thing its proper place in the world. Alternatively, and giving the point a more polemical thrust, if the word 'place' has any real work to do in our language and lives, it *presupposes* the possibility of defining, for each thing, a unique place. And since in the context of this ancient debate, the definition has to be through containers and surroundings, we soon reach the result that the only proper place a thing can have is the narrow circumscribed place which Sextus identifies as the target of his questioning. For, as Aristotle saw, this is the only surrounding container which is not shared with something else. If a man's *place*, as distinct from his city or his house, has to be uniquely *his* place, it can only be that boundary of air or whatever which directly surrounds and contains him and nothing else. This is how Sextus can represent his sceptical doubts about narrow circumscribed place as doubts about the reality of place *tout court* (*PH* III 135, quoted below; *M* X 6).

# VI

We can check this conclusion, which I have so far defended on philological and historical grounds, against Sextus' argumentative practice. *M* X 95

---

assertion that broad place is a Stoic notion. The Stoic contrast is between place (which they define, differently from Aristotle, as the interval occupied by and equal to a body) and room (*PH* III 124–5, *M* X 3–4). Sextus refutes the Stoics separately at *PH* III 124–130 and in the larger work confines himself to the mere mention at *M* X 3–4; in both discussions of place his main target is Aristotle.

introduces a suggestion designed to meet Diodorus Cronus' argument against continuous motion. Diodorus' argument claimed that continuous motion is impossible because a moving object cannot be moving in any place it is not in (obviously), nor in the place where it is (place proper is too narrow to move in), hence it cannot be moving in any place; hence it cannot be moving. The suggested reply is this:

> 'Being contained in place' has two meanings, they say: (i) in place determined broadly, as when we say that someone is in Alexandria, (ii) in place determined exactly, as the air moulded round the surface of my body would be said to be my place and a jar is called the place of what is contained in it. On this basis, then, that there are in fact two senses of 'place', they assert that the moving object can be moving in the place it is in, viz. place determined broadly, which has extension enough for the processes of motion to occur. (*M* X 95)

There is the suggestion: in broad place the moving object has plenty of room to get its moving done. Now observe how Sextus rebuts it:

> Those who say that 'place' has two senses, place taken broadly and place determined exactly, and that because of this motion can occur in place conceived broadly, are not replying to the point. For place conceived exactly is *presupposed by*[20] place conceived broadly, and it is impossible for something to have moved over broad place without first having moved over exact place. For as the latter contains the moving body, so the broad place contains, along with the moving body, the exact place as well. As, then, no-one can move over a distance of a stade without first having moved over a distance of a cubit, so it is impossible to move over broad place without moving over exact place. And when Diodorus propounded the argument against motion which has been set forth, he was keeping to exact place.[21] Accordingly, if in this case motion is done away with, no

---

20. *Proēgeitai*, lit. 'precedes': the context shows that the priority is logical, not temporal.

21. The rebuttal, like the suggestion it rebuts, presupposes that Diodorus' argument is aimed at ordinary objects moving from one Aristotelian place to another. For remarks of Aristotle's which expose him to Diodorus' attack by implying that a body can move in its place, see *Phys.* 211a 35–6, 212a 9–10. At *M* X 85–6, 119–20, the same argument treats of 'partless' bodies moving from one 'partless' place to another. On the latter, atomistic application, see Denyer 1981; on the relation between the two applications, Sedley 1977: 84–6, Sorabji 1983: 17–20, 369–71.

argument is left in the case of broad place. (*M* X 108–10, my emphasis; cf. *PH* III 75)

The contention is that broad place will not save anything that has foundered on considerations drawn from narrow place. It certainly will not save the Aristotelian account of motion from Diodorus' critique, for we have seen that Aristotle states himself in his own terms the premise that broad place presupposes narrow place.[22]

We need not stop to examine ways in which the Aristotelian description of motion could be reformulated to escape the dilemma, nor the ingenious alternative picture which Diodorus offers whereby a body can be first in one place and then in another without our ever being entitled to say of it, in the present tense, 'It is moving'.[23] The question we must ask is whether Sextus accepts the presupposition premise.

In the quoted rebuttal he is speaking on behalf of Diodorus, whom he has cast (*M* X 48) as the dogmatic denier of motion. Sextus' concern is to ensure that the arguments against motion are no less, but also no more, effective than the arguments in favour of it. For this purpose all he needs is that both negative and positive dogmatists accept the premise. However, the reason they accept it is that they regard broad place as derivative from narrow place. In their view, the presupposition is built into the very language of 'place', the proper meaning of which is narrow circumscribed place. In other words, it is in the first instance the dogmatists who would call broad place a catachrestic use of the term.[24] If Sextus does so too (*PH* III 119, quoted above), this can only be because he does not question the dogmatist's analysis of the language of 'place'. What he questions is whether the project for which this language is designed can be successfully carried through. He questions the entire language game (as he would have chuckled to be able to call it) of locating bodies in their places.

22. Add *Phys.* 241a 8–9: 'It is impossible that any moving object should have moved over a distance greater than itself without first having moved over a distance equal to or less than itself'.

23. See references in note 21. Comparisons have been made with Russell's view (1914: 144) that 'nothing happens when a body moves except that it is in different places at different times'. But ancient opinion mostly sides with Russell's opponents in taking this to be a denial of motion rather than a theory of it (Ar. *Phys.* 231b 21 ff., 240b 8 ff., S. E. *M* X 48).

24. Note *PH* I 207: the sceptic uses language 'without distinctions (*adiaphorōs* —n. 33 below) and, if they wish, catachrestically', i.e. if non-sceptics wish to call it a misuse, he admits the charge.

# VII

You are asked to fetch a slab and are told that it is in Alexandria. This just
says that it is somewhere in Alexandria without indicating exactly where.
Locating the slab vaguely in Alexandria presupposes that it can be located
precisely at a particular place which is enclosed within the larger whole of
Alexandria. The same applies if you are told 'It's in the temple' or 'In the
inner shrine'. You can still ask, 'Where in the shrine is it?'. So we reach the
thought that there is exactly one place which is the slab's place and nothing
else's place, and, as Aristotle saw, inevitably this will be narrow place: that
envelope of air which directly surrounds and contains the slab and nothing
else. If this and this alone is place proper, the fact that we can all agree that
the slab is somewhere in Alexandria does not help to show that we can arrive
at a clear notion of the place which is the place where it is. It is this precise
place that we have to get a clear notion of if we are to vindicate our practice of
locating bodies in places.

The pro-arguments in *M* X read quite well as arguments in favour of the
proposition that we can and do locate things in well-defined places. An
important passage not yet quoted is the following:

> Moreover, if where Socrates was another man (such as Plato) now is, Socrates
> being dead, then place exists. For just as, when the liquid in the pitcher has
> been emptied out and other liquid poured in, we declare that the pitcher,
> which is the place both of the former liquid and of that poured in later, exists,
> so likewise, if another man now occupies the place which Socrates occupied
> when he was alive, some place exists. (*M* X 8, tr. Bury 1933–49)

What is being argued for is the legitimacy of quite ordinary locating activities, as well as the more theoretical physicists' doctrine of natural places and
directions. And here again Sextus is following Aristotelian precedent.[25]
Like Sextus' dogmatist, Aristotle mixes considerations drawn from natural
philosophy with arguments based on what is said in the common speech of
ordinary life. Aristotle and Sextus are not country gentlemen; in both
writers the ordinary concern with place and the theoretical concern are seen
as continuous with each other.

Sextus' counter-arguments, urging the denial of place, are compatible
with this. They fall into two classes: (i) rebuttals of the pro-arguments,

---

25. The replacement argument just quoted from *M* X 8 (cf. *PH* III 120) corresponds
to Ar. *Phys.* 208b 1–8.

chiefly on the score that all talk of right and left, or of Plato being where Socrates was, presupposes the existence of place and cannot without circularity establish it (*M* X 13–14); (ii) dilemmas of a typical sceptical kind (though partly derived from Aristotle, *Phys.* 211b 5ff.) to the effect that absurdities follow whether place is body or void, whether it is form or matter or the limit of a body or the extension bounded by those limits (*M* X 20–29). What is important for our purposes is the final upshot of the negative arguments:

> If the place of a thing is neither its matter, nor the form, nor the extension between the limits, nor again the extremities, of the body, and besides these there is nothing else to conceive it as, we must declare place to be nothing. (*M* X 29)

It comes to this, that the legitimacy of locating things in places depends on whether or not we can formulate a coherent conception of place in the proper sense of the word. Both in ordinary life and in doing physical theory we take for granted that we could be more precise if need be. But could we? Can we defend this practice without circularity? Can we formulate a clear and coherent notion of what a thing's place is? Some say 'Yes', some say 'No', but the sceptic remains in doubt and refrains from judging either way. If that is how the question stands, there is no Gassendi-type insulation by subject matter between scepticism and ordinary life.[26]

Finally, it seems to me that only some such interpretation as I have now reached will make adequate sense of the way the topic is concluded in the *PH* version:

> It is possible to adduce many other arguments. But in order to avoid prolonging our exposition, we may conclude by saying that while the Sceptics are put to confusion by the arguments, they are also put to shame by the evidence of experience. Consequently we attach ourselves to neither side, so far as concerns the doctrines of the Dogmatists, but suspend judgement regarding place. (*PH* III 13–15, tr. Bury 1933–49)

26. When Gassendi 1658: Pt. II, Bk. II, Chs. 1–6 (selections in Brush 1972: 383–90) criticizes Aristotelian place, his predominant complaint is that it is bad science and wrong-headed metaphysics. I do not deny that insulation by subject-matter, between the theoretical and the ordinary, is to be found in antiquity also: the obvious example is the Empirical school of medicine (see Deichgräber 1930). But Sextus firmly repudiates the suggestion that the sceptic could consistently be an Empiric (*PH* I 236).

The arguments are the negative arguments which show that no coherent conception of place can be formulated, so that place is unreal, but here they are set against a positive belief suggested by ordinary experience. What belief? Does ordinary experience directly suggest that one can formulate a philosophically defensible conception of place? I think not. What ordinary experience suggests is that one can locate objects in places. Anyone, claims the *PH* dogmatist, can look and *see* the difference between right and left, up and down, and can see that I am now talking just where my teacher used to talk (*PH* III 120). Well might a person be ashamed if it turns out he cannot do that. And if he cannot, then of course it will be inappropriate to talk of the 'evidence' of experience: 'evidence' is the dogmatist's epistemologically loaded description, preparatory to his arguing that ordinary experience *establishes* the reality of place.[27] But what ordinary experience establishes, philosophy must be able to elucidate. Conversely—and this is the sting of the negative critique—what philosophy fails to elucidate, ordinary experience fails to establish (compare *PH* III 65–6). The abstract question of the nature of place and philosophical questions about defining it come into Sextus' discussion, through the presupposition premise, as attempts to make coherent sense of the mundane activity of putting things in their places (saying where they are).

# VIII

I believe that the same conclusion can be drawn from Sextus' discussion of time, but rather than go into further details here I propose to step back to consider the overall strategy within which the debate about time and place is one local scuffle. It is not often that Sextus appears to limit the scope of his scepticism in the way he does with place, which is one reason why I have dwelt on this at length.[28] The overall strategy will show that it would have been very surprising if we had reached any other conclusion than that Pyrrhonian scepticism does not practise insulation by subject matter. Once again, I start with a modern foil.

In his book *Ethics: Inventing Right and Wrong* J. L. Mackie writes:

27. There is no parallel to this in the *M* version, because the pro-arguments in *M* have been regimented into *modus ponens* form, without any indication of the epistemological grounding of the categorical premise.

28. Another case, more commonly cited (e.g. Frede 1979: 114; = chap. 1, 11–12), is Sextus' expression of tolerance towards one kind of sign-inference. On this see Barnes 1982: 12–18 ( = chap. 3, 79–89), where I would be less hesitant than he to ascribe to Sextus a Humean reduction of the inference to psychological habit.

The denial of objective values can carry with it an extreme emotional reaction, a feeling that nothing matters at all, that life has lost its purpose. Of course this does not follow; the lack of objective values is not a good reason for abandoning subjective concern or for ceasing to want anything. (Mackie 1977:34)

Mackie can say this because his whole discussion is based on a very strong version of the modern distinction between first and second order inquiries. He insulates first order moral judgements so securely that he thinks they can survive the second order discovery that all first order value judgements involve error, viz. an erroneous (false) claim to objective truth. The original Pyrrhonists, by contrast, thought that if philosophical argument could cast doubt on the objectivity of values—in their terms, if it could be shown that nothing is good or bad by nature—that would precisely have the effect of making you cease to want anything, or to hope for anything, or to fear anything. Their name for this detached view of one's own life was tranquillity.

The great recommendation of Pyrrhonism is that suspension of judgement on all questions as to what is true and false, good and bad, results in tranquillity—the tranquillity of detachment from striving and ordinary human concerns, of a life lived on after surrendering the hope of finding answers to the questions on which happiness depends. As Sextus explains, it turns out that happiness ensues precisely when that hope is abandoned: tranquillity follows suspension of judgement as a shadow follows its body (*PH* I 25–30). In its own way, Pyrrhonian scepticism offers a recipe for happiness to compete with the cheerful simplicity of Epicureanism and the nobler resignation of the Stoic sage.[29]

Now a recipe for happiness must make contact with the sources of unhappiness. It is above all the judgements which underlie the ordinary man's hopes and fears which must be put in doubt and withdrawn if tranquillity is to be achieved. The target of the sceptical arguments is, first, the ordinary man's ordinary belief that it is good and desirable to have money, say, or fame or pleasure (*M* XI 120–4, 144–6; cf. *PH* I 27–8); and second, the first order judgements of ordinary life about what is happening in the world around, which bear upon our achievement of these goals (if it is good and desirable to have money, it is important to know where the money is). The method of attack is philosophical argument, but the target is our innermost selves

---

29. For more detailed discussions of Pyrrhonian tranquillity, see Hossenfelder 1968, Burnyeat chap. 2, Annas 1986.

and our whole approach to life. Any attempt to insulate our first order judgements would frustrate the sceptic's philanthropic enterprise of bringing us by argument to tranquillity of soul (cf. *PH* III 280).

Sextus' discussion of space and time should be seen in this wider perspective. Nowadays, if someone claims that Aenesidemus lived and worked in the first century B.C. and Sextus Empiricus around 200 A.D., we see a big difference between doubting this claim on empirical grounds concerning the historical evidence—it really is frightfully meagre—and doubting the claim on the basis of a philosophical argument to show that the past is unreal. I do not think Sextus has anything like our sense of this difference. For him, anyone who says that Plato now is in the place where Socrates was when he was alive, and intends thereby to make a truth-claim, says something which is open to inquiry in that he can be challenged to give reasons or evidence for his claim and to defend its legitimacy, where this may include (as we have seen) defending a conception of place or the reality of time. If the defence fails, that has much the same effect as failure to produce decent historical evidence. It begins to look as if there is no good reason to believe the statement. And if you can find no good reason to believe a statement, what can you do but suspend judgement about it? All that remains for you is the standard sceptic retreat to a statement which makes no truth-claim, for which, consequently, reasons and legitimacy cannot be demanded, namely, 'It appears to me that Plato now is in the place where Socrates was when he was alive'.[30] That you can say without opening yourself to the sceptical arguments.

But there are other ways this retreat can express itself. Because the sceptic intends no truth-claim, he can say things which, were they intended as truth-claims, would presuppose something he cannot defend. A simple example from another context in Sextus (*M* VIII 129): in ordinary life one would be happy to say 'I am building a house', but strictly and properly speaking reference to a house presupposes the existence of a house already built. So the phrase is a nonsense, a misuse of language (*katachrēsis*).[31] Nonetheless, people use it, just as they use 'man' for 'human being' (*M* VII 50). And in this detached attitude of the ordinary speaker with respect to the presuppositions of his own language the sceptic finds a model to follow on a larger scale.

30. On the importance of the point that statements recording how things appear do not count as true or false, see chap. 2 and Burnyeat 1982.

31. For the Aristotelian ancestry of this puzzle, and the philosophical depths to which it can reach, see Owen 1978/9.

It is catachrestic to use 'is' for 'appear' (*PH* I 135) and to indulge in assertive discourse without intending to affirm or deny anything (*PH* I 191–2; cf. 207). But the sceptic tells us that, because his sole concern is to indicate how things appear to him (this much, of course, he says in plain language, with the verb 'appear' in its proper meaning), he does not care what expressions he uses (*PH* I 4, 191). He can afford to be indifferent to the commitments and presuppositions of his vocabulary, because the part of the language he is serious about is the part which enables a speaker to express his non-committal indifference to the question whether what he says is true or false, viz. the vocabulary of appearance. The verb 'appear' (in its non-epistemic sense) is a device available within language for detaching oneself from the presuppositions and commitments of the rest of language. But an equally good alternative is to say what anyone else would say, without worrying whether it is true or false, without being serious about the proper application of the concepts involved.

In this spirit, if the sceptic says that the slab is in Alexandria, it will not be because he doubts that broad place presupposes narrow place. On the contrary, the presupposition is part of the normal workings of the language within which he thinks and speaks his scepticism. He can be unconcerned about the presupposition, if and only if he is unconcerned about whether it is true or false that the slab is in Alexandria. He will happily say that the slab is in Alexandria because, as he means it, this amounts to a statement of (non-epistemic) appearance. He thereby avoids rashly committing himself to distinctions which it takes a great deal of theoretical knowledge (virtually the whole Aristotelian cosmology)[32] to be able to draw.[33]

# IX

We are now equipped to re-read Sextus' remark at *PH* I 13 that dogma in the sense in which the sceptic avoids dogma is assent to any of the non-evident matters investigated by the sciences. This looked like support for the country gentleman's interpretation because it could so easily be taken to

32. Cf. ns. 15, 19 above.

33. It fits this conclusion that in the last chapter of *PH* I, where Sextus discusses common ground between Pyrrhonian scepticism and the Methodic school of medicine and says that the Methodic's use of language is as undogmatic and as unconcerned with distinctions (*adiaphoron*) as the sceptic's, he subsumes this under the sceptic life following appearances (*PH* I 236–241). *Adiaphoron* is to be compared with *aphelōs* at *M* X 15, discussed above n. 17. The adverb *adiaphorōs* is coupled with *katachrēstikōs* at *PH* I 191, 207; cf. 188, 195, *M* I 61, IX 333.

confine the sceptic's judgement-suspending to theoretical statements. One major problem for this, the country gentleman's, reading is that Sextus plainly states that the outcome of his critique of the criterion and of truth is that one is forced to suspend judgement about the things which the dogmatists take to be evident as well as about the abstruse matters they describe as non-evident (*PH* II 95, *M* VIII 141–2). All statements about external objects are doubtful, even such simple ones as 'It is day' or 'The stove is warm'.

Does this mean that the latter statements are non-evident, and hence dogma too? I used to think so.[34] But now it appears to me that the distinction between the evident and the non-evident is itself one of those dogmatists' distinctions which the sceptic makes light of (cf. *PH* II 97). The definition of dogma as assent to any of the non-evident matters investigated by the sciences is explicitly taken from someone else (*PH* I 13).[35] Sextus will use it, but not for the purpose of insulating the ordinary from the theoretical. About both sides of the dogmatists' distinction he speaks with a clear voice: it is impossible not to suspend judgement. All we need to add is an explanation of why the distinction makes no difference to the scope of Sextus' scepticism.

The answer, I submit, is the lack of insulation. Every statement making a truth-claim falls within the scope of scientific investigation because, even if the statement itself is not at a theoretical level, it will still use concepts which are the subject of theoretical speculation: concepts such as motion, time, place, body. If these concepts are problematical, which Sextus argues they all are, and no line is drawn between philosophical and empirical doubt, the original statement will be equally problematical. You will have to suspend judgement about whether next year's sabbatical will come for you to work on the philosophy of time—and also, of course, about whether it would matter if it did not.[36]

As I see it, then, the ancient sceptic philosophizes in the same direct manner as G. E. Moore. Moore is notorious for insisting that a philosophical

34. Cf. n. 13 above.
35. Cf. Burnyeat 1980: 47, n. 48 ( = chap. 2, 51).
36. This solution to the problem of the status of ordinary life statements in Sextus is a generalization of that in Barnes 1982: 10–12 ( = chap. 3, 76–78). Barnes works with just one presupposition: the Pyrrhonist will not judge that the stove is warm because he is unable to satisfy himself that he has a criterion of truth to ground his judgement. I add: and also because he is unable to find a satisfactory philosophical elucidation and defence of the concepts involved in or presupposed by the statement that the stove is warm.

thesis such as 'Time is unreal' be taken with a certain sort of seriousness, as entailing, for example, that it is false that I had breakfast earlier today. And he thinks it relevant and important to argue the contrapositive: it is true that I had breakfast earlier today, therefore it is false that time is unreal. People always feel that these arguments and attitudes of Moore's miss the point. That is not the way philosophical questions should be treated; it is a naive and wrong sort of seriousness. But I think that Sextus would recognize a kindred spirit. If we look a third time at the texts before us we can see that Sextus' dogmatist argues in a manner exactly like Moore: One thing is to the right, another to the left, therefore there are places; Plato is where Socrates was, so at least one place exists. Compare: Here is one hand, here is another, so at least two external things exist.[37] Sextus complains that this is circular; he does not complain that it is the wrong *sort* of argument to establish the thesis that place exists. And he propounds a modal version of the same inference in reverse: it is problematic whether place exists, therefore it is problematic whether Plato *is* where Socrates was or whether one thing *is* to the right of another. Similarly: it is problematic whether anything is good or bad by nature, therefore it is problematic whether it was worthwhile to write this paper. Perhaps it appears to me now that it was not worthwhile. Never mind. If I have achieved the sceptic detachment, this will be a non-epistemic appearance: a thought or feeling which I experience without any concern for whether it is founded in truth or reasons, and so without any diminution of my tranquillity.

# X

I have been concerned to show that once upon a time philosophical scepticism had a seriousness which present day philosophy has long forgotten about. It is now time for a broader canvas and the question when, and by whom, and why insulation was invented. To this end I shall take a brief—very brief, and accordingly less documented—glance backwards and forwards from the period (first century B.C. to third century A.D.) in which ancient Pyrrhonism flourished.

First, backwards. The idea that a man's first order judgements are put in doubt if he cannot give a defensible philosophical account of the concepts he is applying is reminiscent of nothing so much as Socrates' well-known

37. For an ancient parallel to Moore's further claim (1939: 148–50, 1953: 119–126) that the premise of this argument is much more certain than any philosophical premise that could be used to prove it true (or false), see Cic. *Acad.* II 17.

habit of insisting that unless Euthyphro, for example, can define piety, he does not know, as he thinks he does, that it is pious to prosecute his father for letting a slave die. The Socratic view that one cannot know any examples falling under a concept unless one can give a definition or account of that concept has been branded 'the Socratic fallacy'.[38] The historical perspective I have been offering might prepare us to take a more sympathetic, or at least a more complex view.[39] It is worth pondering the point that when Socrates' interlocutors fail to come up with a satisfactory definition, he never advises them to leave philosophy to those who are good at it, but rather to continue the search for a definition, in order that their life may be rightly directed.

In due course Socrates' insistence on the priority of definitional knowledge became Plato's thesis that you cannot know anything unless you know the Forms which are what definitions specify. And there are other signs that Plato has no inkling of insulation. He quite regularly insists that a philosophical theory must be able to be stated without infringing itself. The thesis of monism, for example, that only one thing exists, is refuted in the *Sophist* (244bd) on the grounds that it takes more than one word to formulate it. Again, Protagoras' relativist theory of truth, that a proposition is true only for a person who believes it to be true, is made to refute itself in the *Theaetetus* (170e–171c) because it implies that it itself is not true for those who do not believe it to be true. In neither case does it occur to Plato that a philosophical theory might claim a special meta-status exempting it from being counted as one among the propositions with which it deals.

Aristotle might seem a more promising source for insulation. In *Physics* I 2, for example, he says firmly that the natural philosopher does not have to worry about the arguments of Eleatics like Parmenides and Zeno which purport to show that motion is impossible and that only one thing exists. In natural philosophy one takes for granted that motion and plurality exist: that is a first principle or presupposition of the whole inquiry.

But on closer examination it turns out that what Aristotle is insisting upon is not insulation but the departmentalization of inquiry. He does think that the Eleatic conclusions are directly incompatible with the first principles of natural philosophy. It is just that no science examines the principles which are a presupposition of its having a subject matter to study; e.g. geometry does not consider whether there are points nor arithmetic whether numbers exist. These are questions for another study, which Aristotle calls first philosophy

38. Geach 1966.

39. References and discussion in Burnyeat 1977.

(metaphysics). But he thinks of this higher study as delivering conclusions which the sciences subordinate to it can use as first principles. Whereas twentieth-century philosophy has usually thought of science and meta-physics as quite distinct *kinds* of enquiry (because in our world they usually are), for Aristotle natural philosophy is simply 'second philosophy' (e.g. *Met.* 1037a 14–15). It is a less abstract and less general enterprise than first philosophy, because it deals with one part of the subject-matter of first philosophy, and secondary to it, because first philosophy has access to the ultimate principles of explanation (*Met.* E 1). That is all.[40]

The other side of this ancient coin is that it is a mistake to think of Aristotle's *Physics*, in the way twentieth-century philosophical interpreters tend to do, as philosophy *of* science in contrast to science.[41] Aristotle's analysis of the ordinary language meaning of 'place' is as direct a contribu-tion to science as his analysis of the language of pleasure in the *Ethics* is a contribution to practical wisdom. In neither case does Aristotle think of the conceptual analysis as operating independently of first order concerns at a level of its own. It contributes directly to first order knowledge. The reason why conceptual analysis bulks so large in the *Physics* and the *Ethics* is that Aristotle holds a substantive, and in its time revolutionary, thesis to the effect that the ordinary man's ordinary concepts are the best starting point from which to proceed to the understanding of nature, on the one hand, and to the saving of our souls on the other. His very positive dogmatism matches Sextus' scepticism at each uninsulated point.

# XI

So when did things change? Who invented insulation?

It was not, I think, Descartes. Descartes had no patience with Gassendi's attempt to limit the scope of the ancient sceptical materials. Indeed it was Descartes' achievement to see that those materials reach much further than the ancient Pyrrhonist had ever dreamed, that they impugn the very exis-tence of the external world in which the Pyrrhonist had looked to enjoy

40. I do not understand why Kung 1981 thinks that Quine 1951 justifies her finding in Aristotle anticipations of Carnap's distinction between internal and external questions. In any case, the claim depends on ignoring the full range of questions that Aristotle assigns to first philosophy.

41. So Owen 1961: 116, 119, 125–6, Hamlyn 1968: ix, Ackrill 1981: 24, Annas 1981: 286.

tranquillity.[42] Accordingly, when Gassendi, in keeping with his unwillingness to allow Sextus to doubt ordinary truth-claims as well as theoretical ones, was unwilling to accept that the sceptical doubt of the first *Meditation* was seriously meant to have absolutely general scope, Descartes replied:

> My statement *that the entire testimony of the senses must be considered to be uncertain, nay, even false,* is quite serious and so necessary for the comprehension of my meditations, that he who will not or cannot admit that, is unfit to urge any objection to them that merits a reply. (*V Rep.,* HR II 206)[43]

But then he continues:

> But we must note the distinction emphasized by me in various passages, between the practical activities of our life and an enquiry into truth; for, when it is a case of regulating our life, it would assuredly be stupid not to trust the senses, and those sceptics were quite ridiculous who so neglected human affairs that they had to be preserved by their friends from tumbling down precipices.[44] It was for this reason that somewhere I announced *that no one in his sound mind seriously doubted about such matters* [HR I 142–3]; but when we raise an enquiry into what is the surest knowledge which the human mind can obtain, it is clearly unreasonable to refuse to treat them as doubtful, nay even to reject them as false, so as to allow us to become aware that certain other things, which cannot be thus rejected, are for this reason more certain, and in actual truth better known by us.

Thus it is the same range of propositions which Descartes treats as certain for the purposes of practical life and as doubtful for the purpose of an enquiry into truth. There is no insulation of the Gassendi type here. But neither is there any other kind of insulation. Descartes has to insist that his doubt is strictly theoretical and methodological, not practical, precisely because he believes that the judgements of ordinary life really are put in doubt by the sceptical arguments. They are rendered so completely and utterly doubtful that Descartes feels he must construct a provisional code

42. See Burnyeat 1982.

43. HR = Haldane and Ross 1931.

44. The reference is to a story about Pyrrho retailed at DL IX 62. Other references to ancient sceptics actually living their scepticism are HR I 206, II 335.

of conduct to keep his practical life going while he is conducting the enquiry into truth. Imagine a modern philosopher launching a seminar on scepticism by drawing up a set of rules for everybody to live by until the sceptical doubts have been laid to rest. That is what Descartes does, at some considerable length, in Part III of the *Discourse on the Method* (HR I 95 ff.). His distinction between the theoretical and the practical is not insulation but a deliberate abstraction of himself from practical concerns, a resolution to remain noncommittal towards everything in the practical sphere until theory has given him the truth about the world and a morality he can believe in.

If not Descartes, then how about Berkeley? Berkeley knew the Pyrrhonist arguments through Bayle[45] and his response was his well-known abolition of the distinction between appearance and reality. If the distinction is made, then Berkeley agrees that the sceptical arguments show we cannot know the truth of any statement about how things really are. The only answer is to say that the way things really are is nothing over and above the appearances. The question is, does Berkeley think this could or should make a difference to the judgements of ordinary life? The answer seems to be that sometimes he does and sometimes he does not.

When in a mood to accommodate the ordinary man, Berkeley will claim or imply that his immaterialist idealism is not an alternative to, but an analysis of, ordinary discourse. It gives the correct account of what we ordinarily mean by talking of objects, an account whereby our ordinary statements come out true (1710: § 82 *fin.*: cf. §§ 34–5).

But Berkeley is not always so accommodating to ordinary thought. Consider his well-known injunction to 'think with the learned, and speak with the vulgar' (1710: § 51). This is motivated by an admission that on his principles ordinary causal statements like 'Fire heats', 'Water cools', come out false. For in his system only minds have causal efficacy. So if we do continue to say, with the vulgar, 'Fire heats', we will have to do it in much the same spirit as the Copernican continues to speak of the sun rising. Strictly, what the vulgar say is inaccurate, false. This is like Mackie's error theory of moral discourse, but with the crucial difference that Berkeley does not have Mackie's twentieth-century assurance that the distinction between first and second level inquiries smooths over the problem. As Berkeley sees the matter, idealism bears upon at least some ordinary judgements in the way the Copernican theory bears upon the statement that the sun rises.[46]

---

45. See Poplin 1981/2.

46. A nice ancient parallel is Empedocles frag. 9: people speak, incorrectly, of things coming to be and passing away; Empedocles acknowledges that he makes use

Thus Berkeley's progress towards insulation is at best qualified and ambiguous. Hume jumps right back to the position we found in Sextus; or, at least, that is how it first appears. It is quite essential to Hume's programme that Pyrrhonism should clash directly and drastically with our everyday beliefs. For Hume maintains that if we were the rational creatures we fancy ourselves to be, we would give up, for example, the belief in external objects once we were confronted with the sceptical arguments which show the belief to be unfounded. The fact is, however, that we do not give up the belief. Inevitably, it recaptures our mind when we leave our study for everyday pursuits. It is this resistance of our beliefs to the sceptical arguments which demonstrates for Hume the role in our lives of factors other than reason, namely, custom and imagination. They, not reason, must be responsible for our beliefs if the beliefs do not go away when the reasons for them are invalidated by the sceptic's critique. The whole argument would collapse if our everyday beliefs were insulated by some logical device from that critique, from what Hume calls the impossible rigours of Pyrrhonism.

True, one may see a kind of insulation in the very fact that the beliefs do not go away. But what is important about this is that for Hume it is just a fact, a phenomenon that we may detect in ourselves when we leave the study. If Descartes had been aware of the same phenomenon, he would have had no need of his provisional morality.

The next step is not difficult to predict. It is possible to be more impressed with Hume's account of the impotence of scepticism to budge our everyday beliefs than with his argument from that premise to the impotence of reason. If someone could find a way of preserving the premise while denying the conclusion, scepticism would suffer a dramatic loss of significance.

Which brings us, as many will have foreseen, to Kant. It was Kant who persuaded philosophy that one can be, simultaneously and without contradiction, an empirical realist and a transcendental idealist. That is, it was Kant who gave us the idea that there is a way of saying the same sort of thing as real live sceptics like Aenesidemus used to say, namely, 'The knowing subject contributes to what is known', which nevertheless does not impugn the objectivity of the judgements in which the knowledge is expressed. Where Aenesidemus would cite the empirical factors (jaundice and the like) which obstruct objective knowledge, the Kantian principle that objects

---

of this customary mode of speech for the purposes of his own discourse; but he does not retract one iota from his contention that it is mistaken.

have to conform to our understanding is designed to show that our judgements are validated, not impugned, by the contribution of the knowing
mind. But Kant can make this claim, famously difficult as it is, only because
in his philosophy the presupposition link is well and truly broken. 'The stove
is warm', taken empirically, implies no philosophical view at the transcendental level where from now on the philosophical battle will be fought.
Empirical realism is invulnerable to scepticism and compatible with transcendental idealism.[47]

In this way, with the aid of his distinction of levels (insulation *de iure*),
Kant thought to refute scepticism once and for all. The effect, however, was
that scepticism itself moved upstairs to the transcendental level.

I say this because I find it interesting to notice how Thompson Clarke's
sceptic repeats some of what Kant said, but in a quite different tone of voice.
Clarke's sceptic takes up what is called the absolute point of view and
declares that the plain man's knowledge claims are all very well in the
context of ordinary life but they do not embody an absolute knowledge of
things as they are in themselves; they are knowledge only in a manner of
speaking—the plain man's manner of speaking, which has no foundation outside the practices of ordinary life. So we reach the idea that there
are two ways of understanding a statement like 'The stove is warm', the
plain way and the philosophical way, and it is only the philosophical claim
to an absolute knowledge that the sceptic wants to question. What he questions is precisely that 'The stove is warm' can embody any further or deeper
kind of knowledge and truth than the plain man puts into it. Once the
Kantian insulation by levels is established, scepticism itself goes transcendental.

The other important thing about Clarke's sceptic, and about most of the
references to 'the sceptic' in modern philosophical literature, is that this
sceptic has no historical reality. It is a construction of the modern philosophical imagination. The point is that when scepticism goes transcendental, the expression 'the sceptic' has to lose the historical reference it still
carries in Hume, its connection with what certain historical figures actually
said and thought. It becomes the name of something internal to the philosopher's own thinking, his alter ego as it were, with whom he wrestles in a
debate which is now a philosophical debate in the modern sense.

---

47. These sketchy remarks owe much to Stroud 1983, which may be read in
conjunction with Tonelli's (1967) scholarly demonstration that in Kant's day scepticism was still essentially the 'empirical' scepticism of the ancient tradition. For some
relevant connections between Kant and Wittgensteinian insulation, see Lear 1982.

# XII

Now in recent years it has been argued with much skill and scholarship that something very like a transcendental scepticism is to be found in the texts of the ancient Pyrrhonist tradition, above all at *PH* I 13.[48] Sextus, on this interpretation, insulates not between subject matters, as Gassendi thought, but between an ordinary and a philosophical way of understanding statements such as 'The stove is warm'. Sextus describes himself as a defender of the plain man and ordinary life. He has no objection to the plain man's manner of speaking, only to the dogmatist's belief that he can achieve a further or deeper kind of knowledge and truth than the plain man requires for the purposes of ordinary life.

It is an attractive interpretation, but the historical perspective I have tried to present suggests, not that it is simply wrong in the way that Gassendi's insulating interpretation is wrong, but that it is anachronistic. Its anachronism is the other side of the anachronism of G. E. Moore. Moore tried to take scepticism seriously. He refused to consider any insulating device of the kind provided by the Kantian distinction between the transcendental and the empirical. But he succeeded only in sounding peculiarly, even outrageously, naive—just because he was tackling scepticism in pre-Kantian terms, as if Kant had not existed. Moore is naive where Sextus is merely innocent, because of course it is true that when Sextus wrote Kant had not existed. The trouble with innocence—the image is very nearly Kant's own (1781: A761)—is that, once lost, it can never be regained.[49]

## *Bibliography of Modern Works Cited*

Ackrill, J. L. 1981. *Aristotle the Philosopher.* Oxford.

Annas, Julia 1981. *An Introduction to Plato's Republic.* Oxford.

———1986. 'Doing without objective values: ancient and modern strategies', in *The Norms of Nature,* edd. M. Schofield and G. Striker, pp. 3–29. Cambridge.

A shorter version of this paper was published in *Philosophy in History: Essays on the Historiography of Philosophy,* edd. R. Rorky, J. B. Schneewind, and Q. Skinner, (Cambridge University Press 1984), 225–254.

Barnes, Jonathan 1982. 'The beliefs of a Pyrrhonist', *Proceedings of the Cambridge Philological Society,* 208 (N.S. 28): 1–29 ( = chap. 3).

48. Frede, chap. 1, 1979.

49. This paper owes debts to numerous discussions at different times and places. Two particular sources of inspiration that must be acknowledged are the writings of Barry Stroud, and Burton Dreben's Howison Lectures at Berkeley in 1981.

Berkeley, George 1710. *A Treatise Concerning The Principles of Human Knowledge.*

Brochard, Victor 1923.[2] *Les sceptiques grecs,* 2nd edn., Paris.

Brush, Craig B. 1972. *The Selected Works of Pierre Gassendi.* New York and London.

Burnyeat, M. F. 1977. 'Examples in Epistemology: Socrates, Theaetetus and G. E. Moore', *Philosophy,* 52: 381–396.

——1980. 'Can the Sceptic Live His Scepticism?', in *Doubt and Dogmatism: Studies in Hellenistic Epistemology,* edd. M. Schofield, M. Burnyeat, and J. Barnes, 20–53. Oxford ( = chap. 2).

——1982. 'Idealism and Greek Philosophy: What Descartes Saw and Berkeley Missed', *Philosophical Review* 90: 3–40.

——1983. *The Skeptical Tradition.* Berkeley, Los Angeles, and London.

Bury, R. G. 1933–49. *Sextus Empiricus, with an English Translation,* 4 vols. London and Cambridge, Mass., Loeb Classical Library.

Carnap, Rudolf 1950. 'Empiricism, Semantics, and Ontology', *Revue internationale de philosophie,* 11: 20–40. Repr. in *Semantics and the Philosophy of Language,* ed. L. Linsky, pp. 208–228. Urbana 1952.

Cave, Terence 1979. *The Cornucopian Text: Problems of Writing in the French Renaissance.* Oxford.

Cavell, Stanley 1979. *The Claim of Reason: Wittgenstein, Skepticism, Morality and Tragedy.* Oxford and New York.

Clarke, Thompson 1972. 'The Legacy of Scepticism', *Journal of Philosophy,* 69: 754–769.

Couissin, Pierre 1929. 'Le Stoicisme de la Nouvelle Académie', *Revue d'histoire de la philosophie,* 3: 241–276. English translation in Burnyeat ed. 1983: 31–63.

Deichgräber, M. 1930. *Die griechische Empirikerschule.* Berlin.

Denyer, Nicholas 1981. 'The Atomism of Diodorus Cronus', *Prudentia,* 13: 33–45.

Frede, Michael 1979. 'Des Skeptikers Meinungen', *Neue Hefte für Philosophie,* 15/16: 102–129 ( = chap. 1).

——1984. 'The Sceptic's Two Kinds of Assent and the Question of the Possibility of Knowledge', in *Philosophy in History: Essays on the Historiography of Philosophy,* edd. R. Rorty, J. B. Schneewind, and Q. Skinner, pp. 255–278. Cambridge ( = chap. 5).

Gassendi, Pierre 1644. *Metaphysical Colloquy, or Doubts and Rebuttals Concerning the Metaphysics of René Descartes with His Replies.* Selections translated in Brush 1972: 157–278.

——1658. *Syntagma Philosophicum,* in *Opera,* Lyons.

Geach, P. T. 1966. 'Plato's *Euthyphro:* an Analysis and Commentary', *Monist,* 50: 369–382.

Hallie, Philip P. 1967. Article 'Sextus Empiricus', in *The Encyclopedia of Philosophy,* ed. Paul Edwards. New York and London.

Hamlyn, D. W. 1968. *Aristotle's De Anima Books II and III*. Oxford.

Hossenfelder, M. 1968. *Sextus Empiricus, Grundriss der pyrrhonischen Skepsis*, Einleitung und Übersetzung. Frankfurt am Main.

Hussey, Edward 1983. *Aristotle's Physics Books III and IV*. Oxford and New York.

Janáček, K. 1948. *Prolegomena to Sextus Empiricus*. Acta Universitatis Palackianae.

———1979. 'Das Wort *skeptikos* in Philons Schriften', *Listy Filologické*, 101: 65–68.

Kant, Immanuel 1781. *Critique of Pure Reason*. Translated by Norman Kemp Smith. London and New York, corrected edn. 1933.

Kung, Joan 1981. 'Aristotle on Thises, Suches and the Third Man Argument', *Phronesis*, 26: 207–247.

Lear, Jonathan 1982. 'Leaving the World Alone', *Journal of Philosophy*, 79: 382–403.

Mackie, J. L. 1977. *Ethics: Inventing Right and Wrong*. Harmondsworth.

Montaigne, Michel de 1580. *Apologie de Raymond Sebond*, translated in E. J. Trechman, *The Essays of Montaigne*, 2 vols., London 1935.

Moore, G. E. 1925. 'A Defence of Common Sense', in *Contemporary British Philosophy*, Second Series, ed. J. H. Muirhead, pp. 191–223. London and New York. Repr. in G. E. Moore, *Philosophical Papers*, London and New York 1959, 32–59.

———1939. 'Proof of an External World', *Proceedings of the British Academy*, 25: 273–300. Repr. in G. E. Moore, *Philosophical Papers*, London and New York 1959, 127–150.

———1953. *Some Main Problems of Philosophy*. London and New York.

Nagel, Thomas 1979. *Mortal Questions*. Cambridge.

Owen, G.E.L. 1969. 'Tithenaitaphainomena', in *Aristote et les problèmes de méthode*, ed. S. Mansion, pp. 83–103. Louvain. Repr. in *Articles on Aristotle*, edd. J. Barnes, M. Schofield, and R. Sorabji, vol. 1, pp. 113–126. London 1975.

———1970. 'Aristotle: Method, Physics and Cosmology', in *A Dictionary of Scientific Biography*, ed. C. C. Gillespie, vol. I, pp. 250–58. New York.

———1978/9. 'Particular and general', *Proceedings of the Aristotelian Society*, 79: 1–21.

Popkin, Richard H. 1951/2. 'Berkeley and Pyrrhonism', *Review of Metaphysics*, 5:223–246. Repr. in Burnyeat ed. 1983, pp. 377–396.

———1979. *The History of Scepticism: From Erasmus to Spinoza*. Berkeley, Los Angeles, and London.

Quine, W. V. 1951. 'On Carnap's views on ontology', in W. V. Quine, *The Ways of Paradox and Other Essays*, pp. 126–134. New York 1966.

Ross, W. D. 1936. *Aristotle's Physics*. A Revised Text with Introduction and Commentary. Oxford.

Russell, Bertrand 1914. *Our Knowledge of the External World*. London.

Schmitt, C. B. 1983. 'The Rediscovery of Ancient Scepticism in Modern Times', in Burnyeat ed. 1983, pp. 225–252.

Sedley, David 1977. 'Diodorus Cronus and Hellenistic Philosophy', *Proceedings of the Cambridge Philological Society*, 203 (N.S. 23): 74–120.

———1983. 'The Motivation of Greek Scepticism', in Burnyeat ed. 1983, pp. 9–30.

Sorabji, Richard 1983. *Time, Creation and the Continuum.* London.

Striker, Gisela 1980. 'Sceptical Strategies', in *Doubt and Dogmatism: Studies in Hellenistic Epistemology*, edd. M. Schofield, M. Burnyeat, and J. Barnes, pp. 54–83. Oxford.

———1983. 'The Ten Tropes of Aenesidemus', in Burnyeat ed. 1983, pp. 95–116.

Stroud, Barry 1979. 'The Significance of Scepticism', in *Transcendental Arguments and Science*, edd. P. Bieri, R.-P. Horstmann, and L. Krüger, Synthèse Library vol. 133, pp. 277–298. Dordrecht, Boston, and London.

———1983. 'Kant and Skepticism', in Burnyeat ed. 1983, pp. 413–434.

Tarrant, H. 1983. 'The Date of Anon. *In Theaetetum*', *Classical Quarterly*, 33: 161–187.

Tonelli, Giorgio 1967. 'Kant und die antiken Skeptiker', in *Studien zu Kant's philosophischer Entwicklung*, edd. H. Heimsoeth, D. Henrich, and G. Tonelli, pp. 93–123. Hildesheim.

Walker, Ralph 1983. 'Gassendi and Scepticism', in Burnyeat ed. 1983, pp. 319–336.

Wittgenstein, Ludwig 1953. *Philosophical Investigations.* Translated by G.E.M. Anscombe. Oxford.

# 5

# The Sceptic's Two Kinds of Assent and the Question of the Possibility of Knowledge

## Michael Frede

Traditionally one associates scepticism with the position that nothing is, or can be, known for certain. Hence it was only natural that for a long time one should have approached the ancient sceptics with the assumption that they were the first to try to establish or to defend the view that nothing is, or can be, known for certain, especially since there is abundant evidence which would have seemed to bear out the correctness of this approach. After all, extensive arguments to the effect that there is no certain knowledge or that things are unknowable play a central role in our ancient sources on scepticism. And thus Hegel, Brandis, Zeller, and their successors were naturally led to take these arguments at face value and to assume that the sceptics were trying to show that nothing can be known. Closer consideration of the matter, though, shows that it cannot have been the position of the major exponents of ancient scepticism, whether Academic or Pyrrhonean, that nothing is, or can be, known. And this for the simple reason that the major ancient sceptics were not concerned to establish or to defend any position, let alone the position that nothing is, or can be, known. In fact, they went out of their way to point out that, though they produced arguments for it, they did not actually take the position that nothing can be known (cf. *PH* I., 200–1).[1] And they went on to criticize those who did claim that nothing can be known as being as dogmatic as those philosophers who claimed that something can be known, as being pseudo-sceptics (cf. *PH* I., 3, 226; Photius, *Bibl.* 212, 169ᵇ).[2] Hence, in the following I shall call the position they criticize 'dogmatic scepticism', to distinguish it from the scepticism I want to

1. Sextus Empiricus, *Outlines of Pyrrhonism* (hereinafter *PH*).

2. Photius, *Bibliotheke*, ed. R. Henry (Paris, 1959).

attribute to the major ancient sceptics and which I shall call 'classical scepticism'. I do not want to suggest by this that there are no important differences between Arcesilaus, Carneades, and the Pyrrhoneans. It just seems to me that these differences are minor compared to the difference between classical and dogmatic scepticism.

If there should be a substantial difference between classical scepticism and dogmatic scepticism, the questions arise (1) how did it come about that scepticism turned dogmatic, (2) how did it come about that scepticism was identified with dogmatic scepticism, so much so that even classical sceptics came to be interpreted as dogmatic sceptics, and (3) was something philosophically important lost because one was not aware of classical scepticism as an alternative to dogmatic scepticism? It is these questions I am primarily interested in, but since they only arise if there actually is a substantial difference between classical and dogmatic scepticism, I shall first turn to the question whether it can be made out that there is a significant difference.

Traditionally philosophers and historians of philosophy have not seen a substantial difference. For they have treated Arcesilaus, Carneades, and the Pyrrhoneans as if they, just like the dogmatic sceptics, had taken, defended, and argued for the position that nothing can be known. Now this only seems possible if one does not take seriously the classical sceptic's remark that he, unlike the dogmatic sceptic, does not take the position that nothing can be known. And the only reason I can see for not taking this remark seriously is the following: one has reason to believe that the classical sceptic, like the dogmatic sceptic, does have the view that nothing can be known; and thus one thinks that the classical sceptic only says that he does not take this position because he not only cannot consistently claim to know that nothing can be known, but cannot even take the position that nothing can be known, if he wants to preserve consistency with a main tenet of scepticism, namely the principle that one should not commit oneself to any position, that one should suspend judgment, withhold assent on any matter whatsoever. Hence, since I do want to take the classical sceptic's remark seriously, I have to argue either that the classical sceptic does in fact not have the view that nothing can be known or that there is a substantial difference between having a view, on the one hand, and taking a position or making a claim, on the other. Since I believe that there is some sense in which even the classical sceptic might have the view that nothing is, or can be, known, I shall try to argue the latter by distinguishing, following the classical sceptic, two kinds of assent such that having a view involves one kind of assent, whereas taking a position, or making a claim, involves a different kind of assent, namely the kind of assent a sceptic will withhold.

But before we turn to this distinction of two kinds of assent, it will be of use to consider the view that one should withhold assent. For it is this view which, supposedly, the classical sceptic tries to preserve consistency with, in denying that he takes the position that nothing can be known.

What, then, is the status of this view that it is wise to withhold assent? To start with, it is the conclusion of an argument the sceptic produces which is supposed to show that the wise man will always withhold assent. But it clearly is not the case that the sceptic, in arguing this way, thinks that he commits himself to the position that it is wise always to withhold assent. For to commit oneself to this position would be to give assent. In this particular case it is easy to see why the sceptic is not committed to the conclusion of his argument. It is an argument drawn from premises which only his opponent, by granting them, is committed to: an argument designed to show his opponent that he is in a dilemma, that he is committed to conflicting claims and hence had better consider the matter further until he is in a position to decide between them. For it is central to the position of his opponent that the wise man often does have the kind of justification for his views which will allow him to give assent. To be shown then that he also is committed to the view that the wise man will never give assent puts him into a fundamental dilemma.

What is clear in the case of this argument, namely that the sceptic is not committed to its conclusion because he is just trying to show his opponent that he is committed to a claim which conflicts with his original claim, seems to me to be true of all sceptical arguments. The sceptic never tries to argue for a position, he never argues against a claim in the sense that he tries to establish a conflicting claim and thereby tries to show the falsehood of the original claim. He rather thinks of himself as following Socrates, submitting the claims of others to the kind of test Socrates had subjected them to. Socrates saw himself in the unfortunate position of lacking the knowledge and expertise in ethical matters which others claimed to have. He was more than eager to learn from those who were qualified to speak on these matters. But how, given his own ignorance, would he be able to tell whether somebody really had some special qualification to speak on these matters? The method he used was the following: he would ask the person whose qualification he wanted to test a question to which the person would have to know the answer if he were knowledgeable and expert, qualified to speak on the given subject-matter. He would then try to show by an argument drawn for assumptions accepted by his opponent that his opponent also was committed to a belief which was incompatible with his answer to the original question. In case Socrates succeeded, this would have the effect that the opponent would have to admit that by his own standards of rationality he did not have the required qualification, the expertise, or knowledge Socrates was looking for. For if he did have the knowledge he would have sufficient reason to reject one of the two conflicting claims. As it is, he, by his own standards does not even have any reason to maintain one rather than the other of the two claims. For he must have had some reason for his original claim. But this reason is now balanced by another reason which he is shown to have in support of the conflicting claim. And it is because he is not in a position to adjudicate between the two that he ends in an aporia, that he is in a dilemma, that he does not know what to do about the conflict.

For our purposes one crucial feature of this kind of Socratic argument is that all its premises are supplied by the opponent. Socrates does not have to know their truth, he does not even have to have any view as to their truth, nor does he have to know the truth or have a view as to the truth of the conclusion of his argument, to achieve his aim of finding out whether his opponent can be trusted to know the truth on the matters in question. Another crucial feature is that it not only reveals that the opponent by his own standards lacks the knowledge in question, but that it also shows to the opponent that he would have to give the matter further consideration because, as it is, he does not seem to be even in a position to just make the claim.

What I want to suggest is that Arcesilaus and his followers thought of themselves as just following Socratic practice, and that they understood their arguments in the indicated way. In fact, I believe that they went one step further: they not only did not want to be committed themselves to the truth of the premises and the conclusion of their arguments, they also did not want to be committed to the validity of their arguments. More generally, they thought that their opponents had committed themselves to a certain view as to what counts as knowledge, good reason, sufficient reason, justi-fication, and that their opponents had developed something called 'logic' to formulate canons and standards for argument and justification, canons whose strict application would guarantee the truth of the conclusions arrived at in this way. Since the sceptic wants to see whether his opponent at least by his own standards or canons has knowledge, he in his own argu-ments adheres to these standards. But this does not mean that he himself is committed to them. He is aware of the fact, e.g., that ordinarily we do not operate by these standards and that it is because his opponents want more than we ordinarily have that they try to subject themselves to these stricter canons; they want 'real' knowledge, certain knowledge.

For these reasons, then, the sceptics also would see no reason why their arguments that it is wise to always withhold assent would commit them to the position that one should always withhold assent. Their arguments just show that this is a conclusion their opponents are committed to. But the sceptics not only produce arguments to the effect that one should withhold assent, they also, as we can see from Sextus Empiricus, are in the habit of saying, at the conclusion of their various arguments against the various claims they address themselves to, that one ought to suspend judgment, to withhold assent on the matter. Since these remarks are not part of the sceptical arguments themselves, one might think that at least now the sceptics are committing themselves to a position in saying that one should withhold assent on this or that matter. And since the sceptics seem to be willing to make this kind of remark on any subject-matter whatsoever, one might even think that this reflects the general position that one should always withhold assent. But, of course, there is another interpretation of these remarks. Their aim might just be to point out to the opponent that by his own standards it would seem that he ought to withhold assent. But since the sceptic has not committed himself to these standards there is also no reason to think, just on the basis of these remarks, that he is committed to the claim that one ought to withhold assent on a particular subject, let alone to the generalization that one ought always to withhold assent.

What reason, then, do we have at all to assume that the sceptic thinks that one ought to withhold assent? I think that what may allow us to assume after all that the sceptic has the view that one ought to withhold assent is the fact that his opponents try to refute the sceptic by challenging this view and that the sceptic accepts that challenge. But one has to keep in mind that the fact that the sceptic accepts the challenge also admits of a different interpretation. The opponent, in challenging the view that it is wise to withhold assent, may be trying to remove one horn of the dilemma into which he has been put by the sceptical argument that the wise man will not give assent, and the sceptic may be taking up the challenge to show that his opponent is not in a position to rule out this possibility and thus to remove the conflict of his beliefs. In fact, I think that in classical scepticism this is one function of, e.g., the accounts of the so-called practical criterion, i.e., I think that it should not be taken for granted that the sceptical accounts of the practical criterion are just straightforward accounts of how a sceptic may proceed in real life. They, first of all, serve the purpose to show that the possibility that the wise man will not give assent cannot be ruled out just because it would be impossible to lead a life, let alone a wise life, without assent. The accounts without assent. The accounts of the practical criterion are supposed to show that even on the Stoics' own assumptions it might be possible to live without assent. Still, it also seems clear from the way the sceptic's opponents attack the sceptic on this point that they do not regard the sceptic's remarks as just a move in the dialectical game, but think that the sceptic does have the view that one ought to withhold assent. But in what sense could the sceptic have the view that one ought always to withhold assent without involving himself in immediate contradiction? If to have a view is to give assent a sceptic cannot heed his own precept without violating it. Thus we must assume that there is a kind of assent, namely the kind of assent the sceptic will withhold, such that having a view in itself does not involve that kind of assent, if we also want to assume that the sceptic does think that one ought to withhold assent and that he does not thereby involve himself in contradiction.

In what sense, then, could the sceptic have the view that one always ought to withhold assent? The only possibility I see is this: it turns out in his experience, having considered claim after claim, that given certain standards or canons it seems that one ought to withhold assent. And this might suggest to him, leave him with the impression that, given these standards, one ought to withhold assent. But this does not mean that he is ready to make the claim that one ought to withhold assent. For he knows too well that his claim would invite a sceptical counterargument. It would be pointed out to him that his experience was quite limited, that it was possibly quite idiosyncratic, that the future might be radically different, etc. Knowing all this he does not feel in a position to make the claim that one ought to withhold assent, but he also still might have the impression that, given certain canons, one ought to withhold assent, just as he might still have the impression that there is motion, and yet not be ready to make that claim because he acknowledges that there are impressive arguments, like Zeno's paradoxes, on both sides of the question and that he is in no position to adjudicate between them. More generally, the reason why he does not feel like making a claim, let alone a claim to knowledge, is that he thinks that there is a philosophical practice of making claims, and in particular a practice of making claims to knowledge, and that to engage in this practice is to subject oneself to certain canons, and that he has the impression that, given these canons, one ought to withhold assent. To be more precise, according to these canons, one has to have some special reason to make a claim, and given what counts as a reason according to these canons, he does not see himself in a position to make a claim, and thus thinks he ought to withhold assent.

I want to emphasize that this view not only has a rather complicated, tenuous status, it also has this further complexity which tends to be overlooked. It is a view relative to the canons and standards of rationality espoused by dogmatic philosophy, which the dogmatic philosopher insists on applying to any claim whatsoever, whether it be in mathematics or in ordinary life. It is only given these standards that it seems that one should withhold assent. But they are not the sceptic's standards, though he does not reject them, either. And thus Sextus often qualifies his remark that we have to withhold assent by saying that we have to withhold assent as far as this is a matter of reason or philosophical reason (*hoson epi tō philosophō logō; PH* III, 65; 1, 215; II, 26, 104; III, 6, 13, 29, 81, 135, 167). Thus there is room for another kind of assent, though one which will be threatened by the possibility that one ought to conform to the standards postulated by dogmatic philosophy if it should turn out that there is a choice in the matter.

On the basis of this one might try to make a distinction between just having a view and making a claim, taking a position. To just have a view is to find oneself being left with an impression, to find oneself having an impression after having considered the matter, maybe even for a long time, carefully, diligently, the way one considers matters depending on the importance one attaches to them. But however carefully one has considered a matter it does not follow that the impression one is left with is true, nor that one thinks that it is true, let alone that one thinks that it meets the standards which the dogmatic philosophers claim it has to meet if one is to think of it as true. To make a claim, on the other hand, is to subject oneself to certain canons. It does, e.g., require that one should think that one's impression is true and that one has the appropriate kind of reason for thinking it to be true. To be left with the impression or thought that *p*, on the other hand, does not involve the further thought that it is true that *p*, let alone the yet further thought that one has reason to think that *p*, that it is reasonable that *p*. Even on the principles of Stoic logic the propositions (i) that *p*, (ii) that it is true that *p*, and (iii) that it is reasonable that *p*, are different propositions, and hence the corresponding thoughts or impressions are different thoughts. And though the propositions that *p* and that it is true that *p* may be necessarily equivalent, it does not follow from this that the impression that *p* involves, or is identical with, the impression that it is true that *p*.

Now it seems to me that there is such a distinction between having a view and taking a position, but that it is quite difficult to articulate it. And one reason for this seems to be that there is a whole spectrum of distinctions with a very weak notion of having a view at one extreme and a strong notion of taking a position at the other extreme. The problem is to draw the distinction in such a way that it does correspond to the distinction the sceptics actually made.

One way the sceptics draw the distinction is in terms of two kinds of assent, and since I think that it is a difficulty about the way in which the distinction is to be drawn in terms of two kinds of assent which historically give rise to dogmatic scepticism, I focus on the distinction thus drawn. But it is important to realize from the outset that this is just one way in which the sceptics draw the distinction, and that they draw the distinction in this way because their opponents speak about assent in such a way that they are in no position to assail the sceptical distinction.

A clue as to how we might distinguish two kinds of assent for the classical sceptic, we get from Sextus. For Sextus, too, distinguishes two kinds of assent. Though at times he says that the sceptic invariably withholds assent, he also says that the sceptic does give assent to those impressions which are forced upon him (I. 13), or that the sceptic does not want to overturn those views which lead us, having been impressed by things in a certain way, toward assent without our will. The addition 'without our will' is crucial. For it guards this kind of assent against the threat that we might find out we ought to conform to the canons of rationality postulated by dogmatism. This kind of assent is not a matter of choice, unlike the assent of the Stoic wise man. In the first of these passages Sextus also uses the verb *eudokein* as a variant for the verb normally used in this context, *synkatatithesthai*. And indeed, the Suida, the Etymologicum Magnum, and the Lexeis Rhetorikai (*Anecdota Graeca*, I, p. 260)[3] treat *synkatatithesthai* as a synonym of *eudokein*. And if we consider the ordinary use of this verb, it turns out that it might refer to an explicit act of acknowledgment, approval, consent, acceptance, the kind of thing one does for a reason. Or it might refer to a passive acquiescence or acceptance of something, in the way in which a people might accept a ruler, not by some act of approval or acknowledgment, but by acquiescence in his rule, by failing to resist, to effectively reject his rule. Correspondingly there are two ways or senses in which one might accept or approve of an impression. When the Stoics speak of 'assent', they talk of an act of approval, the kind of thing one should do for an appropriate reason; they think that to assent to an impression is to take it to be true, and that one should have good reason for taking something to be true. But there is also the other sense of 'assent'. One might, having considered matters, just acquiesce in the impression one is left with, resign

3.  Ed. I. Bekker (Berlin, 1814).

oneself to it, accept the fact that this is the impression one is left with, without though taking the step to accept the impression positively by thinking the further thought that the impression is true. One might also not acquiesce in the impression one is left with and think that the matter needs further consideration. But whether one does or does not acquiesce in it is not by itself dependent on whether one takes the impression to be true. Assent may be a purely passive matter. It may be the case that human beings work in such a way that impressions are more or less evident to us. Evidence is a purely internal feature of our impressions. Now we also attribute different importance to different questions. We might be constructed in such a way that if we have an impression on a matter whose degree of evidence does not correspond to the degree of importance we attach to the matter, we naturally, unless we are prevented, e.g., by lack of time or energy or have decided to take a risk, go on to consider the matter further till we get an impression which has a sufficient degree of evidence. It would not even have to be the case that at a certain point we decide that we now have a clear enough impression and stop to consider the matter further. It may just be the case that as soon as we have a clear enough impression we, without any further thought, act on it. And this may be all acquiescence and assent consist in.

One might object that both cases of assent constitute some kind of acceptance, and that to accept an impression surely is to accept it as true. After all, how could somebody be said to have the view that $p$ without thinking that it is the case that $p$ or that it is true that $p$?

Here is at least one way in which this might be possible. It might be the case that action does not require that one take the impression one is acting on to be true. It might be the case that action does not, in addition to the impression that $p$, require a positive act of assent or the further thought that it is true that $p$. All that may be needed is one's acquiescence in the impression, and all this may amount to is that in the series of impressions one has reached an impression which produces an action rather than the kind of disquiet which would make one go on to consider the matter further till one reached an impression which one no longer resists and which produces an action. Indeed, one may have the view that $p$ without even entertaining the thought that $p$, let alone the further thought that $p$ is true. Things may have left us with the impression that $p$, and we may act on that view, without being aware of it. We may leave aside here cases in which something prevents us from realizing that this is the view we have (e.g., cases of suppression or self-deception). For even if we know that we have a certain view and on some occasion act on it, it is not necessary that in order to act on it we on that occasion have to entertain explicitly the corresponding thought and to assent positively to it. An expert craftsman is still acting on his expert beliefs, even though he is not actually thinking of what he is doing when he is acting on them. Indeed thinking of them might interfere with his activity. But having finished his work he might well explain to us which views guided his activity. And for some of these views it might be true that this would be the first time he ever formulated them, either to himself or to somebody else. Nevertheless he could properly claim to have acted on them.

The sceptic might think that his opponents will have to grant that there are these kinds of cases and that they can be characterized in terms of assent to an impression. For even the Stoics assume that the wise man will often act, not on the basis of certain knowledge, but of wise conjecture. He is not omniscient, and his rationality and wisdom are characterized exactly by his ability to be rational or reasonable in his assumptions and actions even when he lacks knowledge, as he inevitably will, in the complex situations of everyday life. Nevertheless, he will do what is fitting or appropriate because he will be able, as the Stoics themselves say, to give a reasonable (*eulogon*) account of what he has done. I want to suggest that the past tense of 'what he has done' is to be taken seriously. The view is rather like Aristotle's; the person who has chosen to act in a certain way does not actually have to have gone through some moral reasoning and to have actually decided to act accordingly; what makes the action voluntary, rather, is that one can correctly explain the action after the fact as being done for reasons of a certain kind. Similarly, the Stoic wise man, in order to do what is fitting, does not necessarily actually have to go through some reasoning, overtly accept or assent to the conclusion, and act on the basis of this. It, rather, is that his action in hindsight can be explained in terms of such reasoning. Thus even on the Stoics' theory there will be cases where the wise man, in fact, just acts on an impression of an appropriate kind and where, if we want to talk about assent, the assent consists in nothing but the fact that the wise man does not resist the impression he is acting on, but, in acting on it, implicitly accepts it. This, then, would seem to be a kind of case where acceptance of, or assent to, an impression does not involve taking it to be true. And if this is so, and if withholding assent is counted as an action, one might, e.g., say that the sceptic has the view that one ought to withhold assent in the sense that he might explain his withholding assent in terms of his acquiescence in this impression, pointing out that he is not resisting or fighting against this impression, but implicitly accepts it by acting on it.

Thus the sceptic may have views which account for his behavior. He behaves exactly in the way in which somebody who believed these views to be true would behave. But he insists that there is no need to assume that action, in addition to the appropriate kind of impression, requires the additional belief that the impression is true.

Now one might also ask the sceptic about his view on this or that matter. And he might be ready to try to articulate his view. And in this case it might be objected that he now is taking a position about what he takes to be the truth of the matter. But, as we can see from Sextus, it is open to him to reply that he is merely trying to articulate the views which guide his behavior, he is merely, as it were, giving an autobiographical report, without taking a stand on the truth of his views.

At this point it is also worth taking note of another crucial fact. It is assumed by Greek philosophers that knowledge and truth are correlatives. For them those things count as truths which on the true account of things would come out as truths. But given that dogmatic philosophy has raised the conditions for what is to count as knowledge, it thereby has raised the requirements for what is to count as true. Now things which we ordinarily would count as true no longer necessarily qualify as such. We might think that it is true that this book is brown. But it might turn out that on the true theory of things this is a mere appearance, that, in fact, there only is a certain configuration of atoms which may, or may not, produce this appearance. And similarly for all other ordinary truths. It is in this way that dogmatic philosophy creates a global contrast between appearance and truth or reality. For dogmatic philosophy insists on calling into question all the truths we ordinarily go by.

And given this contrast, the sceptic, of course, does not take his impressions to be true, i.e., he does not think that his impressions are such that they will come out true on the true theory of things. For what reason would he have to think this? And he can point to the fact that not even the Stoic wise man takes all his impressions to be true in this way. The very point of the doctrine of the reasonable is that it allows the wise man to accept impressions and thus not to be reduced to inaction, without thereby taking them to be true. It is in this way that the Stoic wise man avoids having false beliefs, even though some of his impressions, however reasonable, may be false. For though he goes by the impression that $p$, he does not accept it as true, but only as reasonable.

Thus one may argue that the Stoics, given their own theory, can hardly reject the suggestion that there is a difference between having a view and taking a position, between just going by an impression and going by an impression because one takes it to be true, between two kinds of assent, merely passive acceptance and active acceptance as true.

There is one important difference between having a view and taking a position which was emphasized by the sceptics and which is still reflected by our ordinary notion of dogmatism. The sceptic has no stake in the truth of the impression he is left with. He is ever ready to consider the matter further, to change his mind. He has no attachment to the impressions he is left with. He is not responsible for having them, he did not seek them out. He is not out to prove anything, and hence feels no need to defend anything. For the dogmatic, on the other hand, something is at stake. It does make a great difference to him whether his impressions really are true and whether he has made a mistake in taking them to be true. For in actively giving assent to them he has become responsible for them, and hence feels a need to defend them and to prove them to be true. The dogmatic, in taking a position, has made a deliberate choice, a *hairesis*, for which he is accountable. But because so much is at stake for him, he no longer is in a position openly to consider alternatives, to realize and accept the weight of objections; he has become dogmatic in his attitude.

If we now apply this distinction of two kinds of assent and correspondingly the distinction between having a view and taking a position to the question of knowledge, we might say that the classical sceptic perhaps comes to be left with the impression that nothing is, or even can be, known, whereas the dogmatic sceptic takes the position that nothing can be known. How could the classical sceptic come to have this impression? In his experience it turns out that claim after claim does not pass his scrutiny which, at least given the standards his opponents themselves are committed to, these claims should pass if they were made from knowledge. Thus he naturally is left with the impression that, given these standards, nothing will pass the test and hence that nothing is, or even can be, known. And in the course of time he might even acquiesce in this impression. He might stop to think that this cannot be right and that just some further consideration will change his impression. And yet he might not feel the slightest inclination to claim that nothing can be known. He knows the objections too well: limited experience, experience with the wrong claims, experience with the wrong opponents, one day we shall know, etc. And there is, of course, the troublesome tag 'given these standards'. He is not committed to these standards, but he does see their attraction. He himself originally had hoped that by following these standards he would arrive at certain knowledge and thus could adjudicate all the conflicts which were troubling him. But he also knows of powerful arguments against these standards, like the paradox of the liar. He cannot rule out the possibility that other standards would fare better. He is aware of the fact that in ordinary life and in ordinary language we do not subject ourselves to these standards. We do not ordinarily require of somebody who claims to know that he should have the kind of reason and justification for his belief which allows him to rule out all incompatible beliefs, that knowledge has to be firm or certain exactly in the sense that somebody who really knows cannot be argued out of his belief on the basis of assumptions incompatible with it. It seems that ordinarily we only expect satisfaction of these standards to an extent and degree which is proportional to the importance we attribute to the matter in question. And thus, following common usage, a sceptic might well be moved to say, in perfect consistency with his scepticism, that he knows this or that. There is no reason why the sceptic should not follow the common custom to mark the fact that he is saying what he is saying having given the matter appropriate consideration in the way one ordinarily goes about doing this, by using the verb 'to know'. This, in fact, is what we find Sextus doing occasionally (cf. *M* VIII. 157). Aenesidemus obviously was prepared to go so far as to say that a wise man knows that he does not know anything for certain and that if he does know something he is still going to withhold assent (Photius, *Bibl.* 212, 169ᵇ 28ff.). A sceptic might take the view that all one could sensibly do was to follow this very complicated common practice. But if he would follow this practice it would be with the thought that what one said one knew could be radically otherwise, and that the whole practice of using the verb 'to know' the way we ordinarily do could be radically mistaken. For we cannot, e.g., rule out the possibility that we should subject ourselves to the rigorous standards and canons philosophers have been trying to impose, but which their own claims do not meet. There is the possibility that one day they will be able to formulate a set of canons which will find general acceptance. There is the possibility that one day they will make claims which meet these standards and which will pass the test.

It seems to me that this rather differentiated view is quite different from the dogmatic position that nothing can be known. It is a view the classical sceptic finds himself stranded with, not a position he is out to demonstrate, to establish, to defend, not a position he thinks he has reason to adopt and adopts for that reason. He is not out to show that some particular person, or some group of people, or people in general do not have knowledge, he is not out to show anything. He is willing to find out. But so far, all his search has left him with is the impression that nothing is known. If this is correct, then there is a substantial difference between classical scepticism and dogmatic scepticism, and the ancient representatives of classical scepticism were not just deluding themselves when they saw a difference between their own view and that of dogmatic sceptics. But if this is so, then the question does arise how this complex attitude of the classical sceptic collapsed into the dogmatic position that nothing can be known.

It seems that the major step in the direction of a dogmatic scepticism was already taken in antiquity. For, as we saw, in antiquity some sceptics accused other sceptics of being dogmatic in their assertion that nothing can be known. This is the charge Aenesidemus levels against the late Academics (cf. Photius, *Bibl.* 212, 169ᵇ), and a charge, Sextus thinks, which might be leveled against the Academics in general (*PH* I, 226). We find evidence that some late Academics did, in fact, espouse such a dogmatic scepticism. At the end of Cicero's *Academica priora* (II 148), Catulus is made to say:

> I return to the position of my father, which he said to be that of Carneades; I believe that nothing can be known, but I also believe that the wise man will give assent, i.e. will have opinions, but this in such a way that he is aware that he is only opining and that he knows that there is nothing which can be comprehended and known; hence I approve of this kind of withholding assent in all matters, but I vehemently assent to this other view that there is nothing which can be known.

These remarks reveal their dogmatism in the vehemence with which Catulus assents to the impression that nothing can be known, in the strong attachment which he has to this view, attachment of a kind which is quite alien to the classical sceptic and which is explicitly criticized by Sextus Empiricus (*PH* I, 230). Moreover, it reveals its dogmatism in that it allows the sceptic to have opinions, i.e., beliefs on how things are. This passage and its context also supply us with some crucial information about the source of this dogmatism. To start with, it is clear from Cicero's following remarks that he does not think that the view Catulus expresses is the general view of the Academy; Cicero himself thinks that this was not Carneades' view. Second, as we can see from Catulus' own remarks, this view is presented as an interpretation of Carneades, but as one which is controversial.

Now we know from the earlier parts of the *Academica* of at least one respect in which this interpretation of Carneades was controversial among Carneades' pupils. We are told that there was disagreement between Clitomachus, on the one hand, and Metrodorus and Philo, on the other, on whether, in reality and according to Carneades, the wise man will give assent and hence have opinions. The question is whether we can reconstruct enough of this controversy to see how it might have led to the kind of dogmatic scepticism which we find in the later Academy and which is represented by Catulus' remarks. In this case we also would have some explanation why later authors, like Sextus, entertain the possibility, or even assume as a fact, that Academic sceptics in general were dogmatic. For the view presents itself as an interpretation of Carneades and as the position of the Academy in general.

What, then, could have given rise to the view that according to Carneades the wise man will assent to what is not known, i.e., will have opinions, and how could this lead to the kind of dogmatic scepticism we are considering? The following seems to me to be a possibility. The notion of the probable (*pithanon*) plays a central role in Carneades. Among other things it is a matter of probability for Carneades that nothing can be known (Cic., *Acad.* II 110). Now there are two different interpretations of, and attitudes toward, the probable. These seem to correspond to two different interpretations of Carneades' so-called practical criterion. Asked how the sceptic will know what to do if he universally withholds assent, Carneades points out that he will just follow the probable, what seems to be the case, and that depending on the importance of the matter he will go through certain procedures to make sure that his impression is relatively reliable. It is clear that Carneades' account, first of all, is a dialectical move against a dogmatic objection and thus does not commit him to any view at all. But I also think that is does reflect Carneades' view of how people actually go about gaining an impression they are willing to rely on. And taken this way, it admits of two interpretations. It may be taken in just the sense that this is how human beings in general seem to proceed, or it may be taken in the sense that this is how one ought to proceed if one wants to get a reliable impression, one which if not true, at least has a good chance to be true. Whereas on the first interpretation it is just noted that human beings, as a matter of fact, go about considering matters in a certain way when in doubt, on the second interpretation proper consideration is regarded as conferring some epistemological status on the impression thus arrived at: it at least has a good chance to be true. And thus, though it is agreed on all sides that the probable is that which seems to be the case, this is interpreted in two different ways. On one interpretation what on due consideration appears to be the case offers us some guidance about what is actually true. Though we are in no position to say that it is true, we may expect it to have a good chance of being true, to be like the truth (*verisimilis*), or else to be the truth itself (Cic., *Acad.* II 7; 32; 66; 99; 107). On the other interpretation, the fact that something appears to be the case goes no way to show that it is true;

however much it appears to be the case, this does not it itself make it any more likely to be true. The probable is just the plausible, and there is no reason to assume that plausibility and truth, or even evidence and truth, go hand in hand.

Another piece of relevant information seems to be the following: Carneades subscribed to the sceptic tenet that one should always withhold assent. But it also seems to have been agreed that Carneades did say that it is sometimes wise to give assent (Cic., *Acad.* II 67). Obviously, this needed interpretation, because it had to be made compatible with the general sceptical tenet to withhold assent, but presumably also because Arcesilaus had said nothing of the sort and hence Carneades' remark might be taken to indicate a significant departure from the position of Arcesilaus. Thus we find Clitomachus making a distinction of two kinds of assent, obviously trying to give an interpretation of the distinction which will not commit Carneades to the view that it is wise to have mere opinions (Cic., *Acad.* II 104). And it seems clear from Catulus' remarks that the opposing party similarly made a distinction of two kinds of assent, but exactly in such a way that Carneades would be committed to the view that the wise man will have opinions. For Catulus distinguishes between the universal withholding of assent and the vehement assent he gives to the view that nothing can be known and he remarks that the wise man will give some kind of assent, i.e., will have opinions.

Now there is an obvious connection between the two interpretations of the probable and the two interpretations of the two kinds of assent Carneades must already have distinguished. To see this we have to notice that the sceptics sometimes speak of two kinds of assent; at other times they reserve the term 'assent' to the mental act, to something one does for a reason, to the positive acceptance of an impression because one thinks one has reason to take it to be true; and then they refer to the other kind of assent by talking of just following or approving or accepting an impression. At this point they rely on an etymological and conceptual connection between *pithanon* (probable) and *peithesthai* (to follow; cf. *PH* I, 230). It is this connection which Cicero tries to preserve when he renders *pithanon* by *probabile* to make it correspond to the verb for 'approve' or 'accept' which he likes to use, namely *probare* (Cic., *Acad.* II 99; 139). So the probable quite literally is that which invites approval or assent in the sense in which the sceptic is free to give assent. But now there is a disagreement about this sense, and hence about the way the probable is to be understood, and hence a disagreement about whether Carneades allows for mere opinion. The dogmatic sceptic seems to take the view that the only kind of assent which is illegitimate is assent of the kind where one takes something to be true, i.e., commits oneself to a belief about what will come out as true on the true theory of things, about what would turn out to be true if one really knew what things are like. And since it is one thing to take something to be true and quite another to take it to be probable, he thinks it is quite legitimate to give the kind of assent to an impression which would consist in taking it to be probable. And though we may not be able to ascertain what is to count as true, we can consider the matter with appropriate care and thus arrive at an impression which is probable and then assent to it as probable. But to take something to be probable is, on this interpretation of the probable, to take it to be either true or at least sufficiently like what is true. Thus somebody who does give assent in this sense does have beliefs about how things are, i.e., mere opinions.

Clitomachus' interpretation of the two kinds of assent, on the other hand, is very much along the lines of the distinction I earlier on attributed to Sextus, as we can see from Cicero (*Acad.* II 104), who spells out Clitomachus' view in some detail. On this interpretation, a view one acts on and a view one is willing to communicate do not presuppose either that one takes them to be true or that at least one takes them to be likely to be true, because one has considered the matter carefully. It is rather that, as a matter of fact, we sometimes only act on an impression, if we have considered the matter further, but not because we now think it more likely to be true. It surely is relevant to keep in mind in this connection, though this is not pointed out in our ancient texts, that sometimes we, quite reasonably, act on views which we ourselves find less likely to be true than their alternatives.

Now to take something to be true or at least likely to be true is not the same thing as to take it to be true. And thus even the kind of dogmatic Academic sceptic we are considering can insist that he, too, distinguishes between having a view and taking a position if to take a position is to take one's impression to be true, and that he does not take a position in saying that nothing can be known. This is what allows him to think that he is still a sceptic and not dogmatic. But since having a view for him might be a matter of actively adopting a view because he thinks that it is true or at least likely to be true, it is only a thin line which distinguishes him from the dogmatic who adopts a view because he takes it to be true. Both have views on how things are, both may be equally firmly convinced that they are true (remember Catulus' vehement assent), but one believes that the kind of justification or knowledge which would establish the truth of a view is available, whereas the other believes that it is not available. But as for the particular question we are concerned with, namely the possibility of knowledge, one cannot be more dogmatic than our dogmatic sceptic already is. For one cannot consistently claim that on the true account of things, i.e., if we really know how things are, it will turn out that nothing can be known. Thus, though there is a fine distinction between the dogmatism of the dogmatists and the dogmatism of late Academic sceptics, this fine distinction collapses when it comes to the view that nothing can be known. To preserve whatever distinction there is, one might distinguish between adopting a view and taking a position and contrast both with having a view. But I shall in the following use 'taking a position' in a wide sense to cover both, to emphasize the similarity which— in the eyes of the classical sceptic—dogmatic scepticism has with ordinary dogmatism.

If this should be correct, we can see what gives rise to dogmatic scepticism. Having considered a matter carefully, one finds oneself with a view which one finds persuasive. But this is now taken to mean that because one has considered the matter carefully the view has some likelihood of being true, though, of course, there is no guarantee or certainty that it is true. Thus Cicero can talk of the probable as the canon of truth and falsehood (*Acad.* II 32) and can talk of the Academic method of arguing pro and con, of considering a matter from all sides, as a method he pursues in the hope of finding what is true or at least very much like the truth (*Acad.* II 7). Thus the probability of the impression that nothing can be known, too, is interpreted as the likelihood, though not certainty, that nothing can be known, a likelihood one may be so convinced of that one vehemently assents. By contrast, the classical sceptic just finds himself with the view that nothing can be known and may finally acquiesce in it.

Thus a certain interpretation of the Carneadean criterion, and hence the probable, and along with it a certain interpretation of the distinction of two kinds of assent, is the first step on the road to dogmatic scepticism. It allows the sceptic to have opinions about how things are, as long as he is aware that his opinions are not a matter of certain knowledge. And it allows him to take the position that nothing can be known, if only it, too, is qualified by the proviso that it itself is not a matter of certain knowledge. For given his experience with sceptical arguments, it seems at least probable that nothing can be known.

Now the view that, in spite of all the sceptical arguments one has been producing and the effect they have had, one might still be left with an impression of how things are and that, on the basis of this impression, one may take a position, has an effect on the way sceptical arguments in general and the arguments concerning the possibility of knowledge in particular are viewed. On the old view, the sceptical method to argue against any claim and—by implication—for any claim, since one would argue against the contradictory of a claim as much as against the claim itself, was seen as a purely negative, critical method. It might have been granted that the considerations pro and con might still leave one with an impression, that however much one argued for and against the existence of motion one might still be left with the impression that things move. But it was not assumed that this impression gained any epistemological status in virtue of the fact that one was still left with it after having gone through all the arguments pro and con. Now it comes to be assumed that the sceptical method of arguing pro and con is also a method of truth, a method which allows one to approximate the truth, though it does not guarantee the truth of the resulting impression (cf. Cic., *Acad.* II 7). And hence the dogmatic sceptic might well take the view that having carefully considered the Stoic arguments for the possibility of knowledge and the sceptical arguments against it, and finding, on balance, the sceptical arguments to be weightier, he is in a position to claim that nothing can be known.

Moreover, once the sceptic takes the liberty to take positions, his positions, given the eclecticism of the time, tend to become more or less identical to those of the Stoics, except on the question of knowledge itself. Thus he does come to believe in mental items like impressions and mental acts like assents. And he comes to believe in the premises of the arguments the classical sceptics had formulated to show that the Stoics themselves were committed to the view that nothing is, or can be, known. And now these arguments will have a pull on him, which is reflected by the quite unsceptical vehemence with which Catulus assents to the view that nothing can be known. Now sceptical arguments to the effect that nothing can be known can come to be interpreted as arguments which go some way, though not all the way, to establish the truth of the claim that nothing can be known. This, then, is the second major step on the road to dogmatic scepticism. The sceptic now, though qualifiedly, himself espouses the dogmatic framework of concepts and assumptions which seem to make knowledge impossible.

It should be noticed that at this point the classical and the dogmatic sceptic no longer differ only in the kind of assent they might feel free to give, but also in the impressions they give assent to. The difference between classical and dogmatic sceptics does not just consist in the different qualifiers attached to their views. For given his, albeit qualified, trust in the ability of philosophical arguments to get one somewhere, the dogmatic sceptic will have views induced by nothing but such arguments, whereas it would seem that in the case of the classical sceptic such arguments only threaten to undermine even those views which had been induced quite independently of philosophical argument.

Finally, the second step, the acceptance of the dogmatic framework, seems to involve a third step. The classical sceptic had started out being attracted by certain knowledge. He certainly had not committed himself to the view that knowledge is certain knowledge. But the dogmatic sceptic now seems to accept the Stoic view that knowledge has to be certain. In fact, I am inclined to think that Philo provoked such an outcry among dogmatic sceptics because he maintained that though the kind of certain knowledge the Stoics were after was impossible this did not mean that knowledge as such was impossible, that this had never been the position of the Academy, and that hence the supposed break of the New Academy with the Old was an illusion.

In this way, then, we arrive by Cicero's time at the dogmatic sceptical position that since all we ever have are impressions of how things are and since there is nothing to ever guarantee the truth of an impression, nothing about how things are can be known for certain.

The next question I raised was how it happened that scepticism came to be identified with dogmatic scepticism, so much so that even classical scepticism was identified as dogmatic scepticism and that to the present day we associate scepticism with the dogmatic sceptical position. To understand this we have to see that scepticism of any form in antiquity soon came to be a dead issue. Dogmatic scepticism did not have a future in later ancient thought. Rather, it provoked a revival of classical scepticism. For it seems that Pyrrhonism is not so much a revival of Pyrrho's philosophy, but a revival of classical Academic scepticism under the name of Pyrrhonism, to distinguish it from the dogmatism which Aenesidemus and Sextus Empiricus associated with the later sceptical Academy. But neither form of scepticism suited the temper of late antiquity; later antiquity found some form of Platonism or other, in Christian or pagan garb, more congenial, and thus scepticism, with some odd exceptions like Uranius in the sixth century (cf. Agathias, *Historiarum libri quinque* II, 29, 7),[4] came to be a historical position to be vehemently rejected, rather than to be carefully understood. Thus it was largely a matter of ignorance that in late antiquity scepticism came to be identified with dogmatic scepticism. In the Latin West this was, no doubt, in good part due to Cicero's influence, who himself was a dogmatic sceptic and who, moreover, would be the only substantial source concerning scepticism available to those who did not read Greek. And

4. Ed. R. Keydell (Berlin, 1967).

Cicero's influence was magnified by St. Augustine's authority, who for his attack on scepticism in his *Contra Academicos* primarily, if not exclusively, relied on Cicero, but unlike Cicero, gave no indication of the possibility of a nondogmatic scepticism and treated Carneades as taking the kind of position espoused by Cicero. And given Augustine's standing far into early modern times, it is not surprising that the Western view of scepticism should have been determined by him throughout the Middle Ages, especially since for a long time his *Contra Academicos* would have been the only readily available source which discussed scepticism in any detail. And the impression gained from Augustine would be confirmed by the odd remark in the Latin Fathers, Arnobius (*Adv. Nationes* II, 9–10[5] or Lactantius (*Div. Inst.* III. 6),[6] for example. It may also be of relevance in this context that the question of knowledge became a live issue again in the late Middle Ages owing in part to Ockham's doctrine of intuitive cognitions. Ockham took the view that cognitions are entities. He also took the view that God, by his absolute power, can destroy any one of two separate entities, while preserving the other. Thus God could preserve a cognition we have while destroying the object of the cognition. Yet Ockham wanted to maintain that there are cognitions, namely intuitive cognitions, which warrant an evident judgment. Naturally his view raised questions. And at least one author, Nicolaus of Autrecourt, in his letters to Bernhard of Arezzo, took the view that, given the doctrine of cognitions or impressions and the doctrine of divine omnipotence he had to infer 'that every awareness which we have of the existence of objects outside our minds, can be false', and moreover that 'by natural cognitive means we cannot be certain when our awareness of the existence of external objects is true or false' (First Letter, p. 5 11).[7] Thus the question of the possibility of knowledge came to be a live issue again more or less exactly in those terms in which dogmatic scepticism had formulated it. In fact it may well have been this debate kindled by Ockham which created an interest in Cicero's *Academica* and Sextus Empiricus. A fourteenth-century manuscript of a Latin translation of Sextus' *Outlines* and a fifteenth-century manuscript of the same translation in any case show a revival of interest in ancient scepticism which must have been generated by developments in medieval philosophy itself.

Thus the West came to think of scepticism as dogmatic and even thought of classical sceptics as dogmatic sceptics. And the influence of the East

5. Ed. A. Reifferscheid CSEL IV (Vienna, 1875).

6. Ed. S. Brandt, CSEL XIX (Vienna, 1890).

7. In H. Shapiro, *Medieval Philosophy, Selected Reading* (New York, 1964).

during the Renaissance did not change this view. For the Greek East, too, already in antiquity, had settled for a dogmatic interpretation of scepticism. This is true for secular authors as much as ecclesiastical authors. To take the latter first, nobody would be able to gather from Clement's discussion (*Stromateis* VIII, V, 15.2ff.)[8] that not all sceptics asserted it as true that nothing can be known. Similarly, Eusebius (*Praeparatio Evangelica* XIV, 17, 10)[9] talks as if the sceptics took the position that nothing can be known. A particularly striking example of how even classical sceptics are interpreted as dogmatic sceptics is offered by Photius in his report on Aenesidemus' *Pyrrhonean Arguments* (Bibl. cod. 212, 1169[b]). Aenesidemus, in reaction to the dogmatism of the later Academy, had tried to revive classical scepticism under the name of Pyrrhonism. But though Photius tells us in the course of his report that Aenesidemus thought that the Academics had become dogmatic in claiming that nothing can be known, he starts out by telling us that Aenesidemus wrote his book to establish the thesis that nothing is known for certain. As for secular Greek writers one may compare the *Anonymous Prolegomena* (p. 21, 1ff.)[10] and Olympiodorus' *Prolegomena* (3, 32ff.).

Thus it was part of the medieval heritage that scepticism should be thought of as dogmatic scepticism and that even classical sceptics should be considered as dogmatic sceptics. But we have to ask why in early modern times, when most of the evidence concerning classical scepticism was available again, and when Cicero and Sextus Empiricus were reread with a new frame of mind, scepticism continued to be regarded as a dogmatical position, either as the extreme scepticism of the Pyrrhoneans or as the mitigated scepticism of the Academics.

I am not in a position to answer this question, but I do have some suggestions about how it might be answered. There is, first, mere inertia; this notion of scepticism, after all, was the notion inherited from the Middle Ages. Second, the early modern debate concerning the possibility of knowledge must have been a continuation of the medieval debate we referred to earlier. It surely is not accidental that the sceptical arguments against causality found, e.g., in Hume are very much like the arguments to be found in Nicolaus of Autrecourt or in Ghazali and Averroes' refutation of Ghazali. But at issue in this debate was a version of dogmatic scepticism. Third, early modern philosophy, in part in following

8. Ed. O. Stählin, GCS III (Leipzig, 1909).

9. Ed. K. Mras, GCS VIII. I (Berlin, 1954).

10. Ed. L. G. Westerink (Amsterdam, 1962).

the tradition of late medieval epistemology, in part in reaction to Aristotelianism and Scholasticism, came largely to adopt the framework of dogmatic Hellenistic epistemology and thereby invited dogmatic scepticism. The very term 'impressions', for example, may be due to Cicero's influence (*Acad.* II 58). Fourth, dogmatic scepticism satisfied various ideological needs of the time. It could be used to reject Aristotelian science, a curious preoccupation of that period. It could be used to point out the need for faith and revelation. Fifth, the attitude toward historical philosophical texts was very different from ours. Philosophers of the past were studied as paradigmatic philosophers, as authorities, as exponents of a philosophical position worth considering, i.e., they were approached with a preconception of what one expected from them which was determined by one's own needs. Obviously this attitude is not conducive to an understanding of the history of philosophy. One way in which this may be relevant for our question is this: at least on the face of it, classical sceptics seem to differ from dogmatic sceptics primarily in that the latter allowed the sceptic to have beliefs about how things are, whereas the former seem to require a life without beliefs. But this seemed so obviously to be such an untenable position that, until very recently, not even historians of philosophy gave it serious consideration. As a result one focused on the part of classical scepticism which was concerned with the possibility of knowledge, as if that part could be understood in isolation from the classical sceptic's attitude toward belief. But as we have seen, the difference between classical and dogmatic scepticism lies exactly in a different attitude toward belief or assent. Thus we can do justice to the classical sceptic's attitude toward knowledge only if we take his remarks concerning belief seriously. Sixth, when the texts were read again, it must have seemed that there were basically two forms of scepticism in antiquity, Pyrrhonean scepticism, going back to Pyrrho, and Academic scepticism going back to Arcesilaus. Pyrrhonean scepticism seemed hopeless as a philosophical position because one misunderstood the Pyrrhonean attitude toward beliefs and thought that a Pyrrhonean was supposed to live without beliefs. Hence the mitigated scepticism of the late Academy seemed to be the only sceptical position of promise. But remarks in Sextus suggested that the dogmatic scepticism of the late Academy was the position of the Academy in general. For Sextus in part relied on Antiochus for his view of the Academic position, and Antiochus saw Carneades, perhaps Arcesilaus and Carneades, as dogmatic sceptics. Moreover, Sextus himself had a vested interest in seeing the Academy in general as dogmatic. After all, the supposed dogmatism of the Academy is the main rationale for Pyrrhonism. Thus, if one concentrates on Academic scepticism as the viable sceptical position, and under the influ-

ence of Augustine and Sextus interprets Academic scepticism quite generally as dogmatic, one naturally arrives at a dogmatic conception of scepticism. But a more scholarly reading of Sextus or Cicero would have shown
that this was never the position of the Academy.

To turn finally to our last question, it seems to me that early modern
philosophy might have profited from a better historical understanding of
ancient scepticism and the realization that dogmatic scepticism is only a
degenerate form of scepticism. For it was because of this distorted notion of
scepticism that the question at issue was understood as the question how we
ever could be justified, on the basis of the impressions or ideas which are
immediately given to us, to have any views about how things are, let alone to
be certain about how things are. Descartes answered this question very
much along the lines the Stoics had answered it, but Hume, in spite of an
obvious tendency to go in this direction, was prevented from answering it in
the way in which classical scepticism had answered it, since he to a good
extent, too, accepted the dogmatic framework in which the question was
posed by ancient dogmatic scepticism. But once we see that this framework
in which the question is posed is the framework of dogmatic Hellenistic
epistemology, and only thus comes to be the framework of ancient dogmatic
scepticism, it is easy to realize that the classical sceptic will have no part of it.
For all he knows it might be a mistake to distinguish quite generally and
globally between how things appear and how they really are. There are some
cases where it seems to be useful to make such a distinction, e.g., in the case
of illusions, or in the case of deception. But for these cases we have ways to
ascertain what really is the case which allow us in the first place to draw, for
these cases, a reasonably clear distinction between how things appear and
how they really are. But how are we supposed to know what is asked for
when we are asked what things are really like in cases where we have not yet
found that out? In short, I see no reason why a classical sceptic should accept
the global contrast between appearance and reality. I also see no reason why
a classical sceptic would believe in such mental entities as impressions or
ideas. It is not that he is not willing to accept that people have impressions in
the sense that one may have the impression that all this is not very clear, or
that people have a mind. He explicitly says that he accepts this. But it is one
thing to accept this and quite another to believe in mental entities like
impressions. There is no reason to think that he believes in mental acts like
assents. It is true that he talks as if he accepted impressions and assents. But
this is because his opponents believe in these things. And when, for a
change, he does use this language to talk about his own attitude, he is careful
not to commit himself to the dogmatic assumptions associated with this

language. Thus the assent the sceptic is free to give becomes a matter, for example, of his being ready to say 'yes' or 'no' if asked (Cic., *Acad.* II, 104). Moreover, he has no reason to think that impressions are immediately given and unquestionable. Anybody who has written a paper knows how difficult it is to be clear about one's impressions of the subject which one tries to articulate. Similarly, it is by no means easy to tell in detail what the impressions one is acting on actually are like. Again, it is true that the sceptic talks as if there were no question about what our impressions are when he addresses his opponents. Sextus explicitly says that how something appears to one is not an issue. But by good luck we know from two passages in Galen that a radical Pyrrhonean will also challenge reports of impressions if the question should arise (*De diff puls.* VIII, 708ff.; cf. XIV, 628).[11] Moreover, there is no reason why the sceptic should accept what we do not accept in ordinary life, namely that there is a single answer to the question 'what is to count as knowledge?' What we expect from somebody who knows varies enormously from context to context. What counts as knowledge in an ordinary context may not count as such in the context of a scholarly or scientific discussion where we have higher demands. It also varies with the importance we attach to a matter.

So what in good part has happened is that, because one has failed to understand the classical sceptic's attitude toward belief, one also has failed to understand the peculiar nature and status of the arguments of classical scepticism, one has read and keeps reading them as if they represented the sceptical view of the problem of the possibility of knowledge. In fact, their primary function is to present the dogmatic with the difficulties which arise from the framework of notions and assumptions within which the dogmatic moves. And we should expect a proper sceptic to question not only the assumptions arrived at within this framework, but the very framework itself. This is what, from the point of view of classical scepticism, the later sceptical tradition failed to do. A better knowledge of the history of philosophy would have made this failure apparent.[12]

11. *Galeni Opera*, ed. C. G. Kühn (Leipzig, 1821–33).

12. In writing this paper I have been greatly helped by discussions with Myles Burnyeat, John Cooper, Richard Jeffrey, Barry Stroud, and many others, but in particular Charlotte Stough, who took the care to write up her extensive comments on it. For a contrasting view on some of the issues discussed in this chapter, see now M. F. Burnyeat, 'Autipater and Self-Refutation: Elusive Arguments, in Cicero's *Academica*, in Inwood and Mansfeld 1997.

# Select Bibliography of Further Reading

## Texts in Translation

Sextus Empiricus, *Outlines of Scepticism* (transl. J. Annas and J. Barnes). Cambridge 1994.

—— *Against the Mathematicians* (Greek text and transl. R. G. Bury). Loeb Classical Library, 3 vols. London 1935–49.

Cicero, *Academica* (Latin text and transl. H. Rackham). Loeb Classical Library. London 1933.

A most important source of information are Books IV and IX of

Diogenes Laertius, *Lives of Eminent Philosophers* (Greek text and transl. R. D. Hicks). Loeb Classical Library, 2 vols. London 1925.

The most important testimonies concerning ancient scepticism are collected and translated in

A. A. Long and D. Sedley, *The Hellenistic Philosophers*, 2 vols. Cambridge 1987.

## Secondary Literature

The best scholarly history of ancient scepticism remains

V. Brochard, *Les Sceptiques grecs*, (2nd edn., Paris 1923; repr. 1969)

There is a comprehensive bibliography on ancient scepticism prepared by L. Ferraria and G. Santese in G. Giannantoni ed., *Lo scetticismo antico* (Naples 1981), 753–850, and continued by P. Misuri in *Elenchos* 11, 1990, 257–334.

The following books and articles are recommended:

Allen, J. (1994) 'Academic Probabilism and Stoic Epistemology', *Classical Quarterly* 44: 85–113.

Annas, J. (1986) 'Doing without objective values: ancient and modern strategies', in M. Schofield and G. Striker edd., *The Norms of Nature: Studies in Hellenistic Ethics* (Cambridge), 3–29.

———— and Barnes, J. (1985) *The Modes of Scepticism: Ancient Texts and Modern Interpretations.* Cambridge.

Barnes, J. (1980) 'Proof Destroyed', in M. Schofield, M. Burnyeat, and J. Barnes edd., *Doubt and Dogmatism: Studies in Hellenistic Epistemology* (Oxford), 161–81.

————(1983) 'Ancient Scepticism and Causation', in Burnyeat (1983), 149–86.

————(1990) *The Toils of Scepticism.* Cambridge.

Bett, R. (1989) 'Carneades' pithanon', *Oxford Studies in Ancient Philosophy* 7: 59–94.

————(1990) 'Carneades' Distinction between Assent and Approval', *Monist* 73: 3–20.

Brunschwig, J. (1988) 'Sextus Empiricus on the *kritērion:* the Sceptic as conceptual legatee', in J. M. Dillon and A. A. Long edd., *The Question of Eclecticism: Studies in Later Greek Philosophy* (Berkeley), 145–75; reprinted in J. Brunschwig, *Papers in Hellenistic Philosophy* (Cambridge 1994), 224–43.

————(1990) 'La formule ὅσον ἐπὶ τῷ λόγῳ chez Sextus Empiricus', in A. J. Voelké ed., *Le scepticisme antique* (Cahiers de la Revue de Théologie et de Philosophie 13), 107–21; reprinted in English translation in J. Brunschwig, *Papers in Hellenistic Philosophy* (Cambridge 1994), 244–43.

Burnyeat, M. F. (1976) 'Protagoras and Self-Refutation in Later Greek Philosophy', *Philosophical Review* 85: 44–69.

————(1979) 'Conflicting Appearances', *Proceedings of the British Academy* 65: 69–111.

———— (1980) 'Tranquillity without a stop: Timon frag. 68', *Classical Quarterly* 30: 86–93.

———— (1982) 'Idealism and Greek Philosophy: What Descartes Saw and Berkeley Missed', *Philosophical Review* 91: 3–40; also in G. Vesey ed., *Idealism, Past and Present* (Royal Institute of Philosophy Lectures 13, Cambridge 1982), 19–50.

———— ed. (1983) *The Sceptical Tradition.* Berkeley.

Couissin, V. (1929a) 'Le Stoïcisme de la Nouvelle Académie', *Revue d'histoire de la philosophie* 3: 241–76; reprinted in English translation in Burnyeat (1983), 31–63.

———— (1929b) 'L'origine et l'évolution de l'ἐποχή', *Revue des Études Grecques* 42: 373–97.

Fogelin, R. J. (1994) *Pyrrhonian Reflections on Knowledge and Justification.* Oxford.

Foster, M. N. (1989) *Hegel and Scepticism.* Cambridge, Mass.

Frede, M. (1973) Review of Stough 1969, *Journal of Philosophy* 70, 102–29.

———— (1983) 'Stoics and Sceptics on clear and distinct impressions', in Burnyeat (1983), 65–93; reprinted in M. Frede, *Essays in Ancient Philosophy* (Minneapolis and Oxford, 1987), 151–76.

—— (1989) 'A Medieval Source of Modern Scepticism', in R. Claussen and R. Daube-Schackat edd., *Gedankenzeichen* (Düsseldorf), 65–70.

Glidden, D. (1983) 'Sceptic Semiotics', *Phronesis* 18: 213–55.

Glucker, J. (1978) *Antiochus and the Late Academy*. Göttingen.

Hankinson, R. J. (1995) *The Sceptics*. London.

Inwood, B. and Mansfeld, J. edd. (1997) *Assent and Argument: Essays in Cicero's Academica Books*. Brill: Leiden, 277–310.

Ioppolo, A. M. (1993) 'The Academic Position of Favorinus of Arelate', *Phronesis* 38: 183–213.

Long, A. A. (1978) 'Sextus Empiricus on the criterion of truth', *Bulletin of the Institute of Classical Studies* 25: 35–49.

McPherran, M. (1987) 'Sceptical Homeopathy and Self-Refutation', *Phronesis* 32: 290–328.

Naess, A. (1968) *Scepticism*. London.

Penelhum, T. (1992) *God and Scepticism: A Study in Scepticism and Fideism*. Dordrecht and Boston.

Popkin, R. (1979) *The History of Scepticism from Erasmus to Spinoza*. Berkeley and Los Angeles.

Schmitt, C. B. (1983) 'The Rediscovery of ancient scepticism in modern times', in Burnyeat (1983), 225–51.

Sedley, D. (1981) 'The End of the Academy' (Critical Notice of Glucker [1978]), *Phronesis* 26: 67–73.

—— (1983) 'The Motivation of Greek Scepticism', in Burnyeat (1983), 9–29.

Stough, C. L. (1969) *Greek Scepticism: A Study in Epistemology*. Berkeley.

—— (1984) 'Sextus Empiricus on Non-assertion', *Phronesis* 29: 137–64.

Striker, G. (1980) 'Sceptical Strategies', in M. Schofield, M. Burnyeat, and J. Barnes edd., *Doubt and Dogmatism: Studies in Hellenistic Epistemology* (Oxford), 54–83.

—— (1981) 'Über den Unterschied zwischen den Pyrrhoneern und den Akademikern', *Phronesis* 26: 153–69.

—— (1983) 'The Ten Tropes of Aenesidemus', in Burnyeat (1983), 95–115.

—— (1990) 'The Problem of the Criterion', in S. Everson ed., *Epistemology* (Companions to Ancient Thought 1, Cambridge), 143–60.

——(1996) *Essays on Hellenistic Epirtermology and Ethics*. Cambridge. Chap. 4 is Striker 1980; chap. 6 is Striker 1981 in English translation; chap. 5 is Striker 1963; chap. 7 is Striker 1990.